MANCHESTER:
SHAPING THE CITY

© MANCHESTER CITY COUNCIL, 2004

Published by RIBA Enterprises Ltd
15 Bonhill Street
London EC2P 2EA

ISBN 1 85946 157 3

Stock Code 36181

09738081

The right of Manchester City Council to be identified as the Author of this
Work has been asserted in accordance with the Copyright, Design and
Patents Act 1988.

British Library Cataloguing in Publications Data
A catalogue record for this book is available from the British Library

Publisher: Steven Cross
Project Editor: Anna Walters
Editor: Ian McDonald
Designed by Kneath Associates
Printed and bound by Butler and Tanner

While every effort has been made to check the accuracy of the information
given in this book, readers should always make their own checks. Neither
the Authors nor the Publisher accept any responsibility for misstatements
made in it or misunderstandings arising from it.

Photographs and illustrations have been supplied by
picturesofmanchester.com (Len Grant, Jan Chlebik, Shaw &
Shaw, Will Cross/Skycam, David Birchall, Patrick Henry, Clare
Hayes, David Oates and G.ten), Ian Lawson, Marketing
Manchester and Manchester City Council. Additional picture
research was under-taken by Len Grant, with exception of the
case studies in Chapter Three which have been supplied
separately and are credited accordingly within the text.

Cover: Marks & Spencer, Manchester (BDP, 1999).
Photo: Charlotte Wood

i

CONTENTS

MANCHESTER: SHAPING THE CITY

FOREWORD

GEORGE FERGUSON

Royal Institute of British Architects, President 2003 – 2005

PHOTO:
VALERIE BENNETT

Manchester has given me good reason to return time and time again during my Presidency. The highlights have been the presentation of the record number of RIBA national awards for any single city or region outside London, and the first ever RIBA Council meeting outside of the capital. Manchester has earned the right to be held up as an example to others of the way that imaginative masterplanning, fine contemporary architecture, and an entrepreneurial culture can make such a spectacular contribution to environmental and economic revival.

It is therefore with great pleasure and pride that I write this Foreword. The first of what I hope will become a great series of books on the major cities of Britain that will, in partnership with those cities, demonstrate the rich architectural variety, both new and old, that this country enjoys. I would like to thank my predecessor Paul Hyett who – following a meeting with Sir Howard Bernstein – drew up the concept for this book and for the series as a whole.

Personally, I am extremely pleased at how Manchester has greatly encouraged the development of its own architectural talent, and, at the same time, has not been afraid to look for the best from elsewhere – all as evidenced by the impressive array of achievements in this book. The other noticeable trait is the encouragement of a balance of the most prestigious national retailers, alongside a healthy mix of locally grown independent businesses giving Manchester something of a continental quality of 'designer' shops and bars, and reviving the streets, spaces and canals with vibrant new uses.

The Manchester story is a great one to tell. It is a story of adventure and innovation, and of a fierce independent spirit. It is a story of the power of confident and imaginative local leadership to change perceptions, and hence reality. I now find a real local pride in what has been achieved, and a greater understanding of how the power of good architecture, and planning, changes lives for the better.

I look to Manchester to continue to spread this message and to contribute to the development of a visual and environmental literacy across the nation. It is through the healthy competition between our cities that, I believe, this can be fostered, and Manchester has clearly begun to set the standard by which all others may be judged. However, it is important not to merely copy what Manchester has done, but that each city finds its own particular way. It is important that we reinforce regional variety and encourage our own local talent. If this is done, Manchester will have done more than generate its own revival, it will have stimulated others to shape their cities in their own way.

Congratulations to Manchester, and all those involved, on yet another first.

PREFACE

COUNCILLOR RICHARD LEESE
Leader of Manchester City Council

SIR HOWARD BERNSTEIN
Chief Executive of Manchester City Council

We are delighted to work so closely with the RIBA in the joint production of this book, which has evolved into far more than a chronicle of the city's outstanding architecture.

The original idea for *Manchester: Shaping the City* was conceived during discussions between RIBA and the City Council, about exceptional developments emerging all over the city of Manchester. Their range, designated end-use and style was varied, but they were consistent in being architecturally of the highest quality.

We agreed a collection of case studies was worthy of publication and debate. For these analyses demonstrate, unquestionably, a series of constants in Manchester's history – factors that apply whether we look at political, economic, social or architectural influences.

Implicit in all Manchester's major developments have been some key drivers for change – the determination to challenge the norm, a spirit of independence, unshakeable determination, the bravery to think the unthinkable and, vitally, our resilience and ability to deliver a sound product in the face of extreme challenge. Equally, the city is determined that all projects must bring benefits to everyone who lives, learns, works and invests in Manchester.

RIBA has been a constructive and critical friend throughout our progress in recent years, acknowledging our good work in key areas and providing a crucial sounding board. When we received from RIBA the award of Client of the Year in 2003, the title was an honour, not just for us, but for countless organisations and enterprises throughout the city, because nothing happens in Manchester as a result of council action alone – partnership working is the central tenet of all our success.

It is indeed the needs and desires of our constituents and partners that gives to us in the City Council the stamina and the validation to continue the pursuit of quality projects and developments. Making do is not good enough for Manchester; we have the vigour to go the extra distance to deliver for our city the highest quality in every aspect of our lives.

Thank you to RIBA for encouraging us in this quest for excellence, and for helping us to deliver this chronicle of Manchester's development as the original modern city. And thank you also to all those who work with us as we continue our mission to create a sustainable world-class city.

Congratulations to all those who have played a part in shaping our city. We hope sincerely this publication also serves to inspire all those who are still to play their part in future creations.

3

4

ACKNOWLEDGEMENTS

George Ferguson, President of the Royal Institute of British Architects, Councillor Richard Leese, Leader of Manchester City Council, and Sir Howard Bernstein, Chief Executive of Manchester City Council would like to thank the Editorial Team and authors without whom this book would not have been possible.

The members of the Editorial Team are:

> Peter Babb, Head of Planning, Manchester City Council

> Fran Toms, Head of Cultural Strategy, Manchester City Council

> Janine Watson, Head of Press, Manchester City Council

> Steven Cross, Publishing Director, RIBA Enterprises

The Editorial Team would like to thank all those who were interviewed for the book and have helped in formulating and telling this great story, especially:

> Councillor Richard Leese
> Sir Howard Bernstein
> Graham Stringer MP
> Sir Bob Scott

> Sir Alan Cockshaw
> Professor Alan Gilbert
> Tom Bloxham
> Andrew Stokes

> Leslie Chalmers
> Jim Ramsbottom
> Justin O'Connor

The Editorial Team would also like to give special thanks to Jane Price who tirelessly undertook the research for the book and wrote the majority of the text – and all with utmost dedication and attention to detail.

Valuable contributions have also been made by: Jane Ansell; Pat Bartoli; Alan Bellwood; Nigel Bodman; Richard Elliott; John Glester; Alison Gordon; Karen Hibbitt; Martin Kelly; Richard Llewellyn; Maria Price; Warren Marshall; Marilyn McGuinness; Hannah Mummery; Eddie Smith; Simon Warburton; Len Grant; Ian Lawson; and Ian Howarth.

Jane Price writes:

The invaluable support, useful suggestions and continuous direction that I received from the Editorial Team, and all of the contributors, made the challenging task of preparing this work so much easier. I very much appreciate their assistance. I dedicate my role in this work to Tony Cross (1968–2004), a true 'Manchester Man' who, from the age of 15, was a dedicated and radical campaigner for Manchester's residents and the rights of those from marginal groups.

PUBLISHING PARTNERS

We would like to thank all of the companies listed below who have generously supported the publication of this wonderful book.

The development and regeneration of Manchester is a success story for all those involved – from those working within the City Council, the investors, developers, architects and contractors who have supported and backed the redevelopment plans, to, ultimately, the local businesses, people and communities.

None of what you will see and read in this book could have been achieved without the support and encouragement of companies like those listed below. We thank them for their support and look forward to working with them in the future.

George Ferguson, Councillor Richard Leese and Sir Howard Bernstein.

> Alfred McAlpine
> Allied London Properties Ltd
> Argent
> ASK Developments
> Beetham Organization Ltd
> Bovis Lend Lease Ltd
> Co-operative Financial Services
> The Co-operative Group
> Crosby Homes
> GMPTE
> Laing O'Rourke
> MACE
> Manchester Airports Group
> Prudential Property Investment Managers Ltd

TIMELINE

1974	Great Manchester Council (GMC) established.
1982	Haçienda club opened.
1984	City Centre Local Plan adopted.
1986	G-MEX opened.
1986	Greater Manchester Council (GMC) abolished.
1988	CMDC established.
1989	Funding awarded for Phase One: Manchester's LRT – Metrolink.
1990	Manchester's bid for 2000 Olympics announced.
1992	Draft Manchester Unitary Development Plan.
1992	Phase One of Metrolink completed.
1992	East Manchester 10-year Regeneration Strategy published.
1992	Manchester City Council publishes first Arts and Cultural Strategy.
1992	Hulme City Challenge Action Plan launched.
1992	Manchester's Festival of Expressionism.
1992	Victoria Station development, including a new arena.
1994	Velodrome opened (later became known as National Cycling Centre).
1994	Manchester hosted Global Forum.
1994	Manchester was City of Drama.
1994	First City Pride Prospectus published.
1994	Great Northern Initiative established.
1994	Nynex Arena (later the Manchester Evening News Arena) opened.
1995	Manchester awarded £77m for stadium, and £13m for Manchester Aquatics Centre.
1995	Manchester awarded the 2002 Commonwealth Games.
1995	Manchester Unitary Development Plan adopted.
1996	Marketing Manchester established.
1996	CMDC disbanded.
1996	Manchester is a host for Euro '96.
1996	Terrorist bomb explodes in the city centre.
1996	Manchester Millennium Ltd established to oversee rebuilding of the bomb - damaged city centre.
1996	Bridgewater Hall opened.
1996	Great Northern Initiative approved.
1997	City Development Guide adopted.
1997	Spinningfields Initiative established.
1997	Hulme Arch opened Bridge.

1997	MIDAS established.
1997	Piccadilly Regeneration Study.
1998	Millennium Commission awarded £42m for new Millennium Quarter.
1998	Phase Three Metrolink proposals submitted to Government.
1999	City centre officially reopened following bombing.
2000	Manchester Airport's Second Runway opened.
2000	Metrolink: Phase Two completed.
2000	Metrolink: Phase Three, Government agreed further extensions.
2000	Manchester City Centre Management Company Ltd. established.
2000	Southern Gateway Study.
2001	Regeneration Framework for New East Manchester published.
2001	Urban Regeneration Company for New East Manchester established.
2002	Manchester International Convention Centre opened.
2002	City of Manchester Stadium completed.
2002	Manchester's Cultural Strategy – Our Creative City – launched.
2002	Significant projects completed: Urbis, Manchester Art Gallery Extension, Piccadilly Concourse.
2002	Piccadilly Gardens reopened.
2002	Manchester hosts the XVII Commonwealth Games.
2002	Metrolink 'Big Bang' agreement to expansion of network agreed in principle.
2002	Knowledge Capital Prospectus launched.
2003	Manchester hosted Core Cities Conference.
2003	North Manchester Regeneration Framework published.
2003	Wythenshawe Regeneration Framework commissioned.
2003	City of Manchester Stadium handed over to Manchester City Football Club.
2003	RIBA Client of the Year awarded to Manchester City Council.
2003	Eastern Gateway Study.
2004	Radisson Edwardian Manchester opened on Free Trade Hall site.
2004	International Festival approved for 2006.
2004	Northern Way Initiative.
2004	Spinningfields projects opened: Magistrates Court, Number One Spinningfields, MANCAT City Centre campus.
2004	Civil Justice Centre and Hilton Tower commence development.

01
THE FIRST
MODERN CITY

Manchester is a talented and determined city. This radical, gritty northern metropolis initiated a new way of working in the 18th century and created extraordinary wealth for the whole nation. It defined a new way of living, with suburbs for middle-class entrepreneurs and inner-city terraces for the working classes. Even today, in the 21st century, Manchester continues to make its impact as a city undergoing a remarkable renaissance. It sets the national agenda for innovative partnerships, regeneration initiatives and methods of delivering services to its residents. It creates one third of the Northwest region's wealth, is determined to become a leading European city, and has a wide range of imaginative strategies in place to achieve this aim.

fig **1.1**
The Royal
Exchange
Theatre, formally
the first trading
exchange in
Manchester

fig **1.2**
Liverpool Road
Station

fig **1.3**
A Manchester
First: splitting
the atom

1.1   1.2

1.3

Manchester not only embraces change, it drives it. Its entrepreneurs and political leaders strive to stay one step ahead, and therefore maintain a constant and vigilant eye on opportunities for advancement. Manchester doesn't wait to see what others do, it gets out there and delivers. Its people are resilient, demanding and purposeful. There is a feeling of independence, and challenge, bordering on defiance, among those who seek new ways of working and who employ pragmatism and imagination to achieve their goals. It is a 'can-do' city, where public and private partnerships are not new phenomena, but have delivered outstanding achievements for the city and its residents for more than 150 years.

Manchester contributed to world history by becoming the first industrial city. Its list of ground-breaking achievements is remarkable: the first British working canal which reached Manchester in 1763; the first passenger railway station built in 1830; the first British plane, though not officially recorded, designed and flown by Mancunian A V Roe in 1908; the first municipal airport established in 1929. The first permanent fire brigade under the control of a civil authority was created there in 1826; the first free municipal library opened in 1852; the atom was theoretically split for the first time by Ernest Rutherford working at Manchester University in 1919. And the list continues to expand. The city has one of the largest university campuses in Europe; the biggest regeneration initiative, in terms of area covered, in the country; it staged the 'best ever' Commonwealth Games in 2002 and was the first local authority to be nominated RIBA Client of the Year in 2003. It is a city that rightfully boasts outstanding commercial, social and cultural achievements and has abundant awards to prove it.

The transformation of Manchester from a market town with a population of 10,000 to a significant regional centre, and then to a global industrial city, began in the early 1700s. By then, Manchester had already established good market and trading links. These supported the manufacture of silk, woollen and linen cloth, but it was the introduction of cotton, combined with local engineering inventions, that transformed home-based weaving into mill-based mechanised mass production. It was from this base that the city's place in world history was secured.

Cotton manufacturing became the driver of economic growth and Manchester grew with the opportunity by developing the commercial infrastructure to support the trade.

As a result Manchester dominated 19th-century history as the world's first modern city. To capitalise on the popularity of the pure cotton fabric, Sir Oswald Mosley, in 1729, built the first trading exchange, now called the Royal Exchange, where raw cotton was bought and sold. The cotton

fig 1.4
Bridgewater
Canal, Castlefield

fig 1.5
Victoria Station

1.4

1.5

industry needed people to operate machines, to build and to deliver goods. By 1801 Manchester's population was 75,281 and by 1851 it had quadrupled while London's population had merely doubled in the same time. The jobs created were not just for cotton-mill workers, many of whom were children, but also for workers in new factories that were engaged in machine and precision engineering, and the chemical and metal industries. Many of these new industries were dedicated to improving and refining cotton production, while others grew to meet the revolutionary change in Manchester's transportation.

While Liverpool capitalised on its waterfront, Manchester began to use its entrepreneurial skills to position itself as the definitive market centre. Reliable links to the region and other major cities were essential, so the visionaries focused on developing ways for the city to become independently accessible. The transport revolution of the 18th and 19th centuries played a vital role in the development of the city and the Northwest region which had become the core of the cotton industry and a centre for engineering and chemical manufacturing. This, in turn, revolutionised the country's social history and politics. Manchester's development as a transport hub grew in line with its industries, and by the late 18th century it was as if all routes led there. The first achievement came in 1736 with the opening of the Mersey and Irwell Navigation which linked the two important towns of Liverpool and Manchester. Previously the existing roads were unreliable for the transportation of goods, being little more than stretches of deep mud during the wet months and full of potholes in the drier months. A more reliable transport method was required and the opening of the Mersey and Irwell Navigation provided an answer and heralded the dawn of the canal era. It was followed by the Duke of Bridgewater's canal, built to carry coal to Manchester from Worsley in 1763. This made engineering history as the first working canal to cross a river by aqueduct, and, as it did not follow an adapted river course but was an artificially created watercourse, it is often described as England's first canal. Some of the great warehouses built around its basin are standing today and have been converted for modern use. The Rochdale Canal, the first trans-Pennine waterway was completed in 1804 and linked to the Bridgewater Canal at Castlefield. Manchester had become an inland port and lay at the core of a complex of navigable waterways.

As engineers revolutionised transport by water, so it was with the railway. The railway boom was breathtaking in its speed and scope. In 1830, the Liverpool and Manchester Railway opened Liverpool Road Station, terminus of the world's first passenger service. It quickly made a profit and was the model for the global rail revolution. By 1840, London Road (now Piccadilly) and Victoria Stations were operational and associated with warehouse developments that today are intimately

13

1.6

connected with Manchester's past. The warehouses stored the imported materials upon which the textile industry depended, the finished products awaiting export, and the food needed to feed the growing population. The smaller warehouses in the Smithfield and Shudehill districts catered for clothing, boots, shoes and other smallwares produced in Manchester, while the larger warehouses in the Castlefield area handled goods transported by canals and railways.

By the second half of the 19th century Manchester's trade and manufacturing was suffering from crippling transport charges exacted by the railway companies and the Mersey Docks & Harbour Board. Four fifths of Manchester's trade had to pass through Liverpool and independence was needed from this constraint. A proposal to bring in deep-sea shipping directly to Manchester, first mooted in the mid-1820s, was resurrected but there was doubt as to whether or not it could be achieved, given the cost and engineering complexities.

The work was driven by Daniel Adamson, the owner of a Dukinfield engineering business, who called a meeting at his Didsbury home in 1882 to 'consider the practicability of constructing a tidal waterway to Manchester' – and it was he who doggedly persevered and eventually persuaded Parliament to pass a bill authorising its construction in 1885. It was also Daniel Adamson, a man of vision and boldness, who led the promoters and raised five million pounds to allow the work to start, in spite of bitter opposition from Liverpool and the railway companies who feared the competition. This funding arrangement can be regarded as the first of Manchester's very significant public-private partnerships, with the Corporation enabling the realisation of this hugely ambitious project.

The Manchester Ship Canal Company, of which the Corporation became a stakeholder, was formed to administer the construction of the Manchester Ship Canal. In the winter of 1891, violent floods

fig **1.6**
Merchants
Warehouse,
Castlefield

fig **1.7**
Victorian housing
in Ancoats, the
first industrial
suburb

1.7

destroyed months of work. There followed a winter freeze which prevented the use of the Bridgewater Canal, at that time the company's only profit-making asset, and the company became desperately short of money. It was the Corporation that stepped in once again to provide loans to keep the project alive. The canal opened on 1 January 1894 and, to mark the event, a procession of 71 ships travelled its 55 kilometres from Liverpool to Manchester, navigating five sets of massive locks, seven swing road-bridges, the famous world-first swing aqueduct at Barton and five high-level railway viaducts. The construction of the ship canal succeeded in making Manchester one of the major ports of the world, and played a vital role in the development of this determined city.

Manchester – with its excellent transport links, commerce and industries – attracted job seekers who flocked into the city. Early workers were migrants from adjacent regions, followed by Irish immigrants and later Italians, who made their homes around the rows of terraced mill workers' houses in Ancoats. The area subsequently became known as 'Little Italy' as more and more Italian family businesses became established there. Throughout the city there was rapid urban growth but with that came problems of a social nature.

The rapid expansion brought problems with environment and health. Infant mortality was high and adult life expectancy was low. There was a permanent pall of smoke and acid rain, plagues of respiratory diseases and poor sewage disposal. There was no clean drinking water until the delivery of water from Longendale Reservoir in the 1850s. Manchester Corporation recognised the need to supply water to its increasing population and considered bringing it from the Lake District. In 1878, they secured a supply from Thirlmere in Cumberland and construction work for its delivery followed under the direction of the Corporation. By 1890, the water was added to the system and had a significant impact in improving the health of the city's residents. Gas lighting was introduced to the mills by their owners, but it was the Corporation that established Manchester's gas works, which they funded out of the rates, in 1817. It became the first, and for some time the only, municipal gas works in the country, and served as a model for other enterprises such as water works, tramways, electricity stations and the ship canal. In the 1820s, the gas venture faced severe competition from a private company, the Manchester Imperial Oil Gas Company. Manchester Corporation opposed the granting of a charter to its rival and presented its own bill to legitimise its municipal gas enterprise. The city triumphed and its gas enterprise evolved into the largest in the region. While Manchester's private sector encouraged *laissez faire* economics, the Corporation adopted a more philanthropic role and established public services which became models for the rest of the country.

fig 1.8 & 1.9
Chetham's
Library

01

1.8   1.9

The poverty and crowded housing attracted attention from those with a keen interest in political and social reform. Before 1868 there were no building byelaws and speculative builders were free to cram as many houses onto an acre as was physically possible with no restrictions as to light, air or room space. The emerging residential patterns followed the town's business development. German political philosopher and social reformer Frederick Engels (1844) saw a city with a core of buildings for commerce, offices and warehouses together with the nation's worst housing occupied by the very poorest people. This core was surrounded by working-class terraces that, in turn, were encircled by suburbia in which nestled the homes of merchants and middle-class dwellers.

During the first half of the 19th century Manchester was overcrowded and polluted and suffered from technological, social and economic change delivered in an unstructured fashion and at an overheated pace. National government was dominated by land-owning gentry who were determined to maintain the status quo by enforcing repressive laws on the emerging working class. With most workers unable to earn a living wage, civil discontent was not far beneath the surface. Manchester had no representation in Parliament and this – together with the suspension of the Habeas Corpus Act, meaning that people could be arrested without trial – caused working men to gather in secret locations. The Manchester Patriotic Union Society was formed in March 1819 and leading local radicals joined the organisation. They lobbied fiercely against the Corn Laws of 1815 under which British corn rose to prohibitive prices making it impossible for the poor to buy bread. They sought parliamentary reform and organised the famous public meeting which led to the 1819 Peterloo Massacre, a historic event during which protestors suffered loss of life at the hands of law enforcers. The temporary wooden hall, built in Peters Street to hold radical meetings became known as the Free Trade Hall and, later, a stone building replaced the original construction.

Opposition to the Corn Laws continued and, in 1838, the Manchester-based Anti-Corn Law League was founded and soon grew into a national organisation. The campaign for a complete repeal of the Corn Laws was not solely for unrestricted free trade, it also raised a number of constitutional, social, moral and political issues. It developed new techniques in popular politics and was part of the loosely-defined general reformist movements of its time. It believed in a world that permitted unrestricted economic growth under conditions of free exchange. The Corn Laws were repealed in 1846 and free trade was established. The school of thought that favoured unrestricted commerce and the free exchange of goods and labour became known as the 'Manchester school of economics'. By 1850 Manchester was the symbol of a new order of society and economic philosophy. A different breed of businessmen had been created: an urban elite of merchants,

fig 1.10
Manchester Art
Gallery on
Mosley Street

fig 1.11
Hallé orchestra

1.10

1.11

1 Asa Briggs,
Victorian Cities
1963

manufacturers and bankers who became known as the 'Manchester Men' – entrepreneurs who influenced their city, the nation and the world. Once again, Manchester led the way, supporting a later often-quoted belief that what Manchester does today, the rest of the world does tomorrow. This premise could be seen when Manchester cotton workers refused to work with raw cotton produced by slaves working on American plantations. The working people of Manchester supported the Union under President Abraham Lincoln at a time when there was an economic blockade of the Southern states. This caused considerable unemployment throughout the cotton industry in Lancashire, but this belief in equality has always been present in the city's politics.

It wasn't only economics, commerce, urban living and social reform for which Manchester had become known worldwide as the 'shock city'[1] of the 19th century. In tandem came an educational and cultural awareness that influenced debates and thinking nationwide, and cultural endeavours that secured their place in history. The first free public library, Chetham's Library, was founded in 1653; the first meeting of the Trade Union Congress (TUC) was held in 1868 in the Mechanics Institute; the first professional football league was set up in 1888 in the Royal Hotel in Piccadilly. The Manchester Literary and Philosophical Society is the oldest enduring English institution devoted to scientific debate, and one that contributed to the advance of science. The Royal Manchester Institution (1823), now the Art Gallery on Mosley Street, was designed by Charles Barry and devoted to art. Locally founded cultural and scientific societies advanced the city's reputation for ideas and innovation and included the Natural History Society (1821), Botanical Society (1827), Architectural Society (1837) and Geological Society (1838). Alan Kidd in his book *Manchester* describes the first industrial city as one with leaders who were 'not a class of money-grubbing philistines, but an urban "aristocracy" with pretensions to grandeur which reached beyond economics and politics to artistic and intellectual pursuits and which so often found expression in the magnificence of their public buildings'.

Through its diverse population, Manchester emerged with a strong cultural identity. Its musical life was transformed when pianist and conductor Charles Hallé founded what has become Britain's longest-established professional symphony orchestra. The Hallé's first concert took place in Manchester's Free Trade Hall in 1858 and, since that date, it has continued to be regarded as one of the country's best ensembles. A major concern of mid-Victorian Britain was the relationship between art and industry and, in 1856, the city's leading citizens shocked the British establishment by suggesting they hold a massive art exhibition outside of London. The place was to be Manchester and it became the Art Treasures Exhibition of 1857 which brought together 16,000 works of art. The idea was threefold: educate the masses, promote British wealth, and gain royal

1.12

patronage. The exhibition was opened by Queen Victoria and was an enormous success, gaining Manchester national and international prestige. The city provided a fertile intellectual environment that attracted engineers and inventors. Education and research flourished, particularly within the academic halls of Owens College which was established in 1851 and which later became the University of Manchester. Manchester, the 19th-century World City, was at the heart of industry, manufacturing and engineering, and cultural and political thought.

It was not, however, a smooth journey from the 20th to the 21st century. As the production of cotton declined, caused in part by a failure to invest in improved technology and from increasing competition from cheaper markets, the city's fortunes waned. Between the two world wars, employment in textiles was halved and the export of cotton goods fell to one fifth of their pre-war levels. Factories began to shut down or relocate. Increased technology led to job displacement, and people – if they could afford it – moved from the city centre to new suburban estates. By 1950, industrial decline was evident; Manchester had lost its hold on its economic base and began to take on the appearance of what became known as the '*de*industrialised city'.[2] Between 1951 and 1981, the inner city lost more than half its inhabitants while the rate of unemployment grew. Previously vibrant areas such as East Manchester, the epicentre of the first modern city, became wastelands with few job opportunities and crumbling housing occupied by those who remained. By the late 1970s, initiatives to tackle reforms began to be explored by the City Council and these were often assisted by government-generated funds. Between 1961 and 1983, Manchester lost more than 150,000 manufacturing jobs; between 1966 and 1972, one third of its manual manufacturing jobs and a quarter of its factories and workshops disappeared. Vision, tenacity, opportunism, creativity and strong partnerships that have roots in the city's industrial past and are now once again driving the city forward.

fig 1.12
Owens College,
later to become
the University of
Manchester

fig 1.13
Manchester
Airport

1.13

Manchester is experiencing a renaissance and is once again demonstrating its instinctive resilience against adversity. Science-based, creative and service industries, together with a thriving international airport, have replaced older forms of employment. Contemporary Manchester demonstrates that its past is the key to its present. Its 18th and 19th-century entrepreneurs and intellectuals displayed strength and independence, operating to a great extent with collective thought and without self-aggrandizement. Manchester today is a city of bold individuals who come together, as partners, to deliver innovative, and frequently ground-breaking, projects for the city. Just as in the 19th century, when nobody would entertain the idea that a great art exhibition could be held outside of London, modern Manchester pushed the boundary in 2002 and staged the first global multi-sport event ever held outside the capital – the XVII Commonwealth Games.

The ambition of this book is to show the constant spirit and originality of Manchester people. These qualities, so well demonstrated during the 18th and 19th centuries, can still be seen today as Manchester undergoes its renaissance. Regeneration initiatives, producing stunning architecture, physical, social and economic improvements, are driving the city forward today. Chapter Two examines the key opportunities, mechanisms and individuals that were the drivers for this change. Chapter Three demonstrates how Manchester's architects have respected the city's history by bringing back into use many of its original buildings, whilst at the same time delivering iconic new buildings of the highest quality. Chapter Four identifies the network of road, rail, bus and pedestrian ways that enable Manchester to be easily accessible to those who come to the city to work, live and enjoy its many cultural, leisure and retail advantages. The final chapters show how change is being managed as the city moves towards becoming established as a leading European centre with a thriving economy and a good quality of life for its residents.

Peter Hetherington,[3] writing in the *Guardian*, believes 'England is changing. I make one prediction: northern cities, led by Manchester, will increasingly become attractive to young graduates, and others, disillusioned with the prospect of work in the south. Soon we will be talking less about the pull of London and the south. The draw of the north will become fashionable. Manchester's reinvention will be complete.'

Today the city is set on a path to improve its economic competitiveness and become a European regional capital. The signs of it reaching its goal are looking good.

[2] Jamie Peck and Kevin Ward,
City of Revolution: Restructuring Manchester
2002

[3] Peter Hetherington,
Society Guardian
12 May 2004

02
DRIVING
CHANGE

Manchester has realised dramatic achievements within the last 15 years. Industrial decline and the loss of manufacturing, employment and cultural identity from the mid-20th century onward had crippled the city. Nothing short of a radical transformation was required, and, with true Mancunian determination, this is being delivered and Manchester is becoming a thriving, dynamic and modern European city.

fig 2.1 & 2.2
Shopping in
central
Manchester

02

2.1   2.2

This transformation from slump to success is no lucky accident. It is the result of vision, application and hard work. Changes have been masterminded and driven by civic leaders with long-term vision and a determined and positive approach to a new future. The successes – born from foresight, strategies and planning – are clearly visible today. There is a renewed skyline with restored historic buildings and gleaming new structures of high-quality design. Opportunity is for the taking, and Manchester is a place where physical and economic change has been achieved by exploiting every opportunity to the city's advantage.

Manchester is described as a city 'that survives on small acts of defiance' (Peck and Ward 2002), but add up all those 'small acts' with some grand vision, and you arrive at a city that is now named in the top ten European urban locations for business investment. It is in the world's top 50 as a conference destination, with rental values and levels of private investment ranked the highest outside of the UK capital. More people live, learn and work in the city centre as the economy has diversified and grown. There is a new air of confidence and competitiveness and, as a result of the hugely successful 2002 Commonwealth Games, the world is aware of all that has been achieved. Manchester is a creative place and one that has been described as the most 'bohemian' city in the UK. This accolade is according to a creativity index created by Richard Florida,[1] the US economic regeneration expert who looked at the mix of ethnic diversity, gay-friendliness and technological innovation and rated Manchester top of the list of 40 UK cities.

All those who have revisited or returned to the city after an absence of ten years or more stand in amazement at its physical transformation, particularly within the city centre. Whereas the Arndale shopping centre with its external yellow tiles and adjacent grimy streets used to draw comment from visitors, in 2004 Exchange Square, New Cathedral Street and Piccadilly Gardens attract the visitors, and iconic buildings such as Urbis and the Bridgewater Hall feature in their photographs. A cosmopolitan revival has taken place as evidenced by designer-wear shops, restaurants selling world cuisine, boutiques and café-bars. Street wardens in red uniforms walk around the city centre offering help and advice, fast-moving machines gobble up rubbish and chewing gum through the day and night, and office workers hurry purposefully through the streets in the early morning clutching branded containers of coffee as if they were in Berlin or Barcelona.

Over the last two decades, the city's public-sector champion, Manchester City Council, formulated and articulated a vision for the strategic direction of the city. Consistent strong Labour political leadership, with individuals dedicated to the welfare of their citizens, played an essential role in driving change. It was the determination of these individuals to halt Manchester's economic and social decline that led them to adopt a pragmatic approach to the Conservative Government of the

[1] Boho Britain creativity index, using a research tool developed by Richard Florida, links creativity and urban renewal in the UK. Manchester was ranked top city, May 2003

fig 2.3
Manchester
Town Hall,
Albert Square

2.3

*2 Northwest
Business Insider,
July 2003*

1980s. Conservative nationally-imposed initiatives were embraced and developed as agents for change. The same approach was extended to leading commercial interests with whom partnerships were formed to secure high-quality educational, economic and social projects for Manchester's communities. Council leaders saw Manchester as a city where people would choose to live, work, invest and learn. They wanted a competitive city, one that could take its place on the European and international stages. They sought to secure investment and jobs; to strengthen and diversify the economy through the development of leisure, sport and tourism; to capitalise on the city's reputation as a centre for excellence in higher education and to improve the skills base and level of job openings. Every chance to access external money was exploited to the full, and opportunities to improve the city's image were skilfully created.

Crucially, behind the frameworks and strategies for delivery were people whose drive and determination were firmly rooted in the belief that Manchester is a great city and is one that could be even greater. These significant 20th-century leaders included Graham Stringer, Labour Leader of the City Council from 1984 to 1996, who maintained a strong hold on the city's principal projects and demonstrated a masterful ability to develop the city's informal networks. Sir Bob Scott came to the city in 1969 as a theatrical impresario. He founded the most successful repertory theatre in the UK, the Royal Exchange Theatre Company, drove a cultural agenda within the city, and fronted Manchester's two Olympic bids. Dr James Grigor, who was Chair of the Central Manchester Development Corporation (CMDC), and played a critical role in bringing together a Conservative Government and a Labour Council. Sir Alan Cockshaw, who was Chair of AMEC plc for 25 years, also held a number of public appointments throughout his career. Sir Howard Bernstein, Chief Executive of Manchester City Council, is a powerhouse of entrepreneurial drive who consistently appears in the top five of any list identifying the Northwest's most influential operators.[2] Richard Leese, Leader of Manchester City Council from 1996, has enriched the city's partnerships by nurturing a wider network of regeneration deliverers across the Northwest, and Europe, and drives the agenda for social change to improve the lives of Manchester's residents. Jim Ramsbottom, entrepreneur and property developer recognised the potential of Castlefield in the late 1980s following the City Council and Central Manchester Development Corporation's (CMDC) initiatives for the area and invested in the derelict canal site. Dr Patrick Greene recognised the links between culture and tourism long before it was fashionable in the UK. He led the award-winning Museum of Science and Industry and was Chair of the Visitor and Convention Bureau that later became Marketing Manchester. Anthony Wilson understood Manchester culture as expressed through its youth and music, and turned it into a global phenomenon. Then came the next wave of city drivers; property entrepreneurs Carol Ainscow and Tom Bloxham; architects Ian Simpson and Roger

23

fig **2.4**
G-MEX Centre

02

2.4

Stephenson; and a new generation of creative professionals, designers and new media wizards, many of whom emerged from the universities in the city.

These are some of the Manchester people who possessed, or who developed, the Manchester can-do attitude. Sitting at the nucleus of this drive for change is the City Council. Look at the make-up of any partnership charged with delivering a significant project within the city over the past 15 years, and therein lies a dedicated group of civic leaders and council officers. As the judges stated when awarding to the City of Manchester the 2003 RIBA Client of the Year Award,[3] 'The City Council has provided an inspiring example of civic leadership which echoes the spirit in which the city fathers created the great architectural landmarks from the 19th century.' The spirit of the 'Manchester Man'[4] is alive and well and continues to deliver innovation and quality.

In the early 1980s Manchester was suffering acutely from reduced manufacturing, disappearing jobs, a restricted economic base and a dimmed strategic vision. There was an increasing loss of local government power, and competition between cities drove the Conservative Government's public investment programmes. It was at this time that a new group of socialists took control of the City Council and a municipal cultural change ensued. A younger Labour group, whose members had honed their politics and debating skills in an intellectual university environment, replaced the Labour 'Old Guard'. Graham Stringer, who became the city's longest serving Leader, took the helm in 1984 as the Tory Government started their second term of office. Stringer recalls,

> At that time Manchester had an old but quite progressive Labour council with one of the highest council tax rates in the country. After about 12 months, Heseltine[5] started indicating that major changes were afoot as Government indicated that it believed Manchester was spending too much public money, particularly on housing. This led to rate capping, cuts in grants and, in 1988, to the evolution of the Conservative Government's Central Manchester Development Corporation (CMDC). It was then we realised that we had to find ways of working together.

Pragmatism rather than confrontation as a way of delivering objectives became the new approach of Manchester's political leaders, an approach that applied not only to the Conservative Government but also to the city's private-enterprise operators.

The Greater Manchester County Council (GMC) had been established in 1972 and was abolished in 1986. During its 14 years of existence, Manchester felt that it did little to further its emergence as the region's capital. The GMC was responsible for the strategic planning, major developments and transport needs of an area that included the ten districts of Greater Manchester[6] and a population

[3] The City of Manchester wins RIBA Client of the Year Award, MCC press release, October 2003

[4] *Manchester Man* by Mrs Linneaus Banks gave an insight into life in Manchester in the early 1800s

[5] The Rt Hon Michael Heseltine, Secretary of State for the Environment in 1985

[6] Bolton, Bury, Manchester, Oldham, Rochdale, Salford, Stockport, Tameside, Trafford and Wigan

fig 2.5
The Air and
Space Gallery

fig 2.6
Museum of
Science and
Industry in
Manchester

2.5

2.6

of more than two million. The *Greater Manchester Structure Plan* was adopted in 1981 and revised in 1986 just before the GMC was abolished. The plan emphasised development in the region's urban areas to prevent the loss of office-based jobs and the negative effect of suburban superstores and large out-of-town shopping developments that drained business from city centres. Derelict sites from mass industrial-building clearances in the 1970s were earmarked for new developments and redundant buildings were identified for reuse.

The City Council leaders, whilst working with their new partners, began to develop a different way of working. They recognised the need to strengthen and to diversify the city's economic base. There was an urgent need to create jobs for local people and to improve the skills of the workforce to meet the demands of new service industries. Competing in the international market-place was essential if future economic growth was to be achieved. New alliances were developed with local, previously marginalised groups, which gave rise nationally to criticisms that the council was developing a 'looney left' approach. However, at the same time, the city's politicians were developing new relationships within the private sector as they looked to develop tourism, leisure and educational opportunities, while at the same time exploring schemes to attract investment from financial, legal and other service industries. The City Council began to exert its influence on external bodies and, with the aim of creating a leisure and tourism critical mass within the city centre, one of the first public and private-sector partnerships was created to deliver a significant project using the redundant Central Station site.

The proposed redevelopment scheme for Central Station was to include an exhibition hall and conference centre, offices, a hotel and apartments replacing the Great Northern Railway Company's goods warehouse. The original developers went out of business and the site was sold to the GMC in 1980. Previously, the Roman site of Castlefield has been designated a Conservation Area in 1979, and archaeological excavations and restoration work begun. There, the Liverpool Road Passenger Station terminus, a rail link between Liverpool and the city – which once contributed so dynamically to Manchester's industrial success – was identified as a major leisure resource if converted into a railway museum. In 1984 the first phase of the Museum of Science and Industry was completed and the Lower Campfield Market building nearby became the Air and Space Gallery. Central Station was successfully converted into an exhibition centre – G-MEX – in 1986, which added to leisure attractions in the area. Additionally, nearby was the Granada Studio Tours site developed by Granada Television,[7] the nation's longest-established independent broadcaster. The vision of developing a critical mass of attractions to boost the city's tourist trade was becoming a reality.

7 ITV plc companies
Granada Television
and Carlton TV
merged in 2004

25

fig **2.7**
Castlefield from
Merchant's
Bridge

02

2.7

The Council focused on developing the city centre's retail and commercial core, recognising that encouraging and managing change within the centre was essential if economic growth was to be secured. The *City Centre Local Plan* was published in 1984 to supplement the *Greater Manchester Structure Plan*, approved in 1981 by the Secretary of State for the Environment, in which Manchester was recognised as the regional capital. The *City Centre Local Plan* established the framework to support city-centre growth, while at the same time recognising the need to establish a relationship between the centre and adjoining areas. For the first time also, the Local Plan extended the preconceived core of the city centre and made a firm commitment to encourage office and residential developments - either through new-build or the reuse of existing buildings, such as the warehouses that once supported the cotton trade. The Local Plan was a significant document in the Council's move to develop positive planning based upon developing holistic physical and economic frameworks on an area basis. The purpose was to make crucial linkages between economic, social and physical change, and to provide clarity and certainty to private-sector investors.

The Council's concerns over the setting up of the CMDC related to the possibility that the imposed organisation would implement initiatives that were not in the best interests of the city as a whole. Councillors also rejected the Government's view expressed at the time that local authorities could not be trusted to deliver physical and economic change in major cities. However, when the Development Corporation was established in 1988, the Council's political leaders believed that close working between the two organisations would further the vision and delivery framework that they had developed previously for the city centre. The CMDC, charged with focusing on inner-city decline, had statutory planning powers for its designated area, but appointed the Council as their agent for planning. The organisation was given additional powers to promote and assist regeneration through its ability to acquire land by agreement as well as compulsorily, by providing grants to the private sector and by entering joint-venture schemes with the private sector. One of the areas within their remit was Castlefield, and associated with that area was a multi-millionaire who had developed a passion for, and personal aspiration of how the derelict canal-and-warehouse area should look. Jim Ramsbottom, who made his fortune with a successful string of betting shops, one of which was in Castlefield, says,

> *The City Council had already taken the initiative by making it a conservation area and*
> *designating it a Heritage Park. The worry at the time when CMDC came in, was that the two*
> *organisations would be at loggerheads. I feared the City Council would resent Central*
> *Government for interfering on their patch. The reality was that the Council saw the practical*
> *rewards through cooperation and there was no problem. It was part of the new Town Hall*

fig **2.8**
Lockkeeper's
Cottage,
Castlefield.
Formally the
office of
entrepreneur,
Jim Ramsbottom

fig **2.9**
Eastgate and The
Rochdale Canal,
Castlefield

2.8   2.9

8 CMDC,
*Development
Strategy for Central
Manchester*
1990

culture which I read as: whatever works, let's do it.

Jim Ramsbottom describes the Castlefield area at that time as 'a dump' with 'decaying warehouses and a festering canal basin', but he had a plan for the area which included bringing the historic buildings back into use and he was determined to resist any pressure to bring in a quick fix solution. 'My vision', he says, 'was to reinstate the buildings, not because they had great architectural merit, but because they were comfortable and built with traditional materials. I thought that with good architects and designers they could be recycled'. The Castlefield buildings so familiar today – Duke's 92, Castle Quay, Eastgate and Merchants Warehouse – owe much of their reinvention to Jim Ramsbottom, a true 'Manchester Man'. He applauded the arrival of CMDC which supported public subsidy for entrepreneurs, 'they rolled into town on a white charger, with saddlebags full of money and, as the organisation had a short lifespan, they hit the ground running.'

CMDC's *Development Strategy* (1990), which was based on the *City Centre Local Plan*, identified a 'new optimism, a realisation that the time is ripe for Manchester to capitalise on its obvious advantages of location, unique environment, high-quality cultural and educational facilities, commercial strength and more importantly, its people'.[8] Under the stewardship of Dr James Grigor, the board members and executive team contained the familiar names of those that had become established as city drivers: Sir Bob Scott, Graham Stringer and John Glester as its Chief Executive. Stringer states that 'Jimmy Grigor was good because he knew that CMDC couldn't work without the City Council's cooperation, so we worked very closely together. There was full integration between the two organisations. Government kept checking whether or not we were doing the right things and Jimmy Grigor kept reassuring them that we were not loonies.'

The Development Corporation's objectives reflected the City Council's aim to create a world-class regional capital city. The Development Strategy included 'projecting Manchester as an international city of repute: the ideal city in which to live, work and play,' and the projects undertaken by the organisation increased residential accommodation, created office space, achieved environmental improvements and stimulated the creation of nearly 5,000 jobs. Manchester City Council had successfully forged a partnership with a government-imposed organisation to create new wealth and jobs for the people of the city.

As Manchester developed its leisure and tourism industry, an opportunity arose which would change the city's fortunes forever. Sir Bob Scott – who had co-founded the Cornerhouse cinema and exhibition centre, the Royal Exchange Theatre Company, and developed cultural facilities such as the Palace Theatre and Opera House – discovered while listening to a radio programme that the

2.10

Prime Minister would be receptive to a British Olympic bid. Sir Bob swept aside the stated notion that London was the obvious choice to host such a sporting event and, fizzing with energy over the potential rewards to the city, he approached Graham Stringer. Together they assembled the first Manchester Olympic bid which was launched in 1984. The first steps of the city's Olympic bid ambitions are described by Sir Bob today as 'naive', but the visionaries quickly realised that international recognition through the bidding process, combined with the use of a major sporting event to act as a regeneration catalyst, was something that could only be of benefit to local people. The City Council saw it also as an opportunity for developing and expanding partnerships which would prove invaluable over the next decade. The CMDC got behind the bid and, when it failed, they supported the subsequent bid to host the 2000 Olympics. The second bidding process had real substance and a tangible impact within the city, and as Jim Ramsbottom recalls, 'we started to feel proud of ourselves, we started to think of ourselves as being on a world stage.'

One prestigious project, which came to fruition under CMDC as a direct result of the Olympic bids, was the Great Bridgewater Initiative. The Council had been seeking to expand the city's cultural activities and to develop a critical mass of conference, leisure and tourism facilities in the southeast quarter of the city centre. The city's leaders also had aspirations for a new international concert hall that would raise the city's profile worldwide. They identified that £42 million was needed for such a building, but that there was no European regeneration or government money available for cultural projects. Creativity was needed to unlock funding, and the best example of City Council, CMDC and private-sector partnership took shape. The city centre needed prestigious office accommodation for the burgeoning new service industries and, by combining both requirements, an imaginative private and public funding package for the major regeneration was assembled to embrace both the concert hall and associated privately funded office blocks. The Bridgewater

fig 2.10
Bridgewater Hall
under
construction

fig 2.11
The Great
Bridgewater
Development,
including G-MEX,
Manchester
International
Convention
Centre and The
Bridgewater Hall

2.11

Hall opened in 1996 and has become a world-class venue for music and entertainment as well as a home for the Hallé which moved from its outdated premises in the Free Trade Hall. The orchestra took up residence in a hall that had no outstanding debt from its construction, which was unusual for a building of that type. The Bridgewater offices enabled the city's commercial core to be expanded and showed a city that could understand and deliver the kind of workspace required by businesses in order for them to compete in the modern world. The Great Bridgewater development added value to the leisure and tourism activities created in the adjacent museum area of Castlefield and, over the next few years, it became integrated into the new developments surrounding the G-MEX centre.

9 *City Pride:
A focus for the
future*
1994

By now, the Council had successfully acquired a reputation with its private-sector business partners as being an agency with strong and consistent leadership, as a local authority that could get things done in support of entrepreneurial activity within the city, as a reliable partner and as one that could deliver the local planning framework to make things happen. The city's civic leaders had also achieved acceptance locally for their pragmatic approach towards the government of the day, particularly following the Conservative's third-term election victory in 1987. It was partly in recognition of this ongoing cooperative approach that Government designated Manchester a 'City Pride' authority in 1994 – one of only three, alongside London and Birmingham.

The City Pride status further formalised the city's agreed vision, established earlier through previous planning frameworks. In the 1994 *City Pride Prospectus*, the priority was to realise Manchester as a European regional capital; an international city of outstanding commercial, cultural and creative potential and an area distinguished by the quality of life and sense of well-being enjoyed by its residents.[9] More than 150 organisations and agencies, led by Manchester City Council, came together to develop the City Pride prospectus. Graham Stringer says, 'We identified particular projects, replicated what worked in the city and involved interested people with skills on a project by project basis. We started to develop these pools of people from all sectors who were talking to each other and to Government.' City Pride demonstrated to Government that a major city could identify local opportunities and deliver change, that a local authority could influence the national agenda, and that major cities in the UK could collectively contribute to the development of a competitive nation.

The *City Pride Prospectus* proposed the concept of regeneration and partnership, with comprehensive frameworks for local action delivered with funds achieved through the bidding process. By the early 1990s, strategic partnerships were gathering strength within the city and Manchester was gaining the trust of big businesses. As these partnerships developed, the Council pursued its commitment to develop the skills of its residents and to secure local jobs for local

fig **2.12**
Hulme Crescents
before demolition

02

2.12

people. As private-sector businesses sought to relocate to Manchester, the Council worked to secure local employment and skills training as conditions for construction and development approvals, and as incentives for lower land rentals. With 17.5 per cent unemployment in September 1990, together with the recognition that the qualifications and skills of its residents are fundamental to the city's integrated approach to improving competitiveness and employability, the City Council aimed to tailor construction contracts to support local labour. It also developed programmes for skills learning through colleges and on-the-job training schemes, thereby linking local people to physical regeneration opportunities.

The symbiotic growth between the public and private sectors was reaching a new level. Within the partnerships, individuals were becoming 'trusted colleagues' and, as Graham Stringer says, 'that level of trust came from both sides, the Council went out of its way to assist with solutions to business problems and the businesses, in turn, saw we could deliver.' Leading council politicians, including Pat Karney, who was at the forefront of developing the 24-hour city, were getting to know local entrepreneurs, not over a council meeting table, but by meeting them face-to-face in their places of work.

During the early to mid-1990s, Government continued to focus on policies aimed at promoting economic development and investment in some of the country's most deprived urban areas, although their social policies for housing, health, crime, education, skills and unemployment failed to deliver holistic change. Following on from the designation of CMDC within the city centre, Manchester City Council further developed area-based regeneration concepts. One of these focused on Hulme, home to Britain's largest system-built housing estate, which lay only a short distance from the city centre. The Hulme estate was developed in the 1970s and was recognised, and awarded, for its deck-access buildings known as the 'Crescents'. Chair of AMEC, Sir Alan Cockshaw, says, 'I was asked to look at Hulme by Graham Stringer who was concerned about the amount of council resources going into the area and which were bleeding other areas dry.' Richard Leese, at that time Deputy Leader and Chair of the Finance Committee, clearly remembers when AMEC first produced a model for Hulme.

> There was a meeting that myself, Graham Stringer and Dave Lunts [10] had with Alan Cockshaw, John Early, [11] David Taylor [12] and Joe Berridge [13] where they produced a model of what a redeveloped Hulme could look like. The same group met again in Manchester Airport, this time with Secretary of State for the Environment, Michael Heseltine, where we presented the model. It's one of those things you can never prove, but shortly after that, City Challenge as a concept was announced. The City Challenge was almost the response to Hulme, it fitted the circumstances of the area perfectly.'

[10] David Lunts became Chair of the Hulme Committee, the only regeneration project to have its own Council Committee and he is currently Director, Urban Policy Unit, Office of the Deputy Prime Minister

[11] John Early is currently Chair of AMEC Developments Ltd

[12] David Taylor, Former head of English Partnerships and AMEC Developments Ltd

[13] Joe Berridge, planner, originally from the UK, is now a Canadian citizen

fig 2.13
Stretford Road,
Hulme

fig 2.14
Hulme Park

2.13　　　　　　　　　　　　　　　　**2.14**

City Challenge funding was dispensed through competitive processes, as the Government believed that competition encouraged cross-sectoral involvement, produced more positive and imaginative proposals for change and required a commitment to delivery within the specified five-year timescale.

In 1992, Hulme Regeneration Ltd (HRL) was launched, with £37.5 million, by the City Council in partnership with a range of public, private and community interests. John Early, who managed the property sector of AMEC plc, was appointed Joint Chair. Joint Chair also was the Council's lead member on housing, and representative for Hulme Ward, David Lunts. The City Council established a sub-committee specifically for the Hulme area, with full delegated powers to act on all matters such as land ownership and management, planning, development control, highways and housing. The sub-committee, led by Graham Stringer and Richard Leese, was set up to ensure that the City Council could respond speedily and positively to actions requiring council decisions. Both the strategy and the delivery framework were developed by the dedicated team. The development strategy aimed to create a viable new urban neighbourhood by addressing the interlinked physical, social and economic problems of the area. To underpin the strategy a working tool – the *Hulme Design Guide* – was published in 1992 and accompanied the positive planning framework. Richard Leese draws attention to the new determination for high-quality design and says, 'By underpinning development frameworks with robust design guidelines, developers, landowners and residents were provided with clear direction as to our expectations and quality. This integration of planning and design into the process was new.'

The first HRL Chief Executive appointed was Lesley Chalmers (previously Lesley Whitehouse) who steered the country's first holistic regeneration project. She recalls, 'We had a new way of working, we saw the area as a whole and through the agreed strategy we built gradually and carefully, making adjustments where necessary but without compromising the vision.' To deliver the project, short lines of decision-making were seen as essential. The involvement of local politicians and officers facilitated fast-tracking of planning procedures and housing programmes. The contribution of significant private-sector individuals bolstered confidence externally and encouraged inward investment. The involvement of local residents, community and voluntary groups at the concept and design stages, with their views incorporated, created a sense of ownership, local confidence and a continued sense of community throughout a period of disruption and upheaval. The model worked and its success has been described as one of the most ambitious exercises in community architecture ever undertaken in Britain.[14]

The Hulme model was not the only model for local areas in need of regeneration at that time. East Manchester had been identified as a key area for regeneration for some time, but the delivery

14 Claire Hartwell,
*Manchester -
Pevsner
Architectural
Guides,*
2001

31

fig **2.15**
Residents return
to Hulme

02

2.15

mechanism and funding opportunities had not yet presented themselves. Richard Leese recalls,

Hulme was the first place where we developed a comprehensive strategic framework for regeneration, we had a map to work to, but it was not a rigid vision. It was the first place where we tried to link physical development with social issues such as crime, education and so on. Looking back I think we did some of it particularly badly because we didn't get schools fully engaged, we didn't get non-council services as engaged as they should have been, but we did get lots of it right. We learned that regeneration was not done on a monolithic scale, but plot by plot, so if we made a mistake on one plot, we could put it right on the next one. We got the urban feel and density right, but, looking back, we got the housing mix wrong and it's too harsh, it needs softening with trees which we are now doing. The other important thing was that we learnt to say "no". The first housing redevelopment plan presented by developers was horrible and we said "no", which is very difficult to say because the developers had done lots of work with tenants who thought the presented plan was wonderful. So there was a lot of work done with tenants to justify why we didn't want that particular form of development. But the point is, we learned all the time.

Quality was vitally important in Hulme and, as the Council's Chief Executive Sir Howard Bernstein says,

The importance of design and functionality was something we all developed through Hulme. The Hulme Design Guide *gave all of us a very clear understanding about what worked and what didn't work, and Hulme was a classic example of telling us all the things that didn't work. At one level this is simple stuff, but at another level it was quite revolutionary in the way in which we started to introduce a proactive approach to planning. This became positive action, where planning is the driving force for change and is no longer a reactive discipline.*

The *Hulme Design Guide* was the forerunner of the *City Development Guide* which has influenced the development of the city in promoting good-quality design since its adoption, as *Supplementary Planning Guidance*, in 1997. The *City Development Guide* is recognised as being the first of its kind in the country, focusing on good urban design that reflects an appropriate understanding of the character of the area and builds positively on Manchester's uniqueness.

The Hulme City Challenge scheme was completed in 1997, and since that date a total of £24 million of public-sector regeneration money, drawn from three major European Commission and national government programmes, has been invested in the area. It was always intended that the regeneration programme would extend long beyond City Challenge and an estimated total of £400 million of public and private investment has gone into Moss Side and Hulme since 1997.[15]

15 *Hulme,
Ten Years On,*
Report to MCC
2002 by University
of Salford, Centre
for Sustainable
Urban and Regional
Future

fig 2.16 & 2.17
Housing in
Moss Side

2.16   2.17

The physical renewal of Moss Side and Hulme is now regarded in academic circles as a benchmark in urban regeneration and an example of sustainable renewal. The model worked and was applied across the city in a number of area-based schemes. Following City Challenge, the principal funding source that kickstarted subsequent projects was the Government's Single Regeneration Budget (SRB) initiative which ran from 1994 to 2000. Projects in North Manchester, Cheetham and Broughton, Eastlands (Miles Platting and Ancoats), Wythenshawe, A6 Stockport Corridor, East Link Investment Corridor (with Tameside) as well as Moss Side and Hulme, have led to schemes that comprehensively tackle housing, crime, education, health, jobs, skills training and leisure provision. By working with all agencies, and by encouraging existing and new local businesses, a holistic approach to change is achieved through locally based multi-sectoral networks. SRB funding ensured the delivery of area-based schemes, and since its demise there has been a change in public funding initiatives. With new forms of funding such as New Deal for Communities, the regeneration approach taken by Manchester is to focus area-based plans where different needs are targeted in different parts of the city. As Richard Leese says, 'a particular area might have problems with its built environment but it may not necessarily have high crime and this way we can differentiate the ways in which we address those issues.'

By the time *City Pride 2 – Partnerships for a Successful Future* was published in 1997, there had been changes in government and local authority leadership. The Conservatives were replaced by Labour nationally, and Graham Stringer became MP for Manchester Blackley; he was succeeded as Council Leader by Richard Leese.

Key projects in the 1994 *City Pride Prospectus* were delivering results. Significant progress had been made in developing the Great Northern Initiative by securing agreement for an international convention centre next to G-MEX. The Piccadilly Gateway framework was agreed and plans were in place to develop Manchester as a centre for excellence in information and communications technologies. Furthermore, the drive to reposition the city on the international stage had been assisted through the establishment in 1966 of Marketing Manchester, which developed out of the Greater Manchester Visitor and Convention Bureau. Andrew Stokes, Chief Executive of Marketing Manchester, explains that the organisation 'grew out of the two Olympic bids and the realisation that when the city was trying to sell the idea that we could host these sort of events, those involved discovered that people either have a very historic perception of Manchester as a grimy industrial place, or that they had no perceptions at all'. Marketing Manchester was established to promote the city, and Greater Manchester, on the national and international stage. Support was also needed for new businesses looking to invest in the city, and existing businesses seeking to expand links across

fig **2.18**
The Haçienda

02

2.18

16 J.B. Priestley,
English Journey,
an account of
Bradford-born
author's travels
around England in
the 1930s

the world. To meet that need, the Manchester Investment and Development Advisory Service (MIDAS) was established in 1997 as an organisation dedicated to attract and sustain inward investors. These two agencies were considered highly radical proposals in those days. The idea of providing coordinated and sustained promotional activity, not only for the city as a destination for visitors, but as a highly desirable place in which to invest, was a new way of reaching appropriate markets.

Manchester now accepted that energetic international promotion of the city, and the region, was necessary to draw attention to local physical changes and to move external perception away from the city described by Mancunian author and DJ, Dave Haslam, as an 'invariably gloomy' place with 'incessant rain'. Manchester aimed to be perceived, and ultimately to be accepted, as a European city sitting comfortably alongside Berlin, Barcelona and Milan - and to achieve this it was also necessary to get away from the problem of a 'dead' city centre after six in the evening, and the popular external perception that the city's entertainment only occurred in smoky, dingy pubs with their peculiar English curfew hours. The drive to establish Manchester as a '24-hour' 21st-century city was gathering momentum and the Council's licensing department was challenged to keep up with the high demand for new licences restaurants, café-bars and nightclubs.

With the city as the birthplace of globally influential bands such as Oasis, Joy Division and New Order, together with its large student campus, Manchester developed the reputation of being young, culturally dynamic and exciting. Anthony Wilson is a key cultural driver and a living legend in the city with his work celebrated in the film *24-Hour Party People* – the story of Factory Records, of which he was one of five co-founders. He felt and lived the pulse of the bands he promoted. Wilson, a writer, broadcaster, music businessman and opinionator, has an undying and infectious passion for Manchester and promotes the city in many unique ways. 'In the City' is an international popular-music festival, held annually since 1995, which was devised and organised by Wilson and his partner Yvette Livesey. While music moguls debate the essence and the way forward in popular music, a fringe festival has taken root and, once again, young Manchester bands are expressing their urbanity, angst and singular views on life.

Building Manchester's reputation as a cultural capital with a wide range of high-quality entertainment and leisure activities has been a key strategy in the city's drive to identify itself through uniqueness, positive statements and creativity. J. B. Priestley described this culture-economy as 'making money out of the new frivolity of our age',[16] and went on to reminisce,

> *Since I was a boy, Manchester had the best newspaper and the best orchestra in the country,*
> *which is saying something: its citizens, who could read the* Manchester Guardian *in the*

fig 2.19 - 2.21
Manchester, city
of festivals and
carnivals

2.19

2.20

2.21

17 MCC, *Manchester
First: The Cultured
City,* 1 August 1992

18 *The City Centre
Strategic Plan
2004-2007*

*morning and listen to the Hallé under Richter in the evening, were not badly off and could be
said to be in touch with civilisation. (They had too, at that time, the best repertory theatre in the
kingdom, and their own considerable school of dramatists and dramatic critics).*

Manchester City Council commissioned consultants Urban Cultures Ltd in 1991 to undertake a
major study of the cultural policy of the city. The City Council recognised that culture and the arts
should be used as a platform for tourism marketing in Manchester in the early 1990s and they
developed a cultural strategy before most other cities had recognised the economic and social
benefits of investment in culture. Manchester witnessed Barcelona's physical and public-space
growth whilst bidding for the 1996 Olympics, and its successful use of sport within a strategic
regeneration framework. In pulling together the original cultural, arts and sports policy, the views of
Anthony Wilson, architect Ian Simpson, and Graham Stringer – among many others – were sought,
along with those of artists and organisations from the multi-ethnic population of Manchester.
The report recommended that,

*Shops should remain open longer and other mixes of activities should be introduced – cafés,
restaurants, arts venues, gyms, and so on. Public support services such as transport and
policing should adopt more progressive regimes for the evening. More housing could be
provided in city centres. Culture can be used to animate, to put on events and activities which
attract people to visit the centre or perhaps stay longer after work.*[17]

Today it is estimated that 250,000 people travel in to the city centre over a weekend to take
advantage of the theatres, restaurants, cinemas and clubs.[18] To raise the city's cultural profile, large-
scale cultural events were staged, including the 1992 Festival of Expressionism, 1994 City of Drama,
1995/6 British Art Show and, in 2002, the international arts festival 'Cultureshock', which ran in
parallel with Manchester's Commonwealth Games. The recognition that a city's cultural identity and
activities are essential to regeneration programmes was further consolidated in Manchester when the
City Council produced its ten-year cultural strategy in 2002, *Our Creative City.*

A major driver in the expansion of the city's cultural infrastructure was the Commonwealth Games.
The creation of new sports facilities for the Games at Sportcity in East Manchester, combined with
Manchester Art Gallery's extensive restoration and expansion, innovative new visitor attractions such
as Urbis, and the new public spaces of Exchange Square and Cathedral and Piccadilly Gardens
ensured that the cultural strategy moved from vision to reality. The image of the city, increased job
opportunities in the leisure industries and diversification of the economic base were reaping rewards
and Manchester emerged with a reinvigorated sense of identity. With a bulging portfolio of

fig 2.22
Former
department store
Affleck & Brown
is now a mecca
for the young
and trendy

02

2.22

attractions on offer, 18 million people came to experience the city and the Commonwealth Games in 2002, the same year that Manchester, as a result of a public survey, was declared to be the most popular visitor destination in England after the capital.[19] The Commonwealth Games attracted many significant benefits, which are described later in this chapter.

Manchester now has the largest concentration of media, creative, sport and tourism businesses outside London, which contribute £500 million to the economy. It is estimated that some 22,585 people are employed in cultural businesses in Manchester,[20] with Granada Television,[21] and the BBC's growing northern base creating centres of excellence for media production. The Creative Industries Development Service (CIDS) was established in 1999 to assist people who work, or are looking to set up business, in art, music, design, fashion, film, photography, performing arts, digital media and poetry. CIDS, funded by the European Regional Development Fund, the North West Development Agency, Manchester City Council and other regional partners, serves the City Pride area and asks, 'Is it something they pump into the Irwell that filters through into our tea-pots? Is it the communal pride that residents have in what's gone before that spurs them on to create what's going to be next? Or, is it that people in the area just get on with it – taking the risks, talking the talk, moving the shakes, and even walking the walk. It's probably a little bit of all three.'[22]

Nowhere in Manchester has the culture of creativity flourished more than in the district known as the Northern Quarter. The area was once home to textile and cotton industries and - with the opening of the department store, Affleck and Brown, in 1901, and numerous and diverse shops on neighbouring Oldham Street - the area was regarded as the city's prime shopping district. The Arndale – a town centre shopping scheme spread over 12,000m^2 – opened nearby in 1979 and almost one quarter of the smaller traders from Oldham Street moved into the new shopping mall. Competition from the Arndale meant that the Northern Quarter as a shopping destination went into rapid decline. With cheap available space, artists and young entrepreneurs began to move in and the area was reborn with a vibrant mix of independent shops, bars and organisations.[23] Bounded by Swan Street and Great Ancoats Street; Shudehill; Market Street and Piccadilly, and the Rochdale Canal, this fringe zone became a seedbed for innovation, experimentation and risk-taking.

Working in the Northern Quarter in the 1980s was a young entrepreneur who had come to the city to study politics at Manchester University. Tom Bloxham supplemented his student grant by selling posters and, as his business developed, he took a lease in Affleck's Arcade. He acquired units on site to lease to other small traders and soon he was in the property business. He expanded further, founded Urban Spash, of which he is Chair, and bought the formerly prosperous Affleck and Brown department store, housed in Smithfield Buildings. This he turned into high-quality city-centre chic

[19] MORI poll carried out September 2002

[20] MCC, *Our Creative City, Manchester,* 2002, and Regional Intelligence Unit, www.nwriu.co.uk

[21] Granada Television is now part of ITV plc and is the longest-established independant broadcaster

[22] www.cids.co.uk

[23] www.northwest publicart.org.uk

fig 2.23
The Department
Store in the
Northern Quarter

2.23

apartments on the upper floors with shops at street level. Tom Bloxham is an urban entrepreneur for mixed retail and city-centre living, and a person who changed this type of property development in the UK. In those days, he says that city leaders saw him and his colleagues as being 'maverick or slightly Arthur Daley-ish as we didn't come from a traditional property background.' But he recognised Manchester as a city particularly open to opportunity. 'I remember vividly the first time I was invited to the Town Hall to the Lord Mayor's "do",[24] I was really made up. I was really impressed, thinking – here I am nothing more than a kid being invited into the Town Hall – it's not something I thought I would ever do and there I met business people, people from charitable organisations, all sorts of people.' It was at this time that Bloxham became aware 'that the City Council had potential, and that rather than being a bureaucratic organisation stopping development, I saw it as an organisation that was going to embrace new ideas and new things. I think they made a real difference in assisting us directly and also by saying publicly that being a 24-hour city was important and that they wanted Manchester to be a young, ambitious, imaginative and creative city.'

With a creative critical mass in place, it was not long before Northern Quarter traders formed the Northern Quarter Association (NQA) to ensure, among other objectives, that the area's unique identity was protected and developed. The NQA passionately believed that the Northern Quarter could be Manchester's cultural industries quarter, focusing and extending its support for new creative businesses. It saw the area in a threefold way: as an urban training quarter, building links between new businesses, the big cultural production houses and the city's higher and further-education resources; as an intelligence quarter, establishing Manchester at the forefront of the information and communications revolution; and as a creative quarter, linking this creative and innovative sector to the development of the wider city economy.[25] CIDS located its headquarters here in 2003, and in the same year the City Council approved a second development framework to take the area forward. The Council's aim was not only to nurture the creativity that existed in the area, but also to unlock its potential.

Within the cultural framework, sport was recognised as a major factor, one that could have a fundamental impact on the economic profile and activities within the city. With two football clubs, one of which is a global brand, together with the close proximity of the Lancashire Cricket Club, Salford Rugby League FC, Sale Sharks Rugby Union Club and Sale Harriers, Manchester became recognised as a place in which athletes excel and where the wide range of top-level sport inspires its communities. The reputation of a city capable of staging world-class events developed and the city's leaders aimed for the title of 'sporting capital' of the UK. They bid for, and won, the right to stage major sporting events including the World Table Tennis Championships, World Track Cycling

[24] The Lord Mayor's Reception 1998. This is an annual celebration.

[25] Northern Quarter Association, *Vision Statement*, 2003

37

fig 2.24
International
Olympic
Committee
delegates
inspecting
progress on the
indoor arena

02

2.24

events at the National Cycling Centre, and the World Rhythmic Gymnastics Competition, and to host key football matches during the 1996 European Championship. But aiming even higher, the city staged two Olympic bids and became Britain's choice as host city for the 2002 Commonwealth Games.

While the first Olympic bid for the 1996 Games was unsuccessful, the British Olympic Association chose Manchester as contender for the 2000 Olympics. Sir Bob Scott and Graham Stringer led both bids with Sir Bob ruefully describing their first effort: 'We were innocents to the slaughter and pretty ignorant, but it was a tremendous learning curve.' It was at the second attempt that urban regeneration, employment opportunities and land reclamation became key words. The City Council recognised that public funding sources became more numerous and accessible with the 'regeneration' approach, and fitted better with their long-term strategy for significant social and economic regeneration. As the second bid developed, the leaders realised that public government support was critical if the International Olympic Committee (IOC) was to consider their bid seriously. Graham Stringer remembers, 'We went to Tokyo in 1990 to present our first Bid and Chris Patten [26] came with us.' The Minister was impressed and returned to Westminster with positive messages. Michael Heseltine picked up the baton and championed Manchester's second bid within Government, which was publicly endorsed during February 1993 by Prime Minister John Major. By now the city's leaders had their sights firmly set on the lasting benefits for Manchester. A new stadium was needed and it was to be located in East Manchester on a brownfield site close to the city centre, with the venue acting as a catalyst, focus and foundation for regeneration. The opportunity to move forward regeneration plans in that long-neglected area had arrived.

To ensure top-class new sports facilities, Manchester City Council launched an international design-and-build competition aimed at attracting the best architects and developers to the East Manchester sports site. The contract for the new stadium was awarded to AMEC with Sir Norman Foster, Arup Associates and HOK Sport among its world-class team of architects. Laing took over the project, with Ove Arup & Partners as architects and structural engineers. The second Olympic bid had also provided the opportunity to extend the city's leisure and sporting facilities. On the Eastlands site, a design-and-build contract by AMEC, with architects Faulkner Browns and design by HOK Sports Facilities Group realised the Velodrome, a dramatic building which became the National Cycling Centre. Additionally, the Manchester Victoria Station site, a key gateway in the north of the city centre that had been identified in 1989 as a potential development area for office accommodation and an indoor arena, was boosted by the Olympic bid. With a grant of £35 million, then the biggest grant for a single sports facility, the Arena (later known as the Manchester Evening News Arena)

26 Chris Patten MP,
Secretary of State
for the Environment
in 1990

fig 2.25
Demolition of the
old Marks &
Spencer store
following the
terrorist bomb

fig 2.26
Disused Maxwell
House prior to
redevelopment

2.25

2.26

was built alongside office accommodation, a multiplex cinema and a Metrolink interchange. The Manchester Evening News Arena was named International Venue of the Year in 2001 and identified in 2004 as the busiest venue in the world, topping the list of the Top 50 arenas for the first time.

In September 1993, Manchester failed to secure the 2000 Olympics but almost immediately announced it would continue its campaign for world recognition in sport by bidding for a smaller jewel, the 2002 Commonwealth Games. In 1995 the Commonwealth Games Federation selected Manchester as host city. The Games were underwritten by the City Council which, right from the outset, sought government support, recognising it as essential to the success of the 2002 Games and to the delivery of new sports venues. The first public manifestation of that support came in 1996 with Sport England's lottery funds awarded for the stadium and the new swimming complex with its two Olympic-size pools.

But, as the sun shone one Saturday morning and with scores of supporters in town from all over Europe for Euro '96, the largest terrorist bomb ever detonated on the UK mainland exploded in the heart of the city centre on 15 June. The 1,500 kg bomb devastated 49,000 m^2 of shops and 57,000 m^2 of offices in the heart of the city centre. At least 80,000 people were evacuated by Greater Manchester Police, 220 people were injured, and miraculously, none was killed. Within less than 24 hours, a task force was brought together in the Town Hall. Richard Leese had become Leader of Manchester City Council only weeks before and was faced with one of the most devastating situations affecting the city since World War II. Leese, together with Howard Bernstein, immediately looked to the city's established network of key drivers, to solicit their support and to seek the views of these trusted partners. A decision had to be made, and be made quickly, between replacing what had been obliterated or taking this as an opportunity to maximise regeneration benefits.

The key strategies and framework for the city centre had been developed as far back as 1984, but the bomb identified an opportunity for rapid change. The physical renewal of the city centre is consistently and closely linked to Manchester's ongoing economic strategy that reflects the objectives of the *City Pride Economic Development Plan*. The aim to build better businesses, secure continuing and increasing investment, provide a convenient transport system and a good environment in order that industry should flourish and jobs for local people increase, has been a driving force for two decades. The city's retail and business core had been dealt a severe blow but the partnerships agreed that a timescale of three years would be sufficient to restore the viability of the retail core and that, with positive planning, the quality of new build would take the city proudly

fig 2.27- 2.29
Relocation of the
Shambles pubs

02

2.27   2.28   2.29

into the future. Sir Howard remembers this as the most difficult time he has yet faced during his
public-sector career,

> *The city centre, both before and after the bomb, was the most challenging for me for different*
> *reasons. Firstly, failure to succeed would mean a real downturn in the city's fortunes. Secondly,*
> *there was an acute sense that people's livelihoods had been affected and we had to assist in*
> *their relocation, especially because at that same time we were facing the opening of the*
> *Trafford Centre* [27] *which would have been bad enough had we been firing on all cylinders, but*
> *became especially so when you've just lost more than a quarter of your retail space. Thirdly,*
> *there were challenges we set ourselves, with the interdependence of the private and public*
> *sector investments, that were critical to the delivery of every element of the development.*

It was agreed that the centre of Manchester would be reinforced as the retail heart of the region,
both by restoring lost floorspace and by creating a wider range and choice of shopping
opportunities. It was essential to turn the damage to the city's favour and bring real benefits to the
people of Manchester.

The task force, brought together to coordinate the city's recovery, was formalised within two weeks
after the bombing. Manchester Millennium Ltd was established, with Sir Alan Cockshaw leading a
dedicated group of public and private-sector employees. Deputy Chair was Richard Leese, and Chief
Executive of MML was Howard Bernstein. Other board members included Sir David Trippier, then
Chair of Marketing Manchester; Marianne Neville-Rolfe, Regional Director, Government Office North
West; Tony Strachan, Agent for the Bank of England; Kath Robinson, Deputy Leader Manchester City
Council and Pat Karney who was Chair of the City Centre Sub-Committee. With staff seconded from
the City Council, KPMG, National Westminster Bank and Government Office North West and others,
the team took up residence in 81 Fountain Street and embarked upon the most ambitious rebuilding
programme within the city centre.

Howard Bernstein says of that time,

> *The most important thing we did first, apart from oversee the re-organisation of the city centre's*
> *function, was to make certain that people who lost their businesses, or who were in danger of*
> *losing their businesses, were not foreclosed by banks. So the first big test of the 'partnership' was*
> *when I asked the Bank of England to convene a meeting of all the regional directors of the clearing*
> *banks in the city requesting that they do not close down any business until they had consulted*
> *with the task force. It was an exceptional thing we were asking people to do, and all of them,*
> *without hesitation, agreed. This then gave us the opportunity to set up the Lord Mayor's Fund.*

[27] Trafford Centre, a
180,000 m² out-of-town
shopping centre, owned
by the Manchester Ship
Canal Company, opened
September 1998

fig 2.30
M & S's store
rebuild nearing
completion, May
1999

2.30

The Fund, managed by John Glester, was established to get traders back into business using money and the advice, skills and expertise of local firms – bankers, accountants, insurance brokers and property developers – which were given free of charge. The Marks & Spencer store had been severely damaged and, in a demonstration of faith in the city's recovery and future, Sir Richard Greenbury, then Chair of Marks & Spencer unveiled plans in June 1997 for the biggest M & S store in the world. Sir Howard Bernstein emphasises, 'The phased three-year timescale was very important to the Boots', M & S's, and Prudential's of this world, they knew it was going to be a struggle but with them we were able to say to people generally, keep faith in the city, keep faith in the shopping and business.'

Government support was sought and within four weeks Deputy Prime Minister Michael Heseltine visited Manchester and announced £20 million of European aid for the city. At Heseltine's instigation, an international urban design competition was launched to find the world's best team that would be charged with creating the masterplan design for the new city centre. The project was awarded to a consortium headed by London-based masterplanner and landscape architect EDAW. The consortium included architects Benoy, who provided advice on retail proposals; the Manchester-based practice Ian Simpson Architects; and Alan Baxter and Associates, who provided design and consultancy advice on a variety of specialist engineering matters. The winning masterplan was unveiled less than five months after the bomb exploded, and was quickly followed by *Supplementary Planning Guidance* to provide a robust planning framework for the rebuilding programme.

Manchester rapidly secured the bulk of the public funding necessary for the rebuilding. European money was matched by private and public contributions including funds from English Partnerships and Government Office North West. A total of £20 million had been secured from Europe, and in February 1997 Michael Heseltine announced a further £43 million of government capital money. Howard Bernstein confirmed that the public money would lever in £500 million from the private sector and explained, 'we did our sums very carefully and we were able to present a case to Government with which they could not argue.' With the economic, social and physical regeneration and redevelopment based firmly on strategies supported by existing planning frameworks, the vision was translated into a reality. Information about plans was widely conveyed, through positive public relations activities designed to engage media support and to reassure residents, visitors, businesses and investors.

In addition to rebuilding, a key aim was to introduce new public spaces and structures that would ensure that the economic boundaries of the city centre were extended. A vital element was the creation of the new 'Millennium Quarter', in which would sit a world-class visitor attraction. The

41

2.31   2.32

Millennium Commission was investing National Lottery money in buildings and environmental projects, so the city grabbed the opportunity to acquire public funding for a new iconic landmark. The building became Urbis, a museum for the modern city. Its existence acted as an anchor for the emerging area and, through high-quality design, it is today a dramatic new signature building for the city. Within the Millennium Quarter, the Corn Exchange was restored and branded the Triangle and, on its periphery, Marks & Spencer created a new flagship store. The much used Arndale shopping centre lost its impenetrable fortress appearance and opened its shop fronts outwards and onto Cross Street and Market Street. A leisure-and-entertainment centre was developed behind the façade of the Maxwell House (the former *Daily Mirror* regional headquarters), and became known as the Printworks. It overlooked a new civic space, Exchange Square, designed by Martha Schwartz from Massachusetts, USA. Shambles West, a large concrete shopping-and-office complex, which acted as an unnatural city-centre barrier, was demolished, opening up the centre and linking the retail core to the previously isolated Cathedral area. The Shambles' two historic pubs, The Old Wellington Inn and Sinclair's Oyster Bar were taken apart peg by peg and brick by brick and relocated to Exchange Square within the heart of the Millennium Quarter where the Manchester Cathedral Visitor Centre, Cathedral Gardens and Urbis were situated. Linking those elements to the retail core of the city is New Cathedral Street.

As this retail core of the city centre was being rebuilt and extended, other regeneration developments continued uninterrupted. The Great Northern Initiative was progressing through the planning process; the 1997 Piccadilly Regeneration Study, and the Spinningfields development were moving forward.

The Great Northern Initiative had been identified in response to the city's intention to expand tourism and leisure activities, provide jobs and recreation facilities for local people, boost the economy of local

fig 2.31
Urbis

fig 2.32
The Printworks,
opened
November 2000

fig 2.33 & 2.34
Piccadilly
Gardens

2.33

2.34

businesses and attract inward investment. With the Bridgewater Hall in place and the G-MEX Centre attracting significant numbers of businesses and visitors into the city, the key objective of creating a conference, business and leisure area was moving to reality. Adding to G-MEX and The Crowne Plaza Manchester Midland Hotel, a new hotel on the site of the historic Free Trade Hall was in progress, together with a refurbished Great Northern Railway Warehouse with its shops and a multi-screen cinema. Planning approval for the International Convention Centre was secured, and a design team with architects Sheppard Robson and Stephenson Bell were appointed. The regeneration of the warehouse was undertaken with a £100 million development carried out by Morrison Developments and Merlin International Properties in conjunction with English Partnerships and Manchester City Council. The development required the demolition of a Grade II* listed carriage ramp, some of the listed railway viaduct and buildings in Peter Street. Historical and civic societies raised objections to many of the changes, but particularly to the proposals for the Free Trade Hall. A public inquiry was held and the Deputy Prime Minister John Prescott vetoed the hotel plans. Over the years, the Free Trade Hall had been the subject of numerous studies by Manchester City Council as to how to bring it into viable use after the Hallé moved to its new home in the Bridgewater Hall. A third design for the Free Trade Hall – a 16-storey hotel by Stephenson Bell – was accepted by English Heritage, the Manchester Civic Society and the Government in 2000. The original developer, La Sande, remained with the scheme and the new Radisson Edwardian Manchester opened in 2004.

With the prospect of thousands of people arriving in the city for the 2002 Commonwealth Games, it became imperative that the Piccadilly Gateway plans were progressed with urgency. The Piccadilly Regeneration Study included improvement to the appearance of Piccadilly Plaza, the transformation of Piccadilly Gardens and a modernised Piccadilly Station. The Gardens were developed through a team approach, with Manchester City Council, EDAW and Arup as team members. The 4 hectare site included a garden pavilion by Japanese architect Tadao Ando and a large fountain where adults meet and children play in the water. The Gardens project was facilitated by public and private-sector funding, secured partly as a result of the development of a prestigious new office building, One Piccadilly Gardens, a similar arrangement to that which had delivered the Great Bridgewater Initiative. Network Rail completed a £108 million remodelled Piccadilly Station complex with a new covered concourse, the pedestrianisation of Piccadilly Approach and a new station entrance from Fairfield Street. The whole scheme is the result of many years of integrated planning and partnerships that has significantly contributed to a new image for the area, with private enterprise assisting in the delivery of public amenities.

fig 2.35
Preparing for the
Commonwealth
Games 2002

02

2.35

Manchester was also seeking to expand and reinforce its central business district by providing a new focus for modern high-quality office space designed to meet the needs of today's corporate business. The Spinningfields Development Plan, accepted in 1997, is delivering a wholly self-contained business and community environment of the highest quality, and will become one of Europe's most prestigious blends of commercial, retail and residential opportunities. The city previously had enabled projects to be successfully delivered through creative public-private partnerships, but Spinningfields has presented a major opportunity for the city to respond to modern requirements by using its commercial intelligence, and then to change the product in order to attract prestigious 21st-century businesses. The ambitious Spinningfields development is being achieved through a partnership cemented between developer Allied London Properties and Manchester City Council. The six-year programme to regenerate nine hectares off Deansgate in a £650 million mixed-use city-centre regeneration scheme began in 2001. 220,000 m^2 of new office space in 14 signature buildings, two of which are Royal Bank of Scotland administrative centres; 37,250 m^2 of shopping, restaurants and bars; and 391 'Leftbank' luxury apartments overlooking the River Irwell, have provided a major opportunity for investment and jobs. Within the scheme, a £30m Civil Justice Centre – delivered by a partnership between the Department for Constitutional Affairs, Manchester City Council and Allied London Properties – replaces the existing County Court. The scheme provides a cornerstone for regeneration plans for the Spinningfields business quarter, with four new squares planned, and pedestrian walkways designed to make the area more accessible and environmentally friendly.

To realise Spinningfields, the energies of a large number of agencies have been effectively harnessed, and the robust masterplan reinforces the fact that Manchester will accept nothing less than high-quality design for its buildings and public spaces. As Tom Bloxham looks across the modern skyline today from his Manchester headquarters he reflects, 'ten years ago there were few buildings of reasonable quality, it used to be the exception, now it's the norm. The planners want quality, quality, quality and by and large, the planners are good and enlightened, and willing to see high-quality designs.'

With the city working towards the 2002 Commonwealth Games, which provided the unifying theme against which to justify bids for a wider range of regeneration programmes, work on the new City of Manchester Stadium and surrounding area in East Manchester was taking shape. This regeneration programme remains one of the UK's most challenging programmes to date and the comprehensive, integrated and long-term nature of the regeneration of East Manchester makes it unique. As the epicentre of the world's first industrial revolution, the area once provided the industrial base on

fig 2.36
The Runner, a
sculpture by
Colin Spofforth,
stands outside
the English
Insitute of Sport
at Sportcity

2.36

which Manchester's pre-eminence, and that of an industrial nation, was formed. Successive economic recessions and intensive competition from global markets reduced the area to one that became a textbook example of deprivation as a result of industrial and manufacturing decline. The regeneration programme is not just about refurbishment and construction of new homes, expansion of business opportunities and improving transportation – all of which are vital to its success – but is also about investing in the people who live in the area, ensuring the training and job opportunities are lasting and sustainable, as well as achieving significant improvements in the housing, health and education of the local community.

One of the key drivers for change in East Manchester was the XVII Commonwealth Games for which the City of Manchester Stadium within the Sportcity site was constructed. EDAW created the masterplan for Sportcity, and the *East Manchester Regeneration Framework*, published in March 2001, initiated the positive planning for the area, which included *Supplementary Planning Guidance* followed by alterations to the *Unitary Development Plan*. Fundamental to the Regeneration Framework is the belief that interrelated issues and problems – jobs, business development, housing, education, the environment, community facilities – are recognised as such, and are tackled in an integrated manner to build confidence and commitment in a positive future for the area.

Over the next decade it is expected that around £2 billion of private and public funding will come into East Manchester. Today, an unprecedented number of initiatives are focused in the area. Funding sources for the Regeneration Framework are intensely complex and include no less than three SRB partnerships as well as New Deal for Communities, Sure Start, Education Action Zone, Sports Action Zone, European Regional Development, North West Development Agency, Manchester City Council, Greater Manchester Passenger Transport Executive (GMPTE) and – the newest source of funding – the Housing Market Renewal Fund. To these are added a host of private-sector partners, with projects from AMEC, Manchester City Football Club, Ask/Akeler, Countryside, Gleeson, Lovell, Urban Splash, Artisan, Langtree Group and Bond Group, with the list ever growing.

The vision is that East Manchester – which includes Ancoats, Miles Platting, Newton Heath, Beswick, Openshaw, Clayton, Ardwick, Gorton and Belle Vue – will be a stable and successful part of the city, providing a high quality of life for residents, where people choose and aspire to live and work. So complex and comprehensive is the renewal required in East Manchester that it has become one of only four areas in the country to have its own urban regeneration company. The umbrella organisation responsible for co-ordinating the programme is New East Manchester Ltd, a partnership of the City Council, English Partnerships and the North West Development Agency. Launched in 2001, its long-term framework for development in the area builds on renewal activities

fig 2.37
City of
Manchester
Stadium

fig 2.38
East Manchester
residents

02

2.37   2.38

already underway and is underpinned by consultation with local residents, businesses and community groups. Representing those partners was Sir Alan Cockshaw, Chair of English Partnerships, who was appointed Chairman of New East Manchester Ltd when it was established in 1999. Sir Alan retired in 2003 and was replaced by Robert Hough, Chair and Managing Director of the Manchester Ship Canal Company and previously a Joint Chair of Manchester 2002 Commonwealth Games Ltd. The North West Regional Development Agency was represented by its Chief Executive, Mike Shields. Community involvement has been more extensive than in other previous regeneration projects and three New East Manchester Board Directors are appointed by, and from, the community.

Manchester City Council's aim is to address the key social, economic and environmental challenges in the area in order to provide a fresh, dynamic and sustained regeneration to improve the lives of people living and working there. Rather than attempt a 'one size fits all' strategy, the area is split into 16 neighbourhoods with area-based programmes and bespoke packages of economic, social and physical renewal. The regeneration model successful in Hulme, and for the city centre following the bombing, has moved forward and accommodates the unique local differences that exist within the large East Manchester area. Over the next ten years, the many partners will oversee the development of up to 12,500 new homes, the improvement of 7,000 existing homes, a doubling of the population to a total of 60,000 and the creation of 15,000 new jobs. Through the development of Central Park, the UK's first large-scale mixed-use urban business park, the regeneration of the area will lead to increased employment opportunities for local people, as 10,000 jobs are created over a 10-15 year period. With Fujitsu moving their headquarters into newly built premises on the site, new jobs are a reality, and linked to those jobs, are skills and training opportunities provided in new premises in Central Park by the Manchester Science and Enterprise Centre, a co-operative venture between Greater Manchester's four universities and the Manchester College of Arts and Technology.

With the City of Manchester Stadium and adjacent venues ready on time and pre-test events completed, the city welcomed athletes, visitors and international media to the city for the XVII Commonwealth Games. Ten days later, as the glow from the last firework died away on 4 August 2002, the city smiled and was justly proud of delivering what Mike Fennell, Chair of the Commonwealth Games Federation described as the 'best Commonwealth Games ever'. Overseeing the delivery process of the Games was the company Manchester 2002 Ltd, with Charles Allen - the then Chair of Granada Television – as Chair, and Frances Done as Chief Executive. Howard Bernstein played a critical role in the delivery of the Games on behalf the Council, the underwriters of the event. The Games could not have been so successful without the new partnerships that were formed over the seven years of their preparation and the support of old allies who rallied round for their city.

fig 2.39
Regional Athletics
Arena, Sportcity

2.39

Building up the relationships took a great deal of time and extensive behind-the-scenes work, and it was not until 2001 that a formal tripartite funding agreement was signed between Government, through its Department for Culture Media and Sport (DCMS), Sport England and Manchester City Council. The tripartite agreement established a strong financial and strategic foundation that had the skills, expertise and funding to stage a successful Commonwealth Games. The City Council's responsibility was to procure and deliver sporting and non-sporting venues, ensure a high quality of design, deliver a legacy of city image and venues and build on the Games to deliver an economic, social and sporting legacy to the region. Bernstein said that the Games had support within the city but that externally, 'the Manchester Games were viewed with considerable cynicism, people didn't believe we could do it. I always believed we would and we did.' There was a great deal riding on the Games, as Richard Leese explains, 'The successful delivery of such a world class event was not only crucial to the economic and social development of Manchester and the North West, but also to the nation's ability to bid for and stage sporting and cultural events of global significance.'

The legacy of the Games was to be the measure of its success in the eyes of all those who live and work in the city. The hosting of the Games was about much more than raising Manchester's international profile. The City Council was committed to capitalising on the massive investment that the biggest multi-sport event ever seen in the UK would bring to the city, to aid the regeneration process. Some 5,000 new jobs were created; sporting, retail and leisure facilities continue to benefit local people; visitor attractions boost the local economy and the city is recognised worldwide as a place where world-class events are staged. More than £600 million of public and private investment poured into the city and it is estimated that approximately 30 million people will now consider Manchester or the Northwest as a possible business and visitor destination because of the improved image.[28] The legacy issue was always uppermost in the minds of the local stakeholders and when the City of Manchester Stadium and Manchester Aquatics Centre were completed there was criticism from some journalists and international sports organisations, who maintained that the new venues too small for future major competitions such as the Olympic Games. Both Stringer and Leese were adamant that there would be commercial after-use for every venue; they had learned from other cities' multi-sport events, for which award-winning venues had been built, but which later became economic drains on their host cities. The City of Manchester Stadium, through long and hard negotiation, was declared the future home of Manchester City Football Club even before the venue was constructed. The Manchester Aquatics Centre, built as the result of a partnership between Manchester University, UMIST, Manchester Metropolitan University and Manchester City Council – with its two Olympic-size pools, a diving pool and a recreational area with flumes – fulfilled the city's criteria for multi-purpose use. Leese says, 'We had to make sure that everyone benefited from the new venues, not just elite athletes. Every sports venue in Manchester, whatever the standard of the building, has to be one that any resident can use either as an individual or as part of one of our sports development programmes.'

28 Manchester Millennium Ltd *The XVII Commonwealth Games Post Games Report,* 2003

47

2.40

As Manchester City Council pursued its plans for a critical mass in East Manchester, the number of new sports venues increased and collectively became 'Sportcity'. The National Cycling Centre (a direct result of bidding for the Olympic Games) was already in place in East Manchester. Opposite this Velodrome, and adjacent to the City of Manchester Stadium, is the £3.5 million National Squash Centre and, next to this, the indoor Manchester Tennis Centre. An outdoor athletics track, which was the Games' warm-up track, has been transformed into an Athletics Arena and these venues, together with the Manchester Aquatics Centre and the Hockey Centre at Belle Vue, have been awarded English Institute for Sport (EIS) status with the EIS North West team based at Sportcity. This innovative collective of sports venues has played a pivotal role in the city and Bernstein reflects, 'A high quality critical mass of public facilities is fundamental to not only creating a sense of place, but also in creating strong economic linkages to different areas. We have shown that public space can also be fundamental to the re-positioning of areas commercially. Sportcity has done this for East Manchester.' Sportcity continues to hold national and international sports events, pulling in benefits for local people. Negotiations are underway for an adjacent £260 million entertainment complex which will create a further 1,800 jobs in the area.

The Games provided another opportunity for the city to develop the skills of its residents. The Volunteer and Pre-Volunteer Programmes were hugely successful, and provided a ready pool of trained and capable people who could be called upon to participate in future events. The Pre-Volunteer Programme (PVP) was developed as a joint commitment between the Games' organisers, Manchester City Council and Manchester Training and Enterprise Council. The programme delivered a nationally accredited qualification and an enhanced opportunity to become a Games Volunteer. The PVP was based on the philosophy of social inclusion and gave those who attended the courses skills, knowledge and experience and in the long term, through a number

fig **2.40**
Manchester
Aquatics Centre

fig **2.41**
Closing
ceremony,
Commonwealth
Games 2002

2.41

of intermediate measures, access to employment. The Volunteer Programme was a resounding success and the legacy of a well-trained and customer-focused army of volunteers, 80 per cent of which originated from the Northwest, has added to the workforce for the service and tourism industries in the region.

Manchester's image and position as a world city had been enhanced through a television audience of one billion and more than 400,000 Games visitors, but it was quickly recognised that this image had to be maintained and managed. For the first time the Council initiated a central co-ordinating role, to ensure that a strategic branding approach be adopted, and delivered, by all Northwest agencies involved in promoting the city nationally and internationally. Richard Leese reflects, 'The Games provided both an unprecedented opportunity to change the image and perception of the city in the eyes of international investors and visitors, and a world class platform on which to build regeneration and marketing strategies to realise and promote the potential and success of the city.'

Manchester has been spectacularly successful in regenerating areas and delivering complex programmes and events. New standards in high-quality design and partnership working have been established. The delivery of regeneration schemes such as Hulme and the City Centre Rebuilding Programme used a regeneration model that is now recognised in academic circles as the 'Manchester Model' which Professor Brian Robson, co-author of an academic study describes as follows,

> *A delivery body with an executive that has an avowedly semi-autonomous arm's-length relationship with the local authority and is serviced by a dedicated team of officers usually seconded from relevant Council departments. The company owns no assets, but draws together key players from the relevant agencies that can deliver elements of the regeneration programme. It can therefore both develop strategy and provide the framework through which partners deliver specific elements of a coherent programme. Its 'commercial' ethos offers a vehicle through which private-sector interest and contributions can be pulled into the regeneration process on the basis that companies can have some confidence that a private-sector ethos will characterise the delivery of projects and programmes. Above all, the model entails short lines of decision-making that are facilitated by the involvement on the central board of key senior politicians and local authority officers.*

This 'Manchester Model' has been refined and developed so as to be more responsive to community needs, and the area-based local model has become a positive planning process using physical and economic frameworks that are responsive to community differences. Regeneration initiatives and related structures that exemplify the vision and success of meeting regeneration aims are examined in Chapter Three. However, it does not stop there; the city has plans to remain competitive in the international market-place for jobs, investment and visitors (Chapter Five), and seeks to maintain the unprecedented levels of private investment and job creation achieved over the past decade. As Richard Leese says, 'We recognise there is much to be done, but the prospects are good.'

49

03
TRANSFORMING
THE CITY

Manchester has been spectacularly successful in
regenerating areas and delivering building programmes.
These initiatives illustrate the variety, quality and complexity
of work undertaken since the mid-1980s.

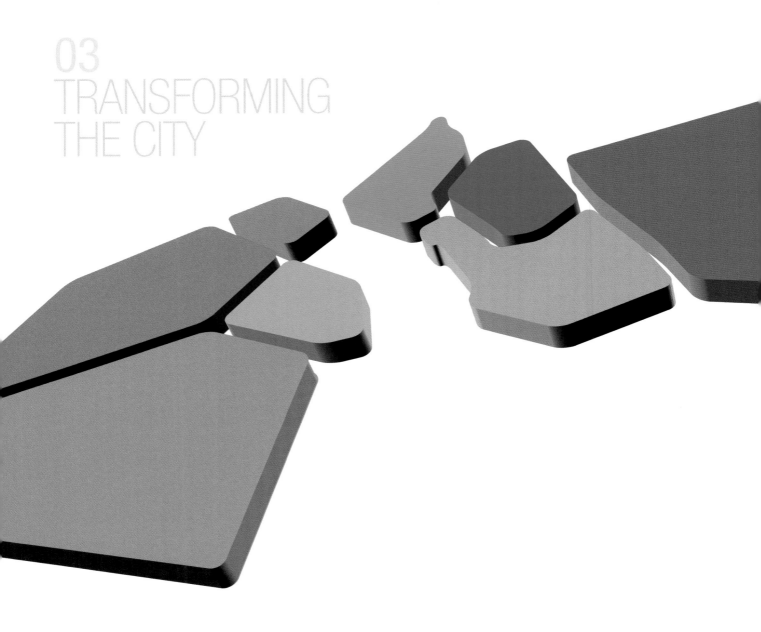

03
TRANSFORMING
THE CITY

CASTLEFIELD

HULME

GREAT NORTHERN INITIATIVE

NORTHERN QUARTER

CITY CENTRE RENEWAL AREA
AND MILLENNIUM QUARTER

PICCADILLY INITIATIVE

NEW EAST MANCHESTER

SPINNINGFIELDS

CASTLEFIELD: The regeneration of historic Castlefield is the result of innovative public-private partnerships and positive planning. It is one of the most exciting areas of the city today.

HULME: The redesign of Hulme set a new standard in inner-city renewal, which became a blueprint for regeneration initiatives throughout the UK.

GREAT NORTHERN INITIATIVE: An area rich in history that today is a world-class conference and leisure destinantion. The new quarter has had a fundamental impact on the economic profile of the city.

NORTHERN QUARTER: An 18th and 19th-century trading centre, an entertainment area and a shopping district – now redefined as a vibrant creative quarter for artists and new media. Independent shops, loft apartments housed in traditional warehouses, and bohemian cafés characterise the area.

CITY CENTRE RENEWAL AREA AND MILLENNIUM QUARTER: A terrorist act in 1996 provided the opportunity to rebuild and dramatically transform the city centre. Multi-skilled, collaborative work delivered a bold and complex project of the highest quality within a remarkably short time-frame.

PICCADILLY INITIATIVE: A key gateway since the early 1800s, revitalised for Manchester's 2002 Commonwealth Games. The remodelled Piccadilly Station and Piccadilly Gardens complement, and reinforce, adjacent regeneration initiatives.

NEW EAST MANCHESTER: Sport has been the driver for change in East Manchester and has served to deliver one of the most complex regeneration initiatives in the UK. The area now has a new sense of place.

SPINNINGFIELDS: The creation of a new city business quarter, one of the largest of its kind in Europe. Private/public partnership is delivering radical economic and physical change within the city centre.

CASTLEFIELD

3.1

The scale and vision of one of the city's earliest regeneration schemes has dramatically transformed the neglected area of historic Castlefield into one of the most attractive and visited parts of the city. The strategic plans for the area restored and conserved the historic district after it had fallen into decay in the 1960s, developing it as a dynamic area for leisure and tourism. The need to diversify the district's activities was addressed by introducing residential and office accommodation. New walkways and bridges linked it to the city-centre core and reduced its isolation.

Nearly 2,000 years ago, the Romans founded a settlement in Mamucium at a site which later became known as the birthplace of Manchester – Castlefield. Its name 'Castle-in-the-Field' dates back more than 400 years. Very little development took place there until the 1700s when it began to increase in importance, developing as a manufacturing centre and market town. To transport coal, a canal was initiated in 1759 and, as the forerunner of all subsequent working canals, the first stage of the Duke of Bridgewater's Canal was completed in 1762 and carried coal to Manchester from Worsley. As Manchester flourished throughout the mid-1890s, Castlefield grew in status owing to Victorian transport links that were developed to support the city's industries.

In 1830 the Liverpool and Manchester Railway opened on Liverpool Road. The rail link, together with the canal system, was instrumental in the growth of Manchester's industrial base in the 19th century. During the late 1800s, at least four railway lines were laid across the Castlefield Basin and, as new railway companies needed to reach the city centre through largely built-up areas, viaducts were built to carry traffic over the city.

Castlefield was a thriving township up to 1900. Then known as Knott Mill, it became home to a community of educated people who built shops, schools, churches and hospitals. With the steady decline in rail and canal transport owing to changes in industry, Castlefield became an area of economic decline in the 1950s and 1960s. By the 1970s, buildings had become dilapidated, piles of scrap metal and cars littered the land, and

fig 3.1
Castlefield
viaduct

fig 3.2
Building new
homes

3.2

the canal arms had become clogged and dirty. The only growing activity in the area at this time was Granada TV which moved to the area in 1956 and occupied warehouses and a newly constructed building.

By the late 1970s, the City Council had already anticipated the potential for regeneration of the area based on its waterways, the railway structures and the remaining warehouses. As a result, Castlefield was designated a Conservation Area in 1979 which gave rise to the opportunity to preserve historic landmarks and to carry out improvements to the environment. Archaeological excavations in the early 1970s had uncovered part of the site of the Roman settlement, and the Council pressed forward with the vision of a critical mass of visitor attractions. The Museum of Science and Industry opened in 1983 on the site of the Liverpool Road Station. Visitors were drawn to the area to visit the Roman and museum attractions and, even more so, when Granada TV opened Granada Studio Tours in 1988 as a response to viewers' interest in the company's productions. So successful were the tours that Granada TV converted old riverside warehouses into the Meridien Victoria and Albert Hotel (1992) with rooms themed according to individual television productions.

The City Council continued to capitalise on the uniqueness of Castlefield, which was designated Britain's first Urban Heritage Park in 1982. Its wealth of industrial heritage in the form of railway viaducts and canal systems together with museums, waterside pubs, walks and boat trips redefined the area. The project, which developed over a period of years, consisted of many partnerships and a constant programme to deliver additional attractions and amenities. The aim was to expand visitor opportunities and preserve and highlight the area's heritage.

In 1988 the newly established Central Manchester Development Corporation (CMDC), working in partnership with Manchester City Council, developed a regeneration programme for Castlefield based on the 1984 City Centre Local Plan, to further develop leisure and tourism and to diversify the economic base of the area. There was a need to create a more favourable climate for private-sector investment in Castlefield and CMDC grants were used to clean up the canals, open up disused canal arms, acquire land in order to carry out environmental improvements, and upgrade

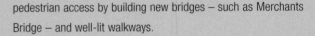

3.3

pedestrian access by building new bridges – such as Merchants Bridge – and well-lit walkways.

As positive public-sector commitment to the area became clearly visible, private-sector entrepreneurs identified investment opportunities and saw value in restoring existing buildings such as Eastgate, once a ragmop factory and now transformed into offices. Warehouses were brought back into use as apartments, offices, restaurants and bars, and the area flourished in the 1990s. The combination of high-quality designer café-bars, a vibrant evening economy and the newly found waterfront made Castlefield the chic place to be. The area continues to develop, and new-build such as Timber Wharf is extending the district's boundary.

As part of the renewal of the Castlefield site, an outdoor arena was built for staging events. It sits overlooking Canal Arms, and captures the feel of an open theatre as in Roman times. Its modern design which is simple and elegant fits well with the surrounding landscape and has been the focal point for many city celebrations including the annual Castlefied Carnival and Manchester's celebrations for the new millennium.

Castlefield is where evidence is still visible of the four important periods in the city's history: the Roman settlement, 18th-century canals, 19th-century Victorian railways, and modern tourism. The regeneration of Castlefield is an example of successful public-private partnership and positive planning. The developments are significant and include the reclamation of a brownfield site, preservation of a historical resource and reuse of buildings. Additionally, the rising numbers of visitors in the city can enjoy the attractions of Castlefield.

fig 3.3
Dukes '92 pub

fig 3.4
Deansgate Quay

3.4

A measure of the success of the regenerated Conservation Area is the influence it has exerted on adjacent parts of the city centre, where conversions of existing buildings and new-build are having a significant impact on the economic well-being of the regional capital.

To illustrate the regeneration of this historic site, case studies include Eastgate, Merchants Bridge and Timber Wharf.

Our adventurous developer client, coupled with a building that already had a strong personality, has allowed us the opportunity to make a place with which the occupants can identify.

EASTGATE

STEPHENSON BELL ARCHITECTS

Castle Street, Manchester

Construction Value: £1.9 million
Completion Date: Spring 1992

Description
Renovation of a five-storey building, 60m long and 10m wide.

History
A former tarpaulin works, built in the 19th-century, it lies between the Rochdale Canal and the Bridgewater Canal in Castlefield and was in poor condition. The building comprised load-bearing masonry and massive timber beams at 2.5m centres spanning between external walls. During its lifetime, due to new and heavier storage requirements, two steel columns per beam were added. There were varying degrees of wet and dry rot in the building and the floor undulated by up to 100mm. Our task was to create 'studio offices' suitable for the artistic end of the working community.

We established that the structure could take the loads required, that the main timber beams had sufficient cross-sectional area to provide fire protection by sacrificial burning and that we would be able to preserve the visual integrity of the steelwork by sandblasting, followed by a careful application of intumescent paint. New plasterboard to the underside of floors and a suspended floor over the top of the existing floor provided floor-to-floor fire protection as well as a level surface.

Design process
The policy we pursued in trying to satisfy the brief was one of careful restoration combined with clear contemporary expression of new uses where appropriate. As found, Eastgate was without an entrance. Our new projecting entrance uses the line of the east wall of the Roman fort that once stood on this site.

Project sign-off
Institutional office space is almost always created for unknown end users and, in consequence, is bland and anonymous. Our adventurous developer client, coupled with a building that already had a strong personality, has allowed us the opportunity to make a place with which the occupants can identify.

58

59

PHOTOS: JAN CHLEBIK

60

PHOTO: ROGER STEPHENSON

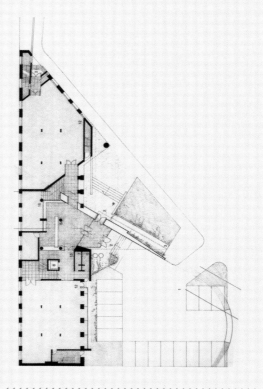

EASTGATE

PROJECT TEAM

Client: **Mark Addy Limited**
Architect: **Stephenson Bell**
Services Engineer: **John Troughear Associates**
Structural Engineer: **Buro Happold**
Contractor: **Fairclough Building & Jackson Construction**
Quantity Surveyor: **Simon Fenton Partnership**

The image desired was that the public were lightly cradled,
as if on the tips of the fingers of an upturned hand.

MERCHANTS BRIDGE
WHITBYBIRD

Spanning the Bridgewater Canal at its junction with the Rochdale Canal, Manchester

Construction Value: £416 thousand
Completion Date: June 1995

Description
This bridge was a product of a design competition and spans the point at which the Bridgewater and Rochdale Canals join.

History
The site is a unique and inspirational location. At ground level the Bridgewater and Rochdale canals join. Over this rides the competing system of railways, which look down on the site of the bridge. Both bridges and canals curve and provide a dramatic backdrop to the new structure.

Client's brief
'The new bridge, as distinct from its predecessors, should be unambiguously a design representative of the late 20th century which will contribute another stratum to the historic layering, which is a feature of Castlefield, and which will reflect the changing pattern of uses that the area is now undergoing.'

Design process
The constraints of the site were analysed as being:
> The wish to not inhibit views of the area from the bridge
> Tight landing zones on either side
> Strict clearance requirements over the canal
> Full disabled access
> Costs

The levels of the ground on both sides of the canal, in conjunction with the clearance requirement, meant that ramps would be needed to get up and over the water. The need to keep the ramps to the minimum for cost and limited land availability led to a requirement that the structure be as thin as possible, i.e. an extra 100mm on the thickness would have led to an extra 2m of ramp each end. The site constraints and the desired lines of pedestrian movement suggested a curved route.

These constraints, combined with the client's brief, and the need to not enclose the public in a structural cage as they crossed over such a wonderful space, implied the final unique structural form.

Using the curved route that is the deck as a torsion box it is possible to support the bridge from a single inclined arch, which in itself is supported by the deck; two mutually compatible structural systems.

Inclining the arch away from the deck counterbalanced the deck, which curves in the opposite direction and developed a sculptural quality to what is, in all respects, a functional bridge. The image desired was that the public were lightly cradled, as if on the tips of the fingers of an upturned hand, rather that contained, as so often with bridges, within a cage of structure.

Engineering has advanced over the last 100 years and our bridge was designed to epitomise this. The computer age makes it possible to combine structural systems that are interdependent, which in any past ages would have been impractical or even impossible to achieve from the viewpoint of analytical effort.

Finite element analysis and 3-d modelling packages came together to make this bridge possible. The bridge is truly a design representative of the late 20th century.

The competition was held at the beginning of 1994. Detailed design happened during the rest of 1994 and the steelwork was fabricated and erected in early 1995. The bridge was open in mid-1995.

Project sign-off
We feel we satisfied the client's aspirations and have provided a bridge that is much used and loved, and has been key to the regeneration of the area.

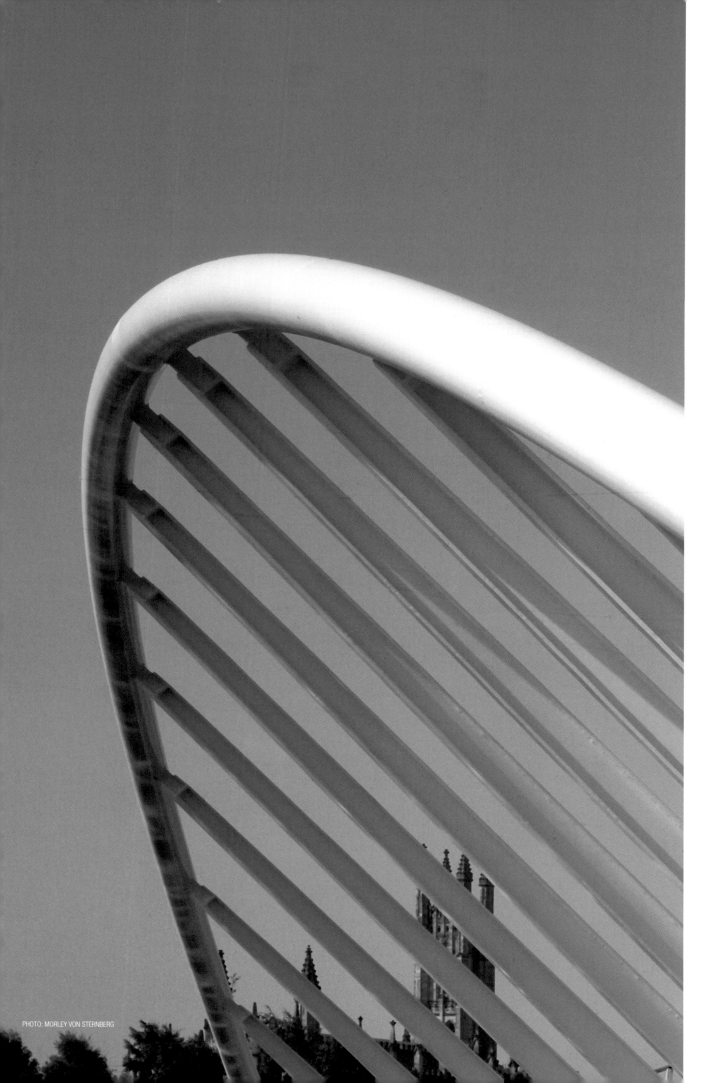

63

PHOTO: MORLEY VON STERNBERG

PHOTO: LEN GRANT

PAINTING: RICHARD CARMAN

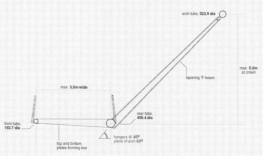

arch tube, **323.9 dia**

max **5.0m**
at crown

tapering 'T'-beam

max **3.0m wide**

rear tube,
406.4 dia

front tube,
193.7 dia

top and bottom
plates forming box

hangers @ 45°
plane of arch 63°

MERCHANTS BRIDGE

PROJECT TEAM

Client: **Central Manchester Development Corporation**
Owner: **Peel Holdings** (Manchester Ship Canal Company)
Designer: **Whitbybird** (then named Whitby & Bird)
Quantity Surveyor: **Davis Langdon**
Steelwork Fabricator: **Watson Steel**

Timber Wharf provides a very strong,
clear identity and achieves optimum
quality of space.

TIMBER WHARF
GLENN HOWELLS ARCHITECTS

Worsley Street, Manchester

Construction Value: £14.8 million
Completion Date: July 2002

Description
Timber Wharf is a nine-storey residential building of precast
concrete crosswall construction, containing 181 apartments and
live-work units at ground floor level.

History
Timber Wharf occupies a site bordering the Bridgewater Canal
and is part of the industrial Britannia Basin/St George's area.
This area already houses Britannia Mills and Box Works, previous
schemes by the developer. It was envisaged that Timber Wharf
would further enhance this new residential and working
community in an area previously home to derelict factories and
warehouses.

Client's brief
An international competition was launched in 1998. The brief
sought to redefine high-density urban housing in the UK,
achieving contemporary designed apartments with a budget
comparable to volume housebuilders.

Design process
Timber Wharf is characterised by a rhythmic layered façade of
full-height natural anodised glazed screens and glazed
balconies, interrupted by a 9-storey off-centred glazed atrium
which forms the principal circulation core for the building.
Corridors from the atrium lead to the apartment entrances, the
palette of concrete, slate chippings and timber are congruous
with the design intent of the building.

The precast concrete crosswall system was designed on a
continuous 6m grid, yet was flexible enough to generate 9
different apartment configurations. These range from small 1-
bay single-aspect units through to larger double-aspect duplex
units at ground floor, used for offices, retail or residential
occupation. Each of these units enjoys a street frontage,
intended to further animate the area.

Within the 181 units, particular attention was paid to the quality
of materials and detailing. The penthouses have a higher
specification of finishes (additional iroko and slate flooring and
granite worktops), although a consistency throughout the

scheme was sought. All apartments have 2650mm high ceilings
and full-height internal doors and all bedrooms and living rooms
have balconies. Electrical sockets and communications are
mostly located within the floor.

The high quality construction components, including factory-
produced concrete wall panels and bespoke glazing systems,
were developed specially for the project. These elements were
subject to strict financial control and delivered through liaison
with the manufacturers and subcontractors at the outset of the
project and throughout the design process. The factory
production of the principal components of the building also
permitted a highly rationalised, fast track construction where the
fit-out was commenced on lower levels as the superstructure
was progressed on upper floors.

Landscape treatment
After the competition, the siting of Timber Wharf relative to the
Bridgewater Canal (a key green route to the city centre), was
reassessed leaving a triangular terraced garden between the
building and the towpath. The towpath gate provides direct
secure access to the canal for the use of all residents. The
landscaped communal gardens running alongside the canal
bring a sense of tranquility rarely available in city-centre
developments.

The natural fall in height between Worsley Street and the canal
advantageously enabled the creation of a naturally ventilated
two-storey basement car park. Cars descend into the car park at
the junction of Arundel Street and Worsley Street, thus minimising
the visual impact of vehicles on site. The well-lit car park also
provides secure cycle storage, recycling facilities and direct
access into the dramatic fully glazed nine-storey circulation core.

Details and materials for the communal gardens are borrowed
from the main building to achieve consistency throughout the site.
The linear bamboo planters provide a visual filter between the
ground-floor-unit terraces and the undulating lawns, which offer
generous recreation space. Non-discriminating access throughout
the garden is also provided in parallel by ramps and steps. An
ongoing programme of artwork installation across the site seeks to
reinforce the elegant simplicity and urban context of the scheme.

URBAN SPLASH

PHOTO: ROD DORLING

PHOTO: URBAN SPLASH

PHOTO: ROD DORLING

Project sign-off

Timber Wharf challenges everyday preconceptions of what housing should be like, achieving optimum quality of space and materials within a modest budget comparable to the volume housebuilders' product. The robust structure provides a very clear strong identity, creating a form which is not immediately recognisable as housing but instead continues the scale and simplicity of an industrial aesthetic, consistent with its surroundings. The project is high density, achieving 367 dwellings per hectare on a derelict brownfield site in inner-city Manchester. However, each unit enjoys external balcony or terrace space, and a generous shared garden with direct access to the Bridgewater Canal. A brief journey along the towpath allows residents access to Metrolink, its route leading through Castlefield to Manchester City Centre and the new cultural facilities at Salford Quays.

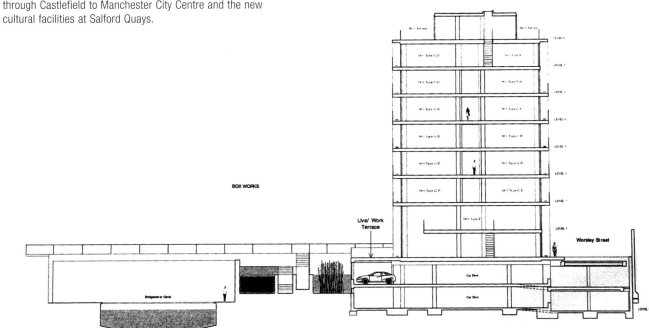

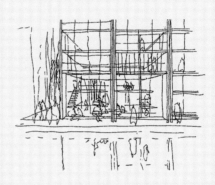

TIMBER WHARF

PROJECT TEAM

Client: **Urban Splash**

Main Contractor: **Urban Splash**

Architect: **Glenn Howells Architects**

Quantity Surveyor: **Simon Fenton Partnership**

Structural Engineer: **Martin Stockley Associates**

Concept Structural Design: **DTA Consultants**
(Competition Stage)

Services Engineer: **Buro Happold**

Landscape Consultants: **Hyland Edgar Driver** (Canalside
Gardens) and **Landscape Projects** (Worsley Street)

HULME

The redevelopment of Hulme has
resulted in one of the most advanced
approaches to inner-city regeneration in
the UK. It is frequently cited as an
example of best practice in creating a
sustainable urban community, and one
in which high-quality design and
positive planning were key drivers in
the programme.

3.5

Hulme in the early 1800s was mostly fields, but with the
rapid increase in the number of factories during
Manchester's industrial and manufacturing era housing for
the working class became essential. Artisan dwellings
sprang up, and by 1851 the district of Hulme had a
population of 53,000. By 1901, the population figures had
risen to 130,000, with many families occupying
overcrowded terraced housing. The area suffered from post-
war depression, and many dwellings, which had become
uninhabitable, were knocked down. In 1934 the district of
Hulme was declared a Clearance Area, but demolition was
not completed until 1960 as a result of other priorities
following World War II.

In the 1960s, razed buildings made way for high-rise towers
and deck-access blocks, the most well-known of which
were the four 'Crescents'. These properties suffered from
chronic damp, condensation and vermin infestation owing to
industrial slab construction, lack of insulation and poor
roofing. A survey conducted in 1975 revealed that 96.3 per
cent of tenants wanted to leave the Crescents. Families
asked to move as severe social problems grew, resulting in
a principally single and shifting population. In the late 1970s
almost half of Manchester's inhabitants lived in council-
rented accommodation, as compared with the national
average of 29 per cent – and a large number of those lived
in Hulme. The area was a drain on stretched Council
resources. In 1986, 69 per cent of adult males in Hulme
were unemployed and the City Council, after moving families

fig 3.5
Inclusive
consultation

fig 3.6
New business
opportunities at
Birleyfields

3.6

to other parts of the city, used the Crescents for housing young childless couples, single people and students.

The area had been the focus of a number of studies as the Council sought to address its physical decline and the social deprivation experienced by its residents. In 1991, the then Environment Secretary, Michael Heseltine, announced the City Challenge programme which offered financial aid to partnerships between local authorities, private-sector firms and community groups to regenerate inner-city areas. The money was awarded through a competitive bidding process and, in April 1992, Hulme City Challenge was launched with £37.5 million.

An arms-length dedicated team of private and public-sector personnel came together under Hulme Regeneration Ltd to develop and manage the City Challenge programme for Hulme. AMEC was appointed as a partner to bring in private-sector knowledge and expertise. Mills Beaumont Leavy became lead design consultants. A key element of the scheme was the re-provision of rented homes for those affected by demolition. This then acted as a magnet for the first ever build-for-sale scheme in Hulme.

The job of Hulme Regeneration Ltd was to combine the efforts of public, private, voluntary and community organisations in strategies to promote economic revival and improve the quality of life. The team developed a holistic approach to urban regeneration and worked to improve the environment; to enhance existing housing, and to build new homes; to tackle crime and vandalism; and to provide jobs, training and leisure for local people. A total of 50 hectares was cleared and replaced with 3,000 new homes, offices and community facilities within the five-year programme. Hulme Regeneration Ltd, at the request of the council-funded tenants' association – Hulme Tenants Participation Project – introduced a phased work approach, which eased the re-housing programme. This approach also led to a sense of continuity, by balancing physical change with stability whilst work was undertaken. It awarded developers the opportunity to learn from experience as each phase was completed. A new model for co-operative social housing was developed with Homes for Change, a housing scheme designed

3.7

with full participation from the community that stands today on the site of the demolished Crescents. On the same site is Rolls Crescent, a residential scheme designed to promote a sense of community. Both schemes are high-quality designs that captured the spirit of a new Hulme.

In 1991 a masterplan for Hulme was introduced and a coherent vision for the area sought. The regeneration team sought to create the appropriate framework in which new development could fit, tenants could be involved and could actively influence decisions and, through high-quality design and confidence in delivery, investors would be drawn to the high-quality urban environment. Following intensive community consultation and numerous meetings with architects and developers, a document was prepared to deliver a sustainable urban neighbourhood. The physical redevelopment was steered by an innovative design guide, *The Guide to Development in Hulme*, published in 1994. This not only directed the delivery of what today is heralded as an example of best practice in inner-city community regeneration, but it was a guide that later was developed to provide a city-wide document.

Since the completion of the City Challenge programme in 1997, the Moss Side and Hulme Partnership (MSHP) managed the continuing regeneration of the area to achieve sustainable economic renewal and to build a competitive inner-city economy. The partnership oversaw the area's various funding programmes including the Moss Side Single Regeneration Budget (SRB) programme (£20 million), the European Urban Community

fig 3.7
New housing
around Chichester
Street

fig 3.8
Pavement cafes
in the new Hulme

3.8

Initiative Programme (£5.39 million) and European Union (EU) Objective 2 Structural Funds (£4 million). Alongside the partnership, the Moss Side and Hulme Agency for Economic Development was established to integrate and improve economic opportunities for the local community and local businesses, and more than £400 million of private and public-sector investment has been levered into the area by the MSHP.

With changes in the local economy and increased levels of economic activity, a number of ambitious regeneration initiatives have taken place. The new bridge that links Hulme to the city centre, Hulme Arch Bridge (1997), is a dramatic architectural landmark spanning Princess Parkway, a major arterial route from the city centre to the main motorway network and Manchester Airport. Along the Princess Road Corridor, shops have been refurbished and frontages renewed as befits a major gateway to the south of the city. Hulme Park is the first large-scale park created in the city since the 19th century, and it provides a safe communal environment in an area previously notorious for crime. A new business park has been built on the site of Birley Fields which has attracted jobs and businesses to the area.

Hulme was the first of the city's area-based regeneration projects and its success became the blueprint for other regeneration initiatives not only within Manchester but in other inner-city areas throughout the UK. The project signified a new era in Manchester's renaissance which strives to make the city a place in which people choose to work and live.

To illustrate Hulme renewal, case studies include Homes for Change, Hulme Arch Bridge, Rolls Crescent and Hulme Park.

A landmark building that is a beacon for change and a
catalyst for social integration and tolerance.

HOMES FOR CHANGE

MBLC

41 Old Birley Street, Manchester
Completion Date: October 1996

Description
A new-build development on a site of 0.63ha of brownfield land
previously used as a brewery.

History
In 1991, Michael Hestletine, then Secretary of State for the
Environment, announced City Challenge. This provided the
potential for the comprehensive redevelopment of an area of the
city that was blighted by 1960s system-built housing. As part of
an overall strategic framework, the site on Old Birley Street was
identified for medium-rise mixed-use development.

Client's brief
A partnership was formed between The Guinness Trust and two
co-operatives, Homes for Change and Work for Change.

The members of the two co-operatives sought a home for their
mixed-use community, providing 50 apartments and duplexes
ranging from one to four bedrooms, together with 1500m² for
studios, workshops, a theatre, gallery, café and retail space, all
to be developed with a varied range of outdoor space.

Design process
The founding principle of Homes for Change is to create a place
for people to successfully be together. The project has come to
life through the collective energy of educated, ecologically
minded, diverse people, most of whom were young Hulme
residents all with a very firm but disparate set of ideas on how
they wanted to live together following the rebuilding of Hulme.
The evolution of the community to include young families and
older residents is a testament to the building's success in
catering for all lifestyles.

Following the creation of a detailed functional brief defining
numbers of dwellings and types, along with the range of varied
uses for the non-residential space, a series of design workshops
was organised to develop the design through the active
involvement of the future occupants. A range of model-making
techniques was used to give hands-on opportunities to

investigate the height, scale, massing and orientation of the
building with its integrated social spaces. When it came to the
apartment layouts themselves, these were constructed full size
in card to allow a clear understanding of the scale of living
space. On such a relatively small site, geometrical shifts to
lengthen views across the courtyard spaces by, in some cases,
up to ten metres have been imaginatively used. There is an
abundant variety of dwelling types – from four-bedroom family
homes, sensibly located at ground level and with small semi-
private gardens, to one-bedroom attic duplexes with open gallery
bedrooms and private sun-trap terraces. The vertical and
horizontal connections provide social linkages in a stepped
terrace arrangement, taking the best aspects of the old deck
access in terms of giving opportunity for informal meeting,
dialogue and interaction yet overcoming the problem of dark,
insecure walkways. Along these 'links' is a diversity of amenity
space located at different levels within the building, diluting its
denseness. These spaces range from large grass roof terraces
all the way down through paved patios to intimate balconies and
delicate cantilevered suntraps.

The building is innovative in a number of areas, both in terms of
the design of the structure and a highly demanding sustainability
brief. It has to be recognised that this level of innovation has
brought challenges that have had to be overcome through the
work of the architects, the construction process and in the
management of the building maintenance. The main structure for
the walls, floor and roofs is a combination of precast and *in situ*
concrete, providing the extremely smooth pre-finished walls
throughout the scheme which allows residents to make a feature
of the raw concrete finish and avoids the need for plastered and
decorated surfaces. The continuous floor-and-wall system gives
the highest possible acoustic separation between dwellings and,
vitally, ensures the privacy of the tenants.

A highly demanding sustainability brief incorporating 21
environmental targets has been met, such as halving normal
carbon dioxide emissions, minimising embodied energy (concrete
ballast from adjacent demolished building, concrete building

PHOTO: ANNE WORTHINGTON

blocks with 80% recycled material and locally produced materials to reduce transport costs), on-site recycling, maximising passive solar gain, reducing car use and promoting the bicycle through to investigating grey-water recycling and encouraging biodiversity by maximising flora and fauna in the courtyard and on the green roofs.

The horseshoe-shaped courtyard created by phase 1 has since been completed, by Harrison Ince and Build for Change, to form the secure unified block of the original vision. Architecturally the building is a landmark within this now vibrant neighbourhood. It is a beacon for change and a catalyst for social integration and tolerance.

Project sign-off

The reshaping of Manchester as it is now perceived owes much to Hulme where MBLC have guided development for over ten years as masterplanners. Homes for Change, the recipient of multiple awards, was at the beginning of the Manchester urban and architectural renaissance and the level of innovation attempted on this project – both architectural and social – means that there are many lessons to be learnt. In this respect the experience and value of the project goes far wider than the regeneration of Hulme, offering a model for urban living that addresses many of the issues that have arisen as we attempt to achieve the 'renaissance' of our cities.

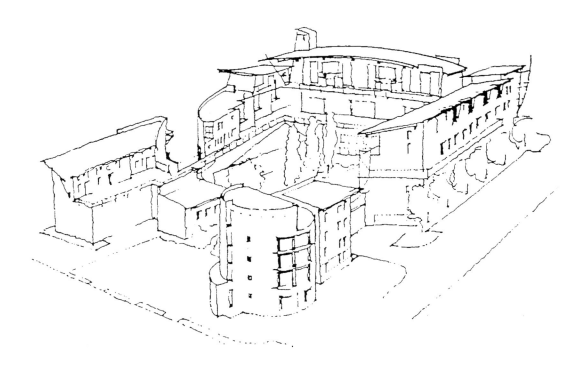

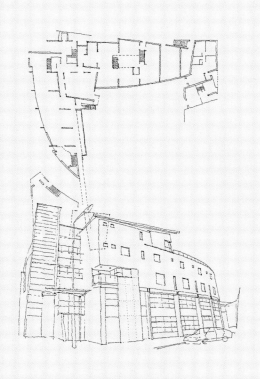

HOMES FOR CHANGE

PROJECT TEAM

Client: **The Guiness Trust**

Architect: **MBLC**

Structural Engineer: **Anthony Hunt & Associates**

Services Engineer: **Steven Hunt & Associates**

Quantity Surveyor: **Tweeds**

Landscape Architect: **Jane Parker Landscapes**

Sustainability Consultant: **Urbed/ECD**

Contractor: **Amey Hynd**

Hulme Arch Bridge forms a landmark on the
main approach to Manchester City Centre.

HULME ARCH BRIDGE
WILKINSON EYRE ARCHITECTS

Stretford Road/Princess Road, Manchester

Construction Value: £2 million
Completion Date: May 1997

Description
An award-winning road bridge connecting a regenerated
community and spanning a major route into Manchester city
centre.

History
Hulme had previously been bisected by a main road into
Manchester city centre for those travelling from the south of the
city and the airport. The new bridge acts as a landmark,
reinforcing the continuity of Stretford Road as it passes over the
Princess Road cutting. It forms a gateway for drivers on both
routes and reunites the community.

Client's brief
The re-establishment of Hulme's former main route is a key
factor in its renewal programme. It had been physically cut in
two by the Princess Road cutting and the brief was therefore for
a bridge to rejoin the two halves. At the same time it would
identify the community with a landmark structure.

Design process
The design features a bridge deck (carrying Stretford Road
traffic) that is supported by cables from a single arch above. The
arch gives the bridge mass and presence, spanning diagonally
across Stretford Road and over Princess Road in the cutting
below, simultaneously providing a gateway in both directions.
The parabolic arch naturally maximises the height in relation to
the relatively modest span of the bridge. Its form, along with a
tapering section and the choice of a reflective material, achieves
a strong visual impact and promotes the structure as an
important landmark for this area.

The bridge is a cable-stayed structure, the bridge deck
supported indirectly from the 25m high arch. Trapezoidal in
section, the steel arch tapers in opposite directions in plan and
elevation. The shiny surface is lit at night and is visible from afar
on both roads.

The two sets of cables that support either side of the 50m long
bridge deck are arranged to interlock and overlap, visually
uniting the two banks and the two halves of Hulme. Tensioned
cables, connecting the bridge deck to the arch, fan out in

opposing directions to resemble a 'cat's cradle' which changes
in complexity and disposition according to the position of the
viewer. By positioning the arch and distributing the cables in this
manner, the structure combines the symmetrical and the
asymmetrical. Visual complexity is achieved from geometric
simplicity.

The steel decking was assembled in the central reservation of
Princess Road below, and was craned into position in three
17m x 17m sections during one weekend. The bridge arch was
prefabricated in six sections for transportation to site and welded
there to form 'halves', which were then installed into their final
position by a tandem lift.

The project has won many awards, including:

> RIBA Award for Architecture, 1998
> Structural Steel Design Awards Commendation, 1998
> Civic Trust Award Commendation, 1998
> Institution of Civil Engineers Merit Award, 1998

Project sign-off
The Hulme Arch Bridge was the culmination of five years
intensive regeneration work in this inner-city community.
With the road link between All Saints and Stretford severed a
generation ago, the bridge represents a new start for a
reconnected area and is an elegant, optimistic and inspirational
symbol for the future. It also represents Hulme on a wider stage,
forming a landmark on the main approach to Manchester city
centre through the area.

79

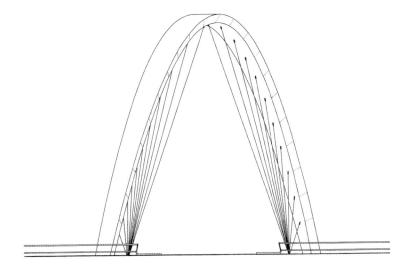

80

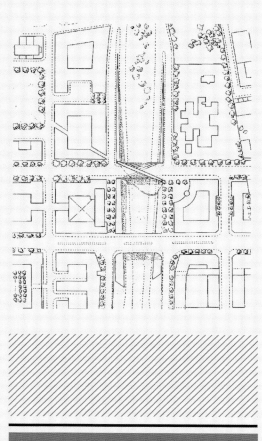

HULME ARCH BRIDGE

PROJECT TEAM

Client: **Hulme Regeneration Ltd /
Manchester City Council**

Architect: **Wilkinson Eyre Architects**

Structural Engineer: **Arup**

Cost Consultant: **Arup**

Contractor: **Henry Boot Limited**

Steelwork Subcontractor: **Watson Steel**

The project has a strong 'urban' presence and the robust materials specified are standing the test of time.

ROLLS CRESCENT
ECD ARCHITECTS

Hulme, Manchester

Construction Value: £4 million
Completion Date: July 1997

Description
This development consisted of 67 new houses for Places for People (formerly North British Housing Association). All the accommodation is for rent and includes a wide range of 2,3,4 and 5-bedroom family houses as well as four 2-bedroom wheelchair bungalows.

History
The site was previously occupied by the curved deck-access 'Crescent' blocks, which were demolished to make way for the new development. It is located in the southern part of the masterplan for Hulme which aimed to re-establish a traditional pattern of streets and urban blocks. Immediately to the south is the Royce County Primary School, a single-storey building, and to the north two-storey terraced housing for sale.

Client's brief
In common with many other schemes in Hulme, the briefing and design process involved close consultation with existing residents of the area. In this case the design team conducted one-to-one interviews with over 50 residents in order to gain views on the preferred form and layout of the development as well as choice of materials and colours. The brief that emerged was for a development with a strong contemporary and European image, in contrast to the traditional red brick architecture of Manchester. It was during this process of consultation that the idea of courtyards and communal gardens emerged as a basis for community life.

Design process
The initial development site was a plot measuring approximately 225m x 60m deep with access roads to north and south. The first move was to subdivide this into three blocks to improve north-south permeability. The design then followed the Hulme Urban Design Code with perimeter buildings fronting the street and small rear gardens opening onto a communal courtyard. The corners of the blocks are celebrated with three-storey elements with distinctive curved metal roofs. The design enables a secure environment for courtyards within the individual courtyards and a high degree of visual surveillance of the public realm. All car parking, with the exception of car ports for wheelchair dwellings, are on-street. The density is 54 dwellings per hectare (233 habitable rooms per hectare). Construction is of traditional load-bearing masonry with facing brickwork at ground level and coloured render on upper levels. The roofing material is silver standing-seam aluminium.

Orientation of dwellings was considered to ensure maximum benefit of the southerly aspect. Bedrooms and living rooms face south along the north boundary whilst three-storey houses were designed on the south boundary with first-floor living rooms facing south. High standards of thermal insulation were incorporated in external walls and roofs, in excess of then current Building Regulations. Ventilation was achieved using whole-house passivents with humidity control. The process began with appointment in 1994, moving to design and planning the following year and construction during 1996 and 1997.

Project sign-off
The project has a strong 'urban' presence and the robust materials specified are standing the test of time. The scale and intimacy of the courtyards has resulted in a good community spirit and the houses are clearly well liked by residents.

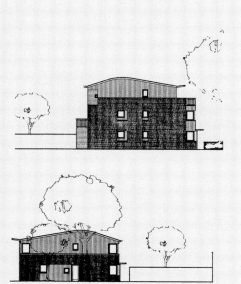

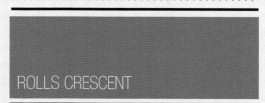

ROLLS CRESCENT

PROJECT TEAM

Client: **North British Housing Association** (Places for People)
Architect: **ECD Architects**
Structural Engineer: **Curtins**
Employer's Agent: **Poole Stokes Wood** (now Davis Langdon)
Design and Build Contractor: **Cruden Construction**

PHOTOS: MARTINE HAMILTON KNIGHT

A show-piece for Hulme, providing
modern and attractive facilities and a
safe and friendly environment.

HULME PARK
LANDSCAPE PROJECTS

Hulme Park, Manchester
Construction Value: £2.67 million
Completion Date: March 2001

Description
A new park forming the primary public open space in the new
urban district of Hulme; provides a place for sports, play, passive
recreation and meeting, and a focus for community events.

History
Hulme Park is located in the heart of new Hulme, overlooked by
the Zion Arts Centre, Royce Road School and Proctors' Youth
Centre. Previously the site had been built over, firstly by Victorian
suburban streets, and later by the infamous 'Crescents', blocks
of flats and maisonettes. The first Rolls Royce Silver Ghost was
built on this site.

Client's brief
The extensive brief for the project was developed through careful
community consultation and planning workshops. The park was
to be a show-piece for Hulme, providing modern and attractive
facilities, simple-to-maintain spaces that would be inclusive and
sustainable, and above all provide a safe and friendly
environment for residents and visitors from the city centre.

Design process
The regeneration of Hulme in the late 1990s grew out of a
fundamental reassessment of the role of public spaces and streets
as the underpinning for the new community. Instead of an excess
of meaningless and undifferentiated green space, new Hulme
would have specific parks and gardens, overlooked and
conveniently connected to surrounding streets. Hulme Park was to
be the largest of these and is some 4ha in extent. It stretches
800m, from the Mancunian Way on the edge of the city centre to
the Stretford Road, the primary east-west route through the district.

Open space in Hulme has had a troubled history. For many it
was where crime and anti-social behaviour took place. The
design of the park had to demonstrate from day one that open
space could be safe and enjoyable and build people's confidence
in using the park. The design is therefore mostly open, with wide
lawns and tree groups in a central band allowing easy short-cuts
and avoiding hidden corners. The park boundary is clearly
marked by a distinctive low wall and horizontal railing, with plentiful

entrances providing convenient short-cuts from the shops to the
school, from the library to home. This helps to maximise casual use
of the park and the self-policing that this brings. Activity areas are
grouped in a series of gardens around its perimeter, overlooked by
the streets, to attract passers-by into the park.

The park has two primary pathways: a direct route from Hulme
to the city centre via a new footbridge over the busy Mancunian
Way, known as the Active Walk; and a slower curving path called
the Promenade which edges the lawns and the perimeter
gardens. Secondary paths crisscross throughout the park.
Activities are organized in three distinctive zones (Sports, Play
and Arts), which relate to nearby community uses.

The gardens include places for skateboarding, made of steel and
mesh; a teenage space in the form of a diving pool, made from
plywood, laminated timber and recycled glass; a sensory garden
made from curved gabion walls; a tree garden with bamboo
groundcover; and a small square designed as a market-place.
Two playgrounds are provided: a small, brightly coloured
toddlers' space, and a larger area designed around ideas
generated by local children from the theme of 'Treasure Island'.
A timber mountain with a steep slide, and a spacenet over a
lagoon complete the play area.

The park has a civic character outside the imposing Zion Arts
Centre, where the park provides a large and simple stone
surface for markets and carnivals, and a place for the dance
groups from the arts centre. Lighting and artwork by local artists
is carefully integrated into the design.

Specific places within the park are marked by distinctive
canopies and shelters, such as the curved timber structure over
the teen space, built by a boatbuilder, and an innovative concrete
structure near the market square. Careful thought was given to
the design of a graphic identity for the park, which appears in
signage and walls throughout the site.

The park was constructed in two phases, in which the
infrastructure of walls, railings, paths and drainage were followed
by the detailed gardens, furniture and artworks. This gave time to
develop collaborations with local artists and residents.

PHOTO: LEN GRANT

Project sign-off

Hulme Park was the first to be constructed in city-centre
Manchester for 50 years. The scheme is highly regarded, and
has been frequently cited as a good example of modern park
design. It is now well-established, and beginning to make a
visual contribution to the streetscape of Hulme. The district is
now one of the city's most desirable inner suburbs, with a wide
and cosmopolitan range of residents. The scheme shows that
contemporary parks make an important contribution to any
modern city, but particularly to places like Hulme, where open
space was seen as threatening and problematic. Since its
completion, the project has become an integral part of Hulme. It
is part of the community's way of life, and is now supported by
an active Friends Group, who are continuing to develop new
ideas for the place. The Park won a Civic Trust Award 2000,
and has been cited by the Design Council as an exemplary
project in its publication *"Design out Crime"*.

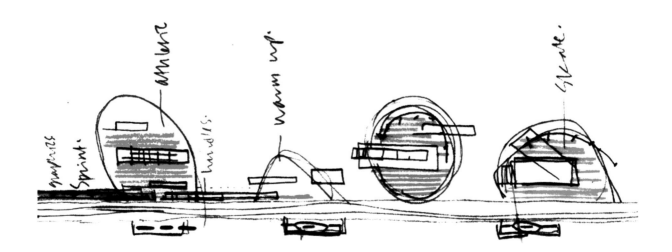

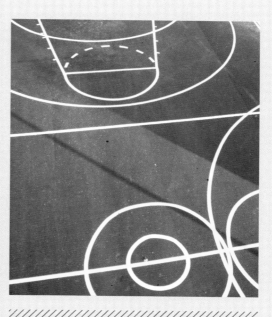

HULME PARK

PROJECT TEAM

Client: **Manchester City Council/Hulme Regeneration Limited/Moss Side and Hulme Partnership**

Landscape Architect: **Landscape Projects**

Architect: **Ian Simpson Architects**

Structural Engineer: **Atelier One, Martin Stockley Associates**

Quantity Surveyor: **Simon Fenton Partnership**

Arts Consultant: **Helen Rudlin/Urbed**

Graphic Designer: **Via Communications**

Building Contractor: **Phases 1&2, P. Casey (Reclamation) Ltd**

Playground Steelwork: **C. Baker & team**

Canopy Construction (Timber): **Miles Boatbuilding**

Canopy Construction (Concrete): **Aura**

GREAT NORTHERN INITIATIVE

3.9

The Great Northern Initiative transformed an inward-looking, derelict, traffic dominated area into a fully-integrated modern district boasting cultural, convention, tourism, leisure, commercial and residential facilities. The 20 hectare site was underused, isolated and neglected, but as a result of many years of integrated planning and private and public-sector partnerships, the physical environment of this southeastern quarter of the city centre has diversified. Today, its components contribute significantly to the economic growth of the city.

The area is a world-class conference and cultural hub that incorporates the Manchester International Convention Centre, G-MEX Centre and Bridgewater Hall. It is linked by public thoroughfares and squares to the visitor attractions in Castlefield and the city-centre retail core. It contains the leisure complex of the Great Northern Experience with a multiplex cinema, adjacent restaurants and bars and, nearby, Deansgate Locks with its conversion of eight railway arches into bars, shops and restaurants. The Crowne Plaza Midland Hotel and the new Radisson Edwardian Manchester on the Free Trade Hall site service the conference and tourism industries. Collectively, these elements dramatically enhance the competitiveness of Manchester within European and global markets.

The area is rich with history. The Central Station Train Shed (1880) and the adjacent Great Northern Railway Warehouse (1898), the Midland Hotel (1903) and the Free Trade Hall (1853) were important locations when Manchester thrived as an industrial and manufacturing centre. The Great Northern Warehouse was originally a three-level transport interchange. At the lowest level was the Manchester and Salford Junction Canal built in 1839 to link the River Irwell and the Manchester, Bolton and Bury Canal to the Rochdale Canal. The waterway continued under Central Station and was used to carry goods to the warehouse and station where they were moved through two lift shafts to warehouse and rail level. At a third level, a ramp connected

fig 3.9
MICC, part of The
Great Northern
Initiative

fig 3.10
Bridgewater Hall

3.10

the warehouse to the highway network. The transport site was noisy and dirty and cut off from surrounding areas by fencing and buildings. Following industrial and manufacturing decline and the closure of Central Station due to transport cutbacks in 1969, the land lay neglected in the 1970s.

Development of Central Station was seen as key to the renewal of the area. Proposals for regeneration put forward the creation of exhibition, cultural and leisure facilities for the station site, commercial facilities in the Great Northern Warehouse and a hotel on the Free Trade Hall site. Outline planning approval for the station was given in 1975 but the project collapsed when the developer went out of business. In 1979, the site was acquired by the Greater Manchester Council (GMC) and – as the result of a joint partnership between GMC, Manchester City Council (MCC) and Commercial Union Properties – regeneration of the site and the adjacent buildings began in 1982. *The City Centre Local Plan* (1984) saw the area as one of the most important opportunities for bringing new activities into the regional centre. It was identified as an area for recreation, exhibition and conference potential – activities that would also act as a catalyst for environmental improvement. The plans were progressed, and in 1986 Central Station became the Greater Manchester Exhibition (G-MEX) Centre.

The Central Manchester Development Corporation (CMDC 1988–96) and the City Council provided the framework to progress schemes within this area. With tourism and leisure acting as a stimulus for regeneration new activities would provide jobs for local people, boost the economy of local businesses and help make the city more attractive. Essential to this vision was the Bridgewater Hall (1996), Manchester's international concert venue, conceived and financed in partnership with Manchester City Council together with substantial backing from the European Regional Development Fund, and delivered on the back of the city's bid for the 2000 Olympics. The funding package gave Manchester a debt-free hall and with a private sector partner appointed as the operating company there was sufficient financial strength to manage the facility without public subsidy. The concert hall, which placed culture at the heart of urban renewal, was one half of a public and private-sector partnership for a scheme that included

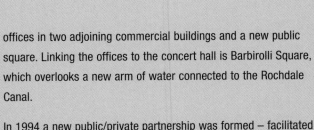

3.11

offices in two adjoining commercial buildings and a new public square. Linking the offices to the concert hall is Barbirolli Square, which overlooks a new arm of water connected to the Rochdale Canal.

In 1994 a new public/private partnership was formed – facilitated by English Partnerships and the City Council – which included CMDC, Merlin International Properties, and G-MEX; Morrison Developments joined the team later. The partnership commissioned a masterplan that produced the Great Northern Warehouse and District Development Strategy in October 1994 which presented the range of uses to be introduced and the development framework for buildings, roads and public spaces. The partnership, underpinned by the masterplan, provided rationalisation of land ownership and gave both confidence to the private sector to invest and the justification for public-sector grant support. The interdependence of the private and public-sector investments was critical to the delivery of every element of the development. When CMDC was disestablished, planning control for the area reverted to the City Council. The Great Northern Experience was given the go-ahead in 1996 and the £100 million development was carried out by Morrison/Merlin in conjunction with MCC and English Partnerships.

The cornerstone of the Great Northern strategy was the Manchester International Convention Centre (MICC), the UK's first purpose-built convention complex linked to an exhibition centre and located in the heart of a city. The £29 million MICC was funded by Manchester City Council, English Partnerships and the European Regional Development Fund and has successfully

fig 3.11
Midland Hotel

fig 3.12
Great Northern
Square

3.12

attracted prestigious national and international conferences.

Opposite MICC, the Free Trade Hall site was being developed as a hotel, and in 1997 Millennium and Copthorne Hotels Group applied for planning permission. A second design was submitted but, following objections, a public inquiry was set up in April 1998. The second design was rejected by the Secretary of State; however a third design was accepted and work started in 2002. The hotel has opened as the Radisson Edwardian Manchester. Linking the hotel, the leisure development and the new bars and restaurants is the Great Northern Square, which opened in 1999. To provide more visitor accommodation for the conference, cultural and leisure services, a dramatic new £150 million, 47-storey glass tower, is set to become the highest living space in the UK. This structure – the Hilton Tower – will feature a 285-bed, five-star hotel to be run by Hilton International with a destination sky bar on the 23rd floor – a city first, which will offer magnificent views across Manchester. The tower will include 219 apartments and penthouses and give an opportunity for 'sky high living'.

There are few examples to be found elsewhere in the region where a single development project, carefully integrated into a holistic approach to redeveloping an entire quarter, has had such a fundamental impact on the economic profile and activities within a city.

To illustrate the interrelated themes and vision for the area, case studies will highlight the Bridgewater Hall, Barbirolli Square and Deansgate Locks; Manchester International Convention Centre; Radisson Edwardian Manchester Hotel and Hilton Tower.

The auditorium has proved to be intimate yet monumental with a fine individual acoustic, much loved by orchestras and soloists.

BRIDGEWATER HALL

RHWL

Lower Mosley Street, Manchester
Construction Value: £32 million
Completion Date: July 1996

Description
Britain's first new stand-alone concert hall since the Royal Festival Hall (1951), the 2,400-seat Bridgewater Hall replaces the existing Free Trade Hall as a concert venue.

History
The City and the Development Corporation jointly launched a developer/architect competition called the 'Bridgewater Initiative' for a new concert hall in the area immediately east of Lower Mosley Street, (then used as a car park), in conjunction with private sector elements potentially to provide cross funding. The surrounding area was ripe for redevelopment with the hall acting as the catalyst for the adjoining sites.

Client's brief
The client required a world-class concert hall for symphonic music as a home for the Hallé, but also to be extensively used by Manchester's other two orchestras, the BBC Philharmonic and the Camerata, together with a range of other musical events. The hall was to be single format with the emphasis on acoustical excellence for orchestral sound, coupled with a new organ. The building needed to be highly accessible both visibly and physically with foyers encouraging a range of uses throughout the day.

Design process
The fundamental relationship between the hall and the city led to the decision to point the public areas back to the city centre, seeking to unite the hall with the town hall and library. The building needed a powerful presence to balance the much larger G-MEX building on the opposite side of Lower Mosley Street. The solution lay in developing the auditorium as a symmetrical stone-clad form rising above the foyers and stage-support accommodation. At the competition stage these were shown in glass to define our principle of the dominating main auditorium. This was subsequently further enhanced by the removal of all plant into a separate plant tower with glass-clad vertical air handling elements acting as a beacon when backlit at night. The roof was developed at all stages throughout as a shell protecting the more delicate animal within, in this case from external sound. The foyers were developed as a prow, accentuating the axis through its innovative delicately hung glass curtain above the entrance.

At the outset we set ourselves the target of achieving a space where there was an appropriate balance between aural and visual criteria, thus providing all members of the audience with a close relationship with the performers on the platform.

A volume of 10 cubic metres per person is a fundamental prerequisite for the design of concert halls. Since we were attempting to achieve close proximity of audience to the platform this resulted in considerable height, somewhat akin to the major ecclesiastical buildings where structure rises to a noble roof form, often in cool stone, whilst the audience sits on a warm toned wooden base. The precedent was adapted to accentuate the contrast in scale between the seated audience and the noble scale for the upper volume. Each surface of the room works to satisfy a range of demands: visually, acoustically, structurally. The introduction of a sequence of materials in layers, coupled with careful use of colour, brings a sense of slight uncertainty and mystery into the room, the subtleties of which one can gently explore visually during a performance.
In addition to the design team four independent artists were commissioned to further enliven and interpret the public spaces. Their work ranges from fluid coloured metal strips suspended under the auditorium in the main foyer, designed by Deryck Healey, to the beautifully calm stone sculpture on the piazza outside the Hall, created by Kan Yasuda.

Project sign-off
The concert hall is a strong statement of the city's cultural aspirations: a landmark building proudly standing in the heart of the city and surrounded by space for public use in a variety of ways. The reintroduction of a length of the Bridgewater Canal into a new basin enhances the importance of the building particularly in its role as a regeneration catalyst, linking through to other canal-side developments. The auditorium has proved to be intimate yet monumental, with a fine individual acoustic much loved by orchestras and soloists. It has gained for Manchester international recognition as one of the world's great concert halls.

95

BRIDGEWATER HALL

PROJECT TEAM

Client: **Manchester City Council**
Architect: **RHWL**
Quantity Surveyor: **Silk & Frazier**
Structural and Services Engineer: **Arup**
Acoustician: **Arup Acoustics**
Lighting Design: **Lighting Design Partnership**
Technical Installation: **Technical Planning International**
Contractor: **John Laing Construction**
Artists: **Kate Egan, Deryck Healey, Jonathan Spiers and Kan Yasuda**

97

Clad in highly polished Italian granite and reflective glass, Barbirolli Square Offices are a commercial development of the highest quality.

BARBIROLLI SQUARE OFFICES

RHWL

Lower Mosley Street, Manchester

Construction Value: £28 million
Completion Date: 1997

Description

The Barbirolli Square Offices form part of Manchester's Great Bridgewater Initiative which includes the Bridgewater Hall.

History

In the initial proposals, the pair of office buildings were angled at the axis of the concert hall, with the larger of the two positioned on Lower Mosley Street. This proposal was abandoned in mid-1992 and a series of design alternatives ranging from high-rise single-building options to rectilinear brick schemes of a more traditional character were examined.

The final proposal, which reversed the direction of access to the buildings so that the main entrances faced inwards towards the concert hall, was generated after detailed dialogue with AMEC Developments Ltd, their agents and a tenant consortium. The agreed massing placed the higher, nine-storey building on the Chepstow Street side of the site, so that when seen from Lower Mosley Street both buildings – stepped also on plan – appeared to be of equal visual status and prestige.

Client's brief

The proposal established, within a development of this size, a sufficient degree of variety in the buildings to avoid setting them apart from the rest of the city, but with enough commonality of design to bring visual cohesion. This has been considered not just in terms of materials but in aspects of the massing and rhythmic quality of the buildings involving both curves and a series of angles.

Design process

Both buildings, which provide a total of 350,000m² of floor space and 213 car parking spaces, were planned generally on a 1.5m planning grid with structural modules of 7.5m and 9m through the central atrium zones. The composition reduces in scale towards the smaller buildings on Bishopsgate which provide access for the servicing and car parking. The new office buildings have double-height marble entrance halls, are fully air-conditioned with suspended ceilings and raised serviced floors, and are arranged with diagonally positioned cores which allow flexible letting arrangements for potentially two tenants per floor.

Stone-clad buildings were a specific requirement of the tenant consortium and the polished Sardinian grey granite was selected to provide, with the semi-reflective glazing (for reduced cooling loads), a smooth-skinned envelope that would blend with the tones and textures of not just the concert hall, but the enormous variety of materials amongst the buildings surrounding and leading up to Great Bridgewater. These ranged from Portland and York stone to faience, stock and red brick, glass and cast iron. The other main cladding material – the metallic 'gunmetal' finish to the column casings, louvres, disc roofs and soffits – is similar to that used on the concert hall.

The overhanging 'floating' roofs at similar heights on both the seven-storey office building on Lower Mosley Street and the ridge of the concert hall, create a further connection which is emphasied at night when floodlit.

The two office buildings have a number of expressed differences apart from their relative sizes, heights and plan shapes – the stronger horizontality and recessed curves of the lower building contrasts with the projecting bays and more 'vertical' nature of the taller building.

At low level the red sandstone that forms the plinth of the concert hall is continued around the quay-side to enclose, with a series of piers, the restaurant, which itself forms the base to the belvedere from which the office buildings rise. The warmth of the traditional brickwork of canal walls and of Chepstow House – newly converted to apartments – is therefore extended into the heart of the development. York stone paving, shot-through with banks of granite emanating from the grid of the office buildings and the radiating axes of the concert hall, creates a further relationship between the buildings. The majority of trees at street level are false acacias with willows and trained false acacias also being used a quayside level.

Project sign-off

The seven and nine-storey Barbirolli Square Offices, clad in highly polished Italian granite and reflective glass, have become an instantly recognisable landmark, and provide the largest and highest quality commercial development in Manchester, with top law and accounting firms as tenants.

99

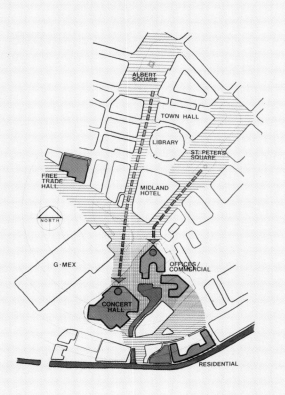

BARBIROLLI SQUARE OFFICES

PROJECT TEAM

Owner: **Hermes Pension Management Ltd**
Architect: **RHWL**
Quantity Surveyor: **Andrews & Boyd**
Structural Engineer: **Arup**
Mechanical & Electrical Engineer: **WSP**
Contractor: **AMEC Construction Ltd**

The refurbishment of 12 brick arch structures
and the addition of new boardwalks has
revitalised this area of the city.

DEANSGATE LOCKS
EGS DESIGN LTD (JEFFERSON SHEARD EGS)

Whitworth Street West, Manchester

Construction Value: £2.8 million
Completion Date: March 2000

Description

Twelve brick arch structures overlooking the Rochdale Canal and
forming part of the original Central Station infrastructure have
been refurbished. The addition of new boardwalks and
pedestrian bridges spanning and exploiting the water elements
of the Rochdale Canal also give direct access to Whitworth
Street West.

History

The Deansgate Locks project falls withtin the overall Central
Station Redevelopment area which occupies over 23 acres
(9.3 hectares) in the city centre. Phase 1 of the development
was created by extensive refurbishment of the original main train
hall.

In order to bring the transport hub into the city, the Victorians
constructed an above-ground infrastructure comprising wrought-
iron bridges, viaducts and brick-arched structures leading
eventually to Central Station. As part of the above-ground
support structure, a section of the Rochdale Canal was sealed
off and a major brick undercroft was created.

The Deansgate Locks project is situated within part of the brick
undercroft overlooking the Rochdale Canal and Whitworth Street
West – a major vehicular artery across the city centre leading
eventually to Piccadilly mainline station.

Client's brief

The client, wished to create within the arch structures a variety
of lettable spaces which could be developed within a flexible
framework.

This flexible approach necessitated some considerable planning
and access requirements to be integrated into the shell scheme
design concepts, thus allowing the full range and and extent of
tenants requirements to be incorporated into the design, as well
as meeting the planning requirements of a major Grade II listed
building.

It was also important that the scheme be integrated into the
fabric of the city by major improvements to access; in particular
pedestrian access from nearby facilities, such as G-MEX and
Bridgewater Hall.

Design process

Examination of the arched structures both internally and
externally indicated that Trafford Street (the original service road)
should be maintained for that purpose, especially as the street
was situated within and beneath major structures forming part of
the railway infrastructure. The open element of the Rochdale
Canal and Whitworth Street West was integrated into the
proposals for the arched structures alongside the canal, bringing
these two elements into the scheme rather than being separated
by the relatively low water level of the canal.

The exploitation of this unused waterside asset formed part of
the design philosophy, and was achieved by building a
continuous boardwalk along the whole length of the development
and, via bridges, across the canal, linking the project both in
visual and actual terms to the Whitworth Street West pavement,
from which pedestrian access to the Bridgewater Hall is easily
achieved.

The creation of the boardwalk allowed access to all twelve
arches enabling the flexibility requirements of the then-unknown
tenants to be achieved without subsequent major alteration to a
planning-approved shell and infrastructure scheme.

Further examination of the arched structures, and in particular
existing cross-arch Gothic forms, allowed integration of one or
more arches with its neighbour without any alteration of the
listed structure. This, together with the excavation of filled
ground, allowed the full height of the arches to be utilised in
what became known as 'the cathedral spaces', and in turn
allowed direct linkage at lower boardwalk level to the canal.

Two boardwalks were thus created, the main one at upper level
linking across the canal to Whitworth Street West and allowing
the canal to function. At canal level a lower boardwalk enabled
pedestrian movement to be achieved, as well as exploiting the
canalside environment.

The use of the boardwalks also provided emergency access and
egress to all areas, linked by an internal staircase to Trafford
Street and a separate external feature staircase to G-MEX and
the Metrolink station.

103

PHOTO: IAN LAWSON

PHOTO: LEN GRANT

Detailed design incorporated key elements; for example use of the massive arch brickwork to support a cantilevered boardwalk steel structure held on feature 'Gothic' brackets. This both respected the listed structures and at the same time provided a feature and interest to the boardwalk areas.

Internally, the arch brickwork is subject to leakages from the filled areas above, and initial consideration was given to cladding the whole interior to give protection below. After considerable thought, and to retain the internal brickwork of the arches (both to respect the listing and at the same time retain a most interesting internal effect), a series of copper removable panels were developed to act as 'umbrellas' to any seepage. These 'umbrellas' were linked to a continuous copper gutter each side of the internal arch strings, the system being able to catch any water seepage and mask the discoloration of brickwork that had occurred.

The result achieves three functions: seepage collector, attractive internal copper features, and importantly, the Victorian brickwork forms a major feature of all internal fit-out design.

Finally, a major feature of the design is to respect and exploit the scale of the massive arched structures without introducing overpowering new elements.

The project commenced on site in 1999 and the shell scheme, achieved in stages, was completed in March 2000 with tenants' fit-out completed over the next six months.

Glazing elements are set back from the arch frontages, to respect and exploit the splendid scale of the Victorian undercroft, and allow the introduction of a brise soleil across each arch to minimise glare.

Project sign-off

The scheme achieves an excellent relationship with the Victorian surrounding infrastructure and has, at the same time, introduced new elements of design to add to the exciting new infrastructure and facilities of the city, exemplified by the adjacent G-MEX and Bridgewater Hall complex.

DEANSGATE LOCKS

PROJECT TEAM

Client: **Westport Developments Ltd**
Architect: **EGS Design Ltd (Jefferson Sheard EGS)**
Structural Engineer: **Mott McDonald**
Quantity Surveyor: **Baker Hollingworth Associates**
Electrical Engineer: **David Belton Associates**
Mechanical Engineer: **Norman Lowe Ltd**
Project Manager: **Axis Project Management Limited**
Building Contractor: **Urbis Construction**

The Manchester International Convention Centre is an exemplary piece of contemporary architecture, providing a well-equipped and comfortable venue for conferences and seminars.

MANCHESTER INTERNATIONAL CONVENTION CENTRE
SHEPPARD ROBSON AND STEPHENSON BELL ARCHITECTS

Windmill Street, Manchester

Construction Value: £21 million
Completion Date: December 2000

Description
The UK's first city-centre purpose-built convention centre.

History
The site is between Watson Street to the south and Windmill Street to the west, adjacent to G-MEX and close to Manchester's Bridgewater Hall. Windmill Street (named after the windmill on the site in 1812) is higher than Watson Street, creating a sloping site.

Client's brief
The brief was for a building that would make a significant contribution to the expanding convention centre as well as to the urban regeneration of the area. The design objective was to produce an exemplary piece of contemporary architecture in the context of a substantially Victorian city and to relate to modern buildings in the vicinity.

Design process
The Manchester International Convention Centre links to the existing G-MEX Centre and was an important venue for the 2002 Commonwealth Games. The building comprises an 800-seat auditorium and an 1800m² banqueting and exhibition hall. Two levels of foyer space with fully glazed façades provide access to the auditorium, which is augmented by associated meeting rooms, administrative offices and other back-of-house facilities.

The project was a collaborative effort by Sheppard Robson and Stephenson Bell and the concept design was developed jointly between the two practices. Stephenson Bell subsequently took responsibility for the external envelope and landscape with Sheppard Robson acting as lead consultant and concentrating on internal design.

The immediate problem facing the architects was the building's location, right in the heart of the city centre but locked away in a 'back street' position overshadowed by immense civic monuments. The team's solution was to opt for a combination of traditional and modern.

To this was added the difficulty of designing for a complex site. G-MEX stands on a low plateau and the Centre site is bounded by two roads. The site is located at the apex of two grid points, creating a triangular-shaped site, further complicated by the angle of the railway station. In addition, the designers had to relate the Convention Centre to several large pavilion buildings (Bridgewater Hall, G-MEX, the Great Northern Warehouse) plus a proposed 14-storey residential building to the south, not yet in existence.

The street geometry, together with the incline of the site, was a key generator of the architectural expression. Site features are expressed by the flat roof plates of the foyer spaces which give focus to the vertically spiralling articulation of the geometric forms. The two major expressed forms of the auditorium and the exhibition hall are articulated by the main services tower and the central circulation spine. Entrance through the lower foyer reveals the powerful form of the building, where the set-back upper level foyer and the roof expose the main underbelly of the auditorium.

The foyers directly feed the auditorium and also lead to the flat floored banqueting and exhibitions hall. On the level above there are a series of seminar rooms connecting directly to the existing G-MEX seminar centre, which enable the two buildings to function together or separately as required.

Ample use of red sandstone cladding makes reference to the and brick from which Victorian Manchester was constructed. Carried through into the foyer, it allows the Centre to harmonise with its neighbours while the aluminium standing-seam roof provides the performance and durability expected for an important new civic building.

Internally, a neutral palette of materials for the circulation areas provides a calm background to the colour and movement of visitors and helps to express the forms, spaces and direction of the building.

The auditorium was designed with excellent sightlines, a traditional proscenium-arched stage and state-of-the-art audio visual and lighting systems. Facilities for up to 24 wheelchair users are provided.

Acoustically the auditorium is designed for speech rather than music, with predominantly absorptive materials and a warm atmosphere. A non-amplified human voice can be heard from the stage in all parts of the space.

The Great Northern Hall is designed to provide both a neutral backdrop for exhibitions and a warmer ambience for banquets. This is achieved by combining neutral tones of painted plaster (both plain and acoustically performing) with lacquered MDF panelling. A variety of lighting systems is available in combination to achieve the desired effect.

Project sign-off

The Centre has been widely acclaimed as a significant contribution to the urban regeneration of the area and a notable addition to the city's cultural quarter. It is a perfect complement to G-MEX, providing a well-equipped, comfortable and pleasantly intimate venue for conferences and seminars.

MANCHESTER INTERNATIONAL CONVENTION CENTRE

PROJECT TEAM

Client: **Manchester City Council**

Public Realm Client: **Manchester Engineering Design Consultancy**

Architects: **Sheppard Robson** (executive and interiors architect)

Stephenson Bell (exterior architect)

Design & Build Contractor: **Carillion**

Quantity Surveyor: **Davis Langdon**

Structural, Services, Acoustic and IT Engineering: **Arup**

Briefing Consultant: **The Right Solution**

Catering Consultant: **Tricon Food Service**

PHOTOS: SHAW + SHAW

The striking modern architecture of the Radisson Edwardian
Manchester Hotel further enhances the 'new' Manchester
ideology as a leading modern European city.

RADISSON EDWARDIAN MANCHESTER HOTEL
STEPHENSON BELL ARCHITECTS

Peter Street, Manchester

Construction Value: £40 million
Completion Date: July 2004

Description
The Radisson Edwardian Manchester Hotel, built on the site of
the historic Free Trade Hall, is a 15-storey contemporary 5 star
hotel in the heart of Manchester.

History
The existing Grade II* listed hall was designed in 1856 by
Edward Walters as a permanent structure for the Free Trade
Movement. Later, it was home to The Hallé for 150 years. It was
bombed in World War II, destroying all but two façades both of
which were retained in the 1950s redevelopment by city
architect Leonard Howitt.

The 'Palazzo' design implicit in the front façade has never been
fully realised in plan form. The proposals for the redevelopment
of the site as a 263-bed 5 star hotel, create a classically
proportioned block from the main Victorian façades
accommodating the appropriate large-volume rooms within. A
cleared site to the rear was created to allow a 15-storey
contemporary accommodation block to be constructed,
principally clad in stone and glass.

Client's brief
In its simplest form, it was to be the best hotel in Manchester with
the finest restaurant. The building needed to respond to the
aspirations of the city, to create a business/conference zone and also
to reflect its location on a busy leisure and entertainment corridor.

Design process
Bomb damage in World War II left two retained façades from the
1860s. The Italianate palazzo references in the Peter Street
façade were skin deep. What lay behind was not the series of
grand spaces that one might expect, but awkward wedge-
shaped slithers of space surrounding an auditorium, shoehorned
onto the site in the 1950s redevelopment by Howitt. It is
acknowledged that such an expression of functionality was not
part of Walters's architectural ethos; however, this did not
preclude the opportunity of enhancing the architectural
expression for the new use of the façades.

The design proposals for the building recognised that the hotel
clearly separated into two very different types of primary space.
This led to a strategic use pattern which firstly put the large-
span public function spaces in a newly created 18m deep
'palazzo' northern block which use the retained 1860s façades
as its principle elevations.

Secondly, the hotel bedrooms which have entirely different
constructional requirements were placed in a clearly expressed
contemporary southern block structure that takes up the
geometry of Windmill Street. Back-of-house accommodation
occupies the less premium spaces.

The symbolism, spirit and social history of the building and site,
which are of enormous importance, are symbolised by retaining
the well-loved Victorian façade. The intention is that the vestigial
'palazzo' Peter Street block will, in effect, be a memorial to the
importance of the site which is furthered by containing the
retained artefacts from the old building. Thus the two parts of
the building reflect and express their functions, in the epitome of
present day architectural credo, and a fitting balance is created
between the old and the new.

The site geometries generated by the intersection of
Manchester's two city grids is expressed in the juxtaposition of
the highly embellished 'palazzo' with the taller unadorned
'contemporary' block.

The triangular fully glazed atrium space between the two blocks
makes for a dramatic entrance foyer. Entered from both Southmill
Street and Peter Street the atrium combines the functional and
symbolic importance of the two differing approaches. The space
is an architectural statement in its own right by linking the two
principal blocks into a cohesive whole allowing appreciation of
the important axial geometries of the blocks.

The ground floor of the 'palazzo' accommodates a two-storey
high grand reception hall, restaurant and bar. The first floor
accommodates an equally grand-scale function room. The upper
two floors have syndicate suites with access to a sheltered
winter garden behind the retained Peter Street façade. The
contemporary block to Windmill Street houses the majority of the
263 bedrooms and suites. The ground floor of this block
incorporates a restaurant/bar. Rooftop plant is masked by an
open-topped glazed enclosure. The basement includes a fitness
spa and the main back-of-house facilities.

An important characteristic of Manchester's architecture is the
tripartite façade composition of base, middle and cap. This has

been respected in the design of the contemporary block, which has a clear two-storey base, a regular homogeneous body and a cap formed by three storeys of lightweight glazed construction. Planning restraints limited the height of the contemporary block to reduce its impact on the Victorian façade, whilst commercial pressure required increased accommodation; space usage is thereby extremely efficient.

The contemporary block, which forms the backdrop to the 'palazzo', is simply detailed and highly glazed, to complement rather than compete with the decorative Victorian detailing. The southern elevation is clad with precast concrete panels faced in honed Jura limestone framed with bronze angles. The same stone is used on the flank walls constructed in an ashlar method. Precast concrete fins project from the façade to aid solar shading. The staircases and fin walls, are expressed in a sandblasted Jura limestone giving a 'white' finish.

City-centre site confinements pushed the design towards fast-track and prefabricated components. The southern contemporary block, using concrete tunnel-form construction, achieved 14 storeys in 14 weeks, constructed simultaneously with the steel frame to the northern block.

Neither the Walters nor Howitt designs successfully turned the corner of Windmill Street and Southmill Street. A characteristic of Manchester buildings is to give architectural expression to such corners. The new building pulls out and expresses the staircase element, divorcing it from the main body of the block at street level by incorporating a double-storey glass link giving street level transparency through the corner.

The post war 1950s redevelopment responded to the 'front & rear' hierarchy of its site context at that time. The blind Windmill Street façade faced onto the railway termini, warehouses and marshalling yards. The new elevation provides an appropriate and balanced solution, which successfully addresses the scale and massing of the grand buildings and public spaces created by the Great Northern Initiative. These, with their civic character, have arguably become more prominent than the Peter Street frontage.

Project sign-off

The completion of the hotel project reunites the people of Manchester with a well-loved and cherished 'friend', the Free Trade Hall. The symbolism inherent in the ornate retained façade will soon become synonymous with the Manchester Radisson Edwardian Hotel on a worldwide scale. The striking modern architecture of the contemporary tower and atrium further enhances the 'new' Manchester ideology as a leading modern European city and an important leisure and business location by placing a much-needed quality hotel and function facility into the city's newly created conference zone.

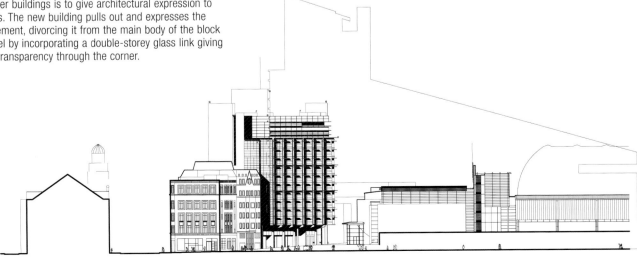

FREE TRADE HALL

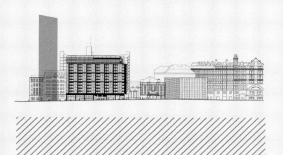

RADISSON EDWARDIAN MANCHESTER HOTEL

PROJECT TEAM

Client: **Riverland Limited**
Architect: **Stephenson Bell**
Hotel Operator: **Radisson Edwardian**
Client Agent: **LaSande**
Service Engineers: **Rodney Environmental Consultants**
Structural Engineer: **Buro Happold**
Interior Design: **SBT Ransley**
Contractor: **McAlpine Laing Joint Venture**
Acoustic Engineer: **AEC**

113

PHOTOS: ROGER STEPHENSON

Hilton Tower will be the tallest residential building in
Europe and its distinctive crystalline blade will become
an iconic landmark.

HILTON TOWER
IAN SIMPSON ARCHITECTS

301 Deansgate, Manchester

Construction Value: £155 million
Completion Date: August 2006

Description
A tall, slender, 47-storey building incorporating a 285-bedroom
Hilton Hotel, 219 residential apartments and on-site parking to
serve all three uses.

History
The building is located on the junction of Deansgate, Liverpool
Road and Great Bridgewater Street and on the site of a
redundant railway viaduct.

Client's brief
A very open brief was outlined: to provide a substantial
integrated mixed-use development of exceptional design quality,
incorporating a Hilton Hotel and as many apartments as
possible, together with a stand-alone commercial office building
of approximately 9,000m². This mix and quantum of uses,
combined with the City Council's aspirations for a landmark
building at a strategic gateway location, determined the form of
development and provide the opportunity to create an elegant
and very beautiful structure.

Design approach
The proposed development is split into three easily identifiable
elements: a 169m-tall tower containing the hotel bedroom and
residential element (hotel guest bedrooms and apartments); a
lower, 'podium', element containing the hotel public areas which
is separated from the tower by a clear glazed atrium through
which the hotel is entered; and a stand-alone office building.

The residential component of the development, comprising 219
apartments, is located within the upper floors of the tower, from
levels 25–47. This accommodation is articulated by cantilevering
the residential levels out beyond the hotel below at level 23, the
floor occupied by the hotel's destination (sky) bar. A dedicated
residential entrance gives access to a lobby and a vertical
circulation core.

The residential tower is set back from Deansgate, opening up
the corner and establishing a new sense of place at the junction
of Deansgate and Great Bridgewater Street. The public space
created will be defined with natural materials and will match the
high standards of design and execution set by other recently
completed public spaces in the city.

A further new public space is created between the eastern
elevation to the tower and the new commercial office entrance.
The tower can, therefore, be read in its entirety – from the
street, from the new public spaces and from within the atrium –
as an element which touches the ground on all four sides. The
small floorplates required for the residential accommodation
have allowed the creation of an elegant tower with a very high
slenderness, (height-to-width) ratio.

The design of the post-tensioned concrete structure to the tower
has been refined to ensure that it is as slender as is physically
possible. The envelope to the tower will be formed as a fully
sealed, unitised, structural silicon-glazed, curtain-walling system,
the design of which will be developed in detail with a specialist
contractor. Where required, the system will incorporate opening
lights and ventilation terminals, but these will be concealed
behind a fixed perforated metal panel, which will be glazed flush
with the adjacent façade.

The façade design is intended to emphasize the verticality of the
building. Elements such as the perforated panels covering the
ventilators and the projecting fins which provide shading to the
areas of clear glazing are aligned vertically, so that they run
across a number of floors and break down the horizontal lines of
the floorplates.

Each of the elevations to the building has a different treatment
according to orientation in order to deal with solar issues. This
provides a richness and individuality to the proposals. This is a
building which is designed specifically to suit this particular
orientation on this particular site. The residential apartments on
the south-facing elevation are protected by a glazed 'buffer'
zone, a semi-external space formed between the inner and outer
skins of the glazed cladding. The inner skin is double-glazed and
the outer skin contains a series of fully openable single-glazed
vertical louvres. The buffer zone provides a useable and flexible
outdoor space at all times of the year, and an extension to the
living accommodation with spectacular views across the city and
the surrounding countryside.

115

IMAGE: WWW.UNIFORM.NET

The areas of clear glazing to the south and west elevations are protected by projecting, anodised-aluminium 'fins' which shade the window adjacent from the morning or evening sun. The lower levels of the building create a place for people to enjoy. The top is light and appears to challenge gravity. The glazed skin of the buffer zone to the south façade cantilevers above roof level to form a crystalline 'blade'. This glazed element blurs the distinction between the building and the surrounding skies and is intended to make the crown of the building appear to dematerialise.

Project sign-off

The project started on site in April 2004 and is due to finish in late 2006. On completion, we believe that we will have created a place for people to enjoy all that is rooted in the life of the city. Equally, the building will be the tallest residential building in Europe, one whose distinctive crystalline blade will become an iconic landmark for the city of Manchester.

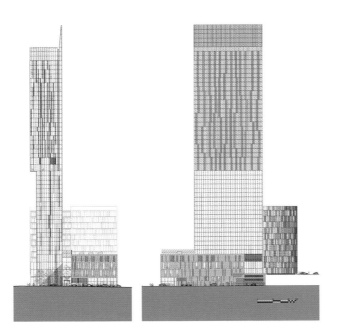

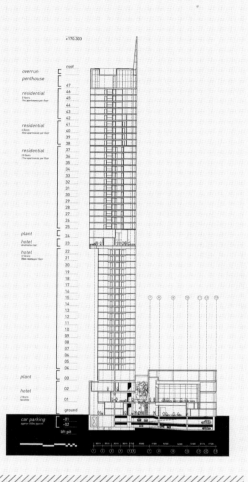

HILTON TOWER

PROJECT TEAM

Client/Owner: **Beetham Organization Ltd**

Architect: **Ian Simpson Architects**

Structural Engineer: **Cantor Seinuk**

Services Engineer: **WSP**

Cost Manager/Client Agent: **Qubed**

Constructor: **Carillion**

Planning Consultant: **Drivers Jonas**

Fire Engineer: **WSP Fire**

117

NORTHERN QUARTER

3.13

The Northern Quarter is strategically placed between Manchester's retail and commercial core and the emerging attractions of Piccadilly Gateway, Ancoats and Shudehill. It is an area different from any other part of the city centre, both in its character and its function, and is of great importance to Manchester as a city of distinctive quarters.

The history of the area is rich and varied. When Manchester dominated the world's textile trade in the 1880s, many warehouses and workshops serving the industry were located in this district. In addition to cotton and textiles, imported food and industrial raw materials were items of commerce, and Manchester's principal wholesale food market was Smithfield Market off Shudehill. An impressive structure of iron and glass, it was purchased by the city in 1846 and by 1897 it covered two hectares. As a trading centre, it quickly became the single largest employer of Irish immigrants, many of whom settled in nearby Ancoats earning their living as traders, porters and labourers.

Although the area then contained some of the worst living conditions in Victorian England, it also had a rich reputation for radical literary and political gatherings, carnivals, music and new fashions. The public houses around Smithfield Market were frequented for their conviviality and live music. One of these was the George and Dragon which, in the 1970s, became the Band on the Wall – today an internationally renowned music venue. Tib Street once specialised in the sale of pets, especially local and exotic birds, while the retail fish-market building of 1895 became home to craft studios and shops in the 1980s.

The main thoroughfare in the 19th century was Oldham Street where the city's reputation for fashion and style was enhanced by Affleck and Brown's department store which opened in 1901 and occupied a group of nine premises

fig 3.13
The ICIAN
development

fig 3.14
Manchester Craft
& Design Centre

3.14

known as Smithfield Buildings. After it closed, the property became British Home Stores, then Littlewoods, both of which relocated to the Arndale shopping centre nearby in the early 1970s. The opening of the Arndale (1976), combined with the closure of Smithfield Market, further marginalised the district and accelerated the decline of commercialism – though textile traders, many of whom today are Asian, still maintain the tradition of fashion import and export.

The recognition of the Northern Quarter as a creative quarter today is therefore not arbitrary. A rich history of popular culture, literature, music and innovation has enabled the Northern Quarter to develop into a zone for experimentation and creativity. The important interplay between the production, showcasing and consumption of cultural goods helps create its unique identity, while the role and prominence of these three activities are encouraged in strategies for the area, as are new developments based on knowledge, new ideas and entrepreneuralism.

By the mid-1980s, the area was characterised by poor environment, high numbers of empty buildings and dilapidated properties. Falling rental values served to encourage small businesses into the area, attracted by low rents in a fringe city-centre location and rich traditional architecture. Although the area was designated as a Commercial Improvement Area in the mid-1980s and the Council provided grants to improve shops and commercial premises, the decline continued. As befitting a city that believes partnership working brings sustainable results, local businesses and residents in the early 1990s began to work together, seeking to influence decisions made about their area. The Eastside Partnership was established, which in 1993 became the Northern Quarter Association (NQA). Through this body local entrepreneurs progressed the aim of improving the area, while maintaining its unique character as the city's cultural district.

The City Council, working with the NQA, commissioned the Northern Quarter Regeneration Study (1995). The report identified that large-scale private-sector investors were unlikely to be drawn to the area, but by attracting small businesses it could evolve at a relatively slower pace as compared with the rapid developments taking place in other parts of the city. The

3.15

study further recommended improvements to public spaces and the need to encourage residential developments and a lively night-time economy. Manchester's booming music scene in the 1980s encouraged musicians and musical entrepreneurs to find bases in cheap accommodation. The disused warehouses and workshops, together with the creative ambiance of the area, were ideal for both pocket and image. One of Manchester's first design-led bars, Dry 201 (1989), was situated on Oldham Street. It was originally conceived as a pre-club bar and remains just as contemporary today, with its Manchester industrial character. A decaying cotton warehouse on Thomas Street is now Europe's largest Buddhist Centre. The Buddhists renovated the building themselves with the assistance of volunteers and a local architect.

Following the 1995 regeneration study, the Council and its partners delivered a number of projects including a public art scheme, footway and street-lighting improvements and the development of 'affordable' housing. One of the earliest residential developments was the conversion of Smithfield Buildings into loft apartments with specialist shops at street level. The development, completed in 1997, heralded a new way of city-centre living in Manchester, one that combined chic loft living with trendy individual retail and modern cafés beneath.

While there has been significant investment in the physical aspects of the area, the Northern Quarter is still perceived by many as being marginal to the rest of the city centre. It is also an area where crime and anti-social behaviour has persisted, in

fig **3.15**
Tib Street

fig **3.16**
Church Street
Market

3.16

spite of significant changes and environmental improvements over the past eight years. It was against this background that a team of consultants, led by Regeneris Consulting, were commissioned to take stock on progress since 1995. The *Northern Quarter Development Framework*, published in October 2003, conducted a baseline analysis and suggested proposals to manage incremental change up to 2008.

The Northern Quarter continues to be a magnet for dynamic independent companies including design studios, companies involved in television and film, recording studios and specialist music shops. It is the home of the Creative Industries Development Service (CIDS), the Manchester Craft and Design Centre and the new location of the Chinese Arts Centre. It has also become a successful secondary office location for companies in the financial and legal services sector. Over the next five years, the full potential of the area is being sought in order to maximise the benefits for the Northern Quarter and for Manchester generally as a growing city of global importance. Through managed incremental change, a balance will be struck between nurturing existing creative and innovative enterprises, capitalising on regeneration activity on the periphery of the area – especially that associated with the borders of New East Manchester and the Piccadilly Gateway – and exploiting opportunities linked to Manchester's future as a 'Knowledge Capital'.

To illustrate this dynamic creative quarter, case studies include Dry 201, Buddhist Centre and the Smithfield Buildings.

Our inspiration for Dry 201 were the bars of Europe where café culture is ingrained as part of society. We wanted to create a new hybrid social environment.

DRY 201

BEN KELLY DESIGN

28–30 Oldham Street, Manchester

Construction Value: £400 thousand
Completion Date: July 1989

Description

Conversion of former furniture showroom in a neglected Victorian five-story building on ground floor and basement level. The upper floors remained empty awaiting future expansion of the bar.

History

The site on Oldham Street in 1989 was run-down and dilapidated. Oldham Street had formerly been one of Manchester's primary shopping streets prior to the development of the Arndale Centre which devastated trade on Oldham Street. The development of Dry 201 initiated the beginning of the redevelopment of the street.

Client's brief

To convert the site into a bar/restaurant with capacity for 500 people to extend the 'Factory' culture and to provide the Haçienda club clientele with somewhere to go outside of Haçienda opening hours.

Design process

Having designed the Haçienda seven years earlier for the same group of clients, it was decided from the outset that a detailed client brief was essential to the success of the project. Feasibility schemes were produced to decide on the extent of the building to be included in the scheme. An early scheme was designed to include three floors. However, this proved to be cost prohibitive. The final scheme was carried out on two floors – ground and basement.

Lengthy discussions took place with the Council's Planning Department regarding the frontage of the building. This was due to the fact that a new design was required for the shop front. Extensive research was carried out into the history of retail units on Oldham Street and this project eventually sowed the seed for a much greater urban regeneration programme within the city centre. Dry 201 became the first new bar of its kind and initiated a trend of bars across the UK.

The 450m² allowed the design team to insert a 24m long slate and stainless-steel bar. Three telegraph poles were inserted near the entrance acting as a screening device to the bar and a support for drinking ledges. A kitchen block subdivided the main front bar from a rear 'lounge bar'. An overhead linear lighting rig linked the bars, running the full depth of the interior from Oldham Street at the front to Spear Street at the rear. Furniture, including settees, chairs, tables and stools were custom designed by Jasper Morrison – this being his first major commission. A large red fibrous plaster curtain (found in the building, left over from the premises' days in the 1950s and 1960s as a furniture showroom) was renovated and set as a backdrop behind the front section of the main bar.

Project sign-off

Our inspiration for the project was the bars of Europe where café culture is ingrained as part of society. We wanted to create a new hybrid social environment.

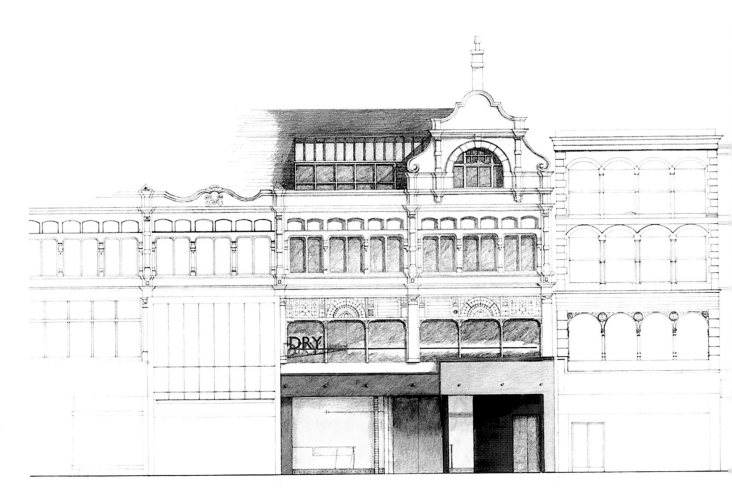

124

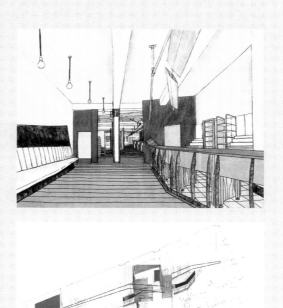

DRY 201

PROJECT TEAM

Client/Building Owner:
Factory Communications & Gainwest Ltd (New Order)
Design team: **Ben Kelly Design**
Quantity Surveyor: **Speakes Hollingworth**
Structural Engineer: **Bailey, Johnson, Hayes**
Main Contractor: **Irwins**
Architectural Metalwork: **Esmanco Construction**

One principle teaching of Buddhism
is that everything changes and our
building surely reflects that.

THE BUDDHIST CENTRE
FRIENDS OF THE WESTERN BUDDHIST ORDER (WITH SAGAR STEPHENSON ARCHITECTS)

Turner Street, Manchester

Construction Value: £350 thousand
Completion Date: July 1996

Description
Conversion of an old four-storey 1,300m² warehouse in a then largely derelict area of the city. The building has a 'z' footprint being made up of four separate warehouses constructed in 1867.

History
Turner Street and its first buildings were marked out, paved and built on Turner's Meadow in 1753 by Thomas Torkinton. In 1867 Bernard Duckworth built the existing buildings, one of which was a cotton waste warehouse. In 1929 Hobday Bros Ltd occupied the property for a motorcycle, wireless and electrical accessories business until their liquidation in 1962. The rag trade bought the building for £8,000 in a public auction but the space was left mostly empty for the next 30 years. During the 1970s and 1980s the rag trade started to leave the area due to the parking and unloading difficulties, and an already neglected environment deteriorated further.

In 1984 members of the Western Buddhist Order based in Chorlton started looking for a city location for a new public Buddhist Centre, and they identified this building and bought it for £92,000.

Design process
The building was to be converted with very little capital by the Buddhists themselves using reclaimed materials wherever possible. The plan was to 'provide a "retreat" from the city's noise, grime, bustle, distraction and materialism to a place that is friendly, warm, peaceful, beautiful and relaxing. A spiritual oasis'. The main elements would be: a reception, a bookshop, two shrine halls, a library, meeting rooms, an alternative health centre, a yoga studio, offices, a video production centre, a residential community and a vegetarian café.

The Northern Quarter was quickly identified as an ideal location: it was central, there were many empty buildings, the area was on the verge of regeneration and grants were available for restoration. Only a little imagination was needed to see what the 1,300m² of worn floorboards, white brick walls and bright green window frames could become. To many it seemed a crazy undertaking – we were going to do nearly all the renovation and

conversion work ourselves, learning the skills as we went along and grasping what advice we could lay our hands on. Dominic Sagar, our original architect, found another helpful and talented young architect, Tony Mead, to work with us on the designs whilst Dominic helped secure generous grants from the City Council for external work, internal refurbishment and art works for the front elevation. He also helped us secure £30,000 from English Heritage for various renovation details. With their help and many very generous gifts and loans from friends as well as a substantial loan from Triodos Bank we kept steadily working and spending over a two-year period rather than the estimated six months.

The building posed a seemingly endless list of questions, difficulties and opportunities. We were creating the biggest urban Buddhist Centre in Europe – a Buddhist Centre in England for Western Buddhists. What should such a centre look like? How could we successfully adapt a neglected Victorian warehouse, especially given our tiny budget? Buddhism has yet to make its mark in Europe and it will probably take hundreds of years for Western Buddhism to define itself in terms of art and architecture. In the meantime we can design buildings that will hopefully reflect the beautiful aesthetic sensibility of the Buddhist tradition, buildings that will inspire and delight, offer tranquillity and stimulation as well as comfort. The building itself should affect our minds for the better. Its exterior should proclaim the 'Truths' of Buddhism to passers-by and, when we enter, we should feel at ease and welcome. The design should reflect the positive mental states we are working to develop. The challenge was to give the tired, worn fabric of the building a completely new role.

Despite the huge labour involved, we decided to reveal the building's structural beauty. We stripped and varnished all the woodwork; sandblasted all the painted brick walls, so allowing the beautiful red Cheshire brick to glow; and exposed the natural materials wherever possible. The simple beauty of the building's raw materials could stand by itself – why hide it? The metal shutters were replaced with decorative metal grilles with designs which represent a movement away from the murky waters of worldly troubles towards the clear bright light of spiritual development and fulfilment. Through raising awareness of the

building's original structure and concerns, and then embellishing it with original Western Buddhist artwork, the very design itself could provide an example – on the material plane – of conversion and the renewal towards which – on the spiritual plane – all Buddhists aspire. The design had to be faithful to the historical context of the building's architecture and use but also offer inspiration - a vision of something beyond it.

We gathered materials from demolition sites. We bartered for fire doors and frames, light fittings, cupboards, maple and beech floors. All the radiators were bought from an old hospital and were stripped and repainted. Then we gutted the warehouse, got rid of the old walls and ceilings, laid it bare and began to realise just how many structural repairs were needed. The winter months of 1994–95 were spent on scaffolding in biting wind, snow, hail and rain stripping, sanding, repairing, treating and varnishing window frames: cold and tedious work requiring a small army of men and women, some financially supported but most just volunteers. The heroic dedication of the streams of people who have helped this renovation lends a unique quality to the finished building. Restoring all the front sash windows, stripping the paint off the huge beams and wooden staircases, repairing all the rear windows, sandblasting all the walls; these were labours of love which could only be given rather than paid for.

Keeping volunteers inspired and engaged as the project's completion disappeared into a misty future was challenging and sometimes a skeleton core team were heard rattling around a cold and drafty building. Money sometimes ran out and so refurbishment grants were desperately sought and local fund-raising prioritised.

Project sign-off

One principal teaching of Buddhism is that everything changes and our building surely reflects that. In the two-year conversion project it changed remarkably, as did all the men and women who put so much time into creating that change. Already it seems too small but it stands as a milestone for the Friends of the Western Buddhist Order. It is a symbol of our faith in the teachings of the Buddha. It is a place where many people encounter Buddhism, learn how to meditate, practise yoga, have lunch and meet up with friends. In our small way we are trying to make Manchester more beautiful, and set an example by creating a caring community in the heart of a modern city.

THE BUDDHIST CENTRE

PROJECT TEAM

Client/Building Owner: **Friends of the Western Buddhist Order**

Architect: **Sagar Stephenson Architects**

Structural Engineer: **Healy Brown Partnership**

A landmark building providing exciting and innovative urban apartments.

SMITHFIELD BUILDINGS
STEPHENSON BELL ARCHITECTS

Oldham Street, Manchester

Construction Value: £6.67 million
Completion Date: September 1998

Description
Smithfield Buildings is the renovation and conversion of a group of buildings, formerly used as a department store, to residential and retail use.

History
The city block is made up of nine buildings, some of which were originally built for the Affleck and Brown department store. Eventually Afflecks expanded into the whole block, altering as it developed. During the 1970s, as a result of the development of the Arndale Centre, Afflecks closed down and the building was occupied by various retailers such as British Home Stores and eventually, prior to its conversion to residential use, a series of small retailers.

Client's brief
The Client, Urban Splash, provided a fairly loose brief which proposed exciting and innovative urban residential apartments and a variety of public-access uses. Over a period of time, the brief evolved into a more definitive requirement for one, two and three-bedroom apartments over a largely retail-orientated ground and basement floor. The retail spaces remained fairly fluid to allow flexibility for occupation by various sizes of retailer.

Design process
A basic plan form was developed which utilised the existing stairways, conveniently sited to provide the vertical escape provision. A proposal was developed whereby the stairways were linked by internal streets on three levels within two lightwells. The lightwells developed into an exciting communal space, one of which is based on a remodelled existing arcade retained from the Affleck and Brown days – the trusses and columns which support the lightwell roof are as originally found. The lightwells function as a winter (and summer) garden, provide the means by which passive smoke extraction of the common spaces is achieved and they also help create useful, useable space at the rear of the apartments, enabling apartment interiors to be fully exploited and dual aspect in nature. Construction work commenced on site without working drawings and the design process proceeded more or less in line with the construction process. As the design evolved, more detailed examinations of the spaces took place, enabling a more thoughtful and more radical design solution to emerge.

A thorough examination of the column grid arrangements within the properties revealed the opportunity for a reasonably optimal configuration of apartments whereby the majority of existing cast-iron, pitch-pine and masonry elements are retained within spaces, and new walls are inserted where necessary.

Apartments surround both lightwells and are generally planned to enable living at the front (street side) and sleeping at the rear (lightwell side). Kitchens and bathrooms sit between living and sleeping and, on the third floor, bed decks straddle the wet areas, set within the roof trusses above. No two apartments are the same although many have similar attributes. All apartments are split level, having a floor deck raised above the existing floor construction over the rear third of the apartment, enabling services from the main distribution area within the lightwells to enter each apartment at low level. Single-storey two-bedroom apartments predominate, with bed decks in roof spaces on the third and fourth floors, although two duplex and one triplex apartment have been created.

Meetings with the planners at early stages enabled significant design and planning issues to be dealt with in a positive manner, and where changes in form or materials were required as a result of the discovery of new aspects of the existing buildings the planners adopted a very positive attitude, recognising the dynamics of the situation we were in.

Wherever possible, existing structure, form and materials were retained. New materials were introduced sparingly and only as required. Existing cast-iron columns, pitch-pine and wrought-iron beams and masonry walls were complemented by new pitch pine, white planes (walls and soffits), natural grey metal and galvanised metal fixtures and fittings.

The project commenced in early 1994 with a planning application and a submission for an English Partnerships Grant. It moved onto site in 1995 and the first occupation took place in September 1997. Final completion took place in September 1998.

The project was granted aided and work was carried out within rigid budgetary constraints based on a cost plan of £6.67 million. The work was carried out within budget.

Project sign-off

Smithfield Buildings is a landmark building within the Northern Quarter. The project was instrumental in the continuing regeneration of this area on the east side of Manchester city centre. The client's brief was to provide exciting and innovative urban apartments and this has been achieved not only in the apartments themselves but also in the unique entrance sequence and interior winter garden that we believe is the first of its kind. The project has won numerous awards including two Housing Design Awards, a RIBA Award and a Civic Trust Award. The scheme was sold completely off-plan and the apartments have realised significantly increased values. Partially as a result of the significant impact of Smithfield Buildings, the Northern Quarter goes from strength to strength.

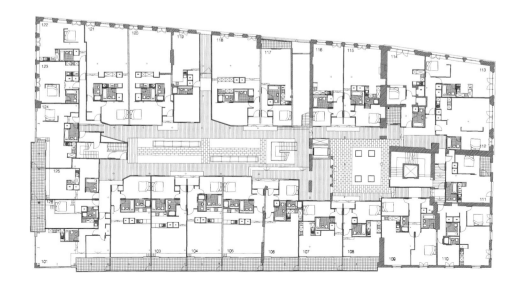

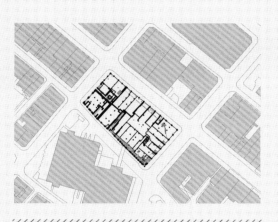

SMITHFIELD BUILDINGS

PROJECT TEAM

Client: **Urban Splash Limited**
Architect: **Stephenson Bell Limited**
Engineer Service: **John Troughear Associates**
Structural Engineer: **Eric Bassett Associates**
Contractor: **Urban Splash Projects**

133

PHOTOS: DAVID GRANDORGE

CITY CENTRE RENEWAL AREA AND MILLENNIUM QUARTER

3.17

On Saturday 15 June 1996, at peak shopping time and on a day when the city was filled with football supporters attending Euro '96, a 1,500 kg terrorist bomb exploded in the heart of Manchester's retail centre. Miraculously no one was killed, but more than 200 people were injured, and damage to shops and buildings was extensive.

The radius of the blast destruction extended over three quarters of a kilometre. The area close to the epicentre of the explosion included the Marks & Spencer store, the Arndale Centre, Corn Exchange, Royal Exchange and Royal Insurance's Longridge House. Longridge House and the adjacent Marks & Spencer building had to be demolished in order to build a new store across both sites. Shops and offices on Corporation Street, Cross Street and Canon Street suffered damage while Manchester Cathedral, Chetham's School, St Ann's Church and other historic buildings were also affected by the blast.

Strategic plans for extending, enhancing and repopulating the city centre had been established and agreed with the 1984 *City Centre Local Plan* and the 1994 *City Pride Prospectus*. The opportunity to significantly accelerate those plans came as a consequence of the bombing.

Within days, the City Council, working with its network of private-sector partners and Government, held detailed discussions on renewal proposals. A 'task force' was formed (which later became Manchester Millennium Ltd) and a number of objectives for the rebuilding programme were established. Many of the objectives existed in the previously published City Centre Local Plan and, with this in mind, it was agreed that the task would not be to simply rebuild and regenerate the area, but to drive forward a more radical scheme to replan and rebuild the heart of the city centre on an unprecedented scale.

fig 3.17
Cathedral
Gardens

fig 3.18
Selfridges

3.18

The proposal was comprehensive, bold and ambitious. It would restore, extend and enhance the retail core; stimulate and diversify the economic base; encourage linkages with fringe areas; develop an integrated transport strategy; and create a high-quality physical environment including the creation of a distinctive Millennium Quarter which would be anchored by a visitor attraction – Urbis – and include Exchange Square, a Cathedral Visitor Centre and Cathedral Gardens. The plan aimed to increase the resident population of the city centre, promote public and investor confidence and deliver and manage the reconstruction process.

Manchester Millennium Limited (MML) oversaw the relocation of businesses affected, and managed and delivered the rebuilding programme. Within its three-year existence, MML secured £83 million of public-sector funding and levered-in £500 million of private-sector investment. To underpin the restoration, and enhance the retail core, an international urban design competition was launched in September and the masterplan winners announced in November. The winning team included landscape architects and masterplanners EDAW; Ian Simpson Architects; Alan Baxter for transport and engineering; and Benoy, who provided information on retail development. The masterplanners worked with MML, whose staff were seconded from the City Council, and private-sector businesses. The masterplan was rapidly followed by supplementary planning guidance to provide a robust planning framework for the rebuilding programme. The team worked closely with landowners and, in addition to their many tasks, they promoted the masterplan to investors, and engaged Government, local people and media. The work was challenging and complex.

The world's largest state-of-the art Marks & Spencer flagship store was built, forming one side of the new Exchange Square. Today it shares the site with the prestige department store, Selfridges, and, with Harvey Nichols opposite, it is a shopping experience of excellence. A bridge, which today is an award-winning construction, was built to link Marks & Spencer and the Arndale Centre across Corporation Street. The Corporation Street Bridge is another world first for Manchester; its double-curving cylindrical structure is a strikingly modern hour-glass-shaped dynamic spiral of steel and glass.

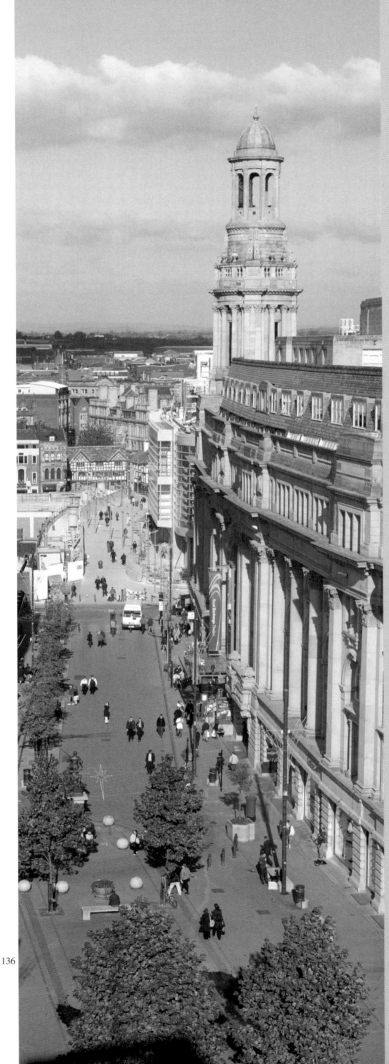

3.19

The Arndale was badly damaged along Corporation Street, but the decision was taken by the owners to reinstate the building rather than to replace it. What did change was its blank frontage, which was unfriendly to those walking along its adjacent streets. The opportunity to create better access to the shopping centre was grasped and new store entrances, accessible from the street, were introduced. The northern end of the Arndale was completely demolished, as was its bus station. The adjacent Cannon Street will now become a covered area within the new Arndale North complex. The Royal Exchange, with its famous repertory theatre, and the Corn Exchange – rebranded the Triangle – are both Grade II listed buildings that required extensive renovation.

To achieve the aim of extending the retail core of the city centre and of linking it to the previously isolated Cathedral area, a pedestrianised route was created. New Cathedral Street now runs from St Ann's Square to the Cathedral and draws people into Exchange Square – a new public space – and a park next to the historic buildings of Chetham's School and the Cathedral. The new route is on the site of the demolished Shambles West, a 1970s concrete square which contained two listed public houses – Sinclair's Oyster Bar and the Old Wellington Inn. These pubs were meticulously dismantled and relocated to Exchange Square within the newly created Millennium Quarter.

The Millennium Quarter contains a significant cultural building of the highest design quality, one that is a signature building and a symbol for the regenerated city centre. Urbis, the £30 million cultural centre is a landmark project for the Millennium Commission who provided the majority of the funding. The building opened in June 2002 to critical acclaim and the innovative exhibits

fig 3.19
By 1999 New
Cathedral Street
had linked St
Ann's Square to
the Cathedral

fig 3.20
The Printworks

3.20

celebrate and explore urban culture. Urbis is an integral part of Cathedral Gardens, a landscaped public space developed as part of the £42 million Millennium Quarter which also includes a new Cathedral Visitors' Centre. Cathedral Gardens, designed by landscape architects and engineers BDP, won the Design Award in the national BCSC Town Centre Environment Awards. Urbis received an RIBA award in 2003 and the Millennium Quarter gained The Civic Trust Urban Design Award in 2004. Overlooking Exchange Square is the Printworks, a popular leisure complex which opened to the public in November 2000. In addition to nightclubs, restaurants and bars, built around a cobbled street that recreates the flavour of the area when it was a flourishing national newspaper centre, there is The Filmworks which contains the Northwest's first IMAX screen.

To fulfil one of the masterplan's aims, the residential population of the city centre has been increased by the construction of No 1 Deansgate. This majestic building is a radical glass 22-storey residential block, overlooking St Ann's Square. It is designed by Ian Simpson and marks a significant departure from the traditional approach to inner-city housing.

Some traffic has been reduced within the city centre as a result of completing key elements of the inner relief route, and the rebuilding programme enabled bus and car journeys to be rerouted to create a congenial and accessible environment. A transport interchange with bus concourse, passenger stops, a new Metrolink stop and a multi-storey car park, is under construction at Shudehill, close to the Printworks. The creation of a safe, friendly and accessible city centre which appeals to shoppers, visitors and workers is critical to the growth of the regional capital.

The rebuilding of the city centre resulted from multi-skilled, collaborative work that delivered a bold and hugely complex project. The high design quality of the public spaces together with the new and restored buildings has significantly furthered Manchester's aim to be a leading European city, and one of which local people are proud and keen to be part.

To illustrate the success of the renewal programme case studies include the City Centre Masterplan, Marks & Spencer store, Corporation Street Footbridge, Exchange Square, No 1 Deansgate, Cathedral Gardens, Urbis, Arndale North, Manchester Transport Interchange and then also Century Buildings.

137

From broad urban design principles through to detailed
architectural solutions, the City Centre Masterplan sets the
aspiration for nothing short of the highest quality of design.

CITY CENTRE MASTERPLAN
EDAW

City Centre, Manchester

Description

The rebuilding and reconfiguration of the city centre retail core
following a terrorist bomb in June 1996, covering an area
between the River Irwell, St.Ann's Square, High Street and
Victoria Railway Station. The Manchester City Centre Masterplan
has served to guide this work resulting in new and improved
buildings; new streets, squares and gardens; a new landmark
cultural centre and leisure facilities; the introduction of housing
into this core area; and a reconfigured transport network,
achieved by promoting public transport while retaining and
managing private car access and servicing requirements.

History

Prior to the 1996 bomb damage, the retail core suffered from
the impact of dysfunctional 1960s and 1970s developments that
had been exacerbated by the impact of traffic growth.

Immediately to the north, the medieval core of the city and Victoria
Railway Station were largely cut off, both physically and
perceptually, from the modern retail core by a combination of busy
roads, awkward level changes and the mostly impenetrable and
blank elevations of the introverted Arndale and Shambles shopping
centres. The listed Shambles public houses (Sinclair's Oyster Bar
and Old Wellington Inn) found themselves isolated within the poor-
quality environment at the core of the Shambles Centre.

This limited north-south permeability, the urban wall created by
the post-war developments and the unattractiveness of the link
routes that did exist contributed to stifle the northward
expansion and regeneration of the retail core. Corporation Street
was a dull but busy traffic route also dominated by the blank
Arndale Centre elevations. Certain parts of the core exhibited
decline, there was minimal open space, and the area had an
uninviting night-time environment with limited activity.

The City Centre Masterplan followed an international design
competition. It acted as a framework for the rebuilding
programme while also setting out a vision for the new city
centre, raising the level of expectation and aspiration and giving
impetus to the continued regeneration of the wider city area.
This whole process was undertaken in consultation with the
various private, public, voluntary and community city-centre
stakeholders.

Client's brief

Rather than merely repairing and reinstating the damage the
underlying principle of the Masterplan was to be one of seizing
the opportunity to transform the city centre to meet the needs of
a 21st-century european city and regional capital. Coupled with
a sense of realism in order to ensure the phased delivery of a
new city centre by the new millennium, the Masterplan focused
on a number of key requirements:

> Creating interesting and active streets together with new and
  enhanced civic spaces

> Securing strong and diverse development

> Providing for an integrated transport system

> Recreating and reinforcing the relationship, including physical
  and economic linkages, with surrounding areas

The Masterplan was not intended to be a blueprint for
development, but a flexible framework to inform and guide
development – both public and private – and the key principles
and integrity of the Masterplan provided the certainty, clarity and
expectation necessary to secure private-sector commitment and
investment and guide public-sector decision making and
spending in all of the key projects in the Masterplan area.

Design process

The Masterplan was inherently very simple. The key elements
were to reconnect previously isolated areas of the city, with the
existing building stock defining the spatial and qualitative
characteristics of the plan, and priority for pedestrian spaces
over road areas in order to create active streets, squares and
gardens. This physical plan was wedded to a use and activity
strategy for a vibrant city centre that would appeal to a broad
range of people both day and night. Critical to this was the
creation of places that were for people to enjoy – places that
were distinctively city places that engendered ownership.

Two north-south streets (one new, one rediscovered) and the
creation of two new civic spaces created a framework that the
private sector responded to with enthusiasm and great
commitment.

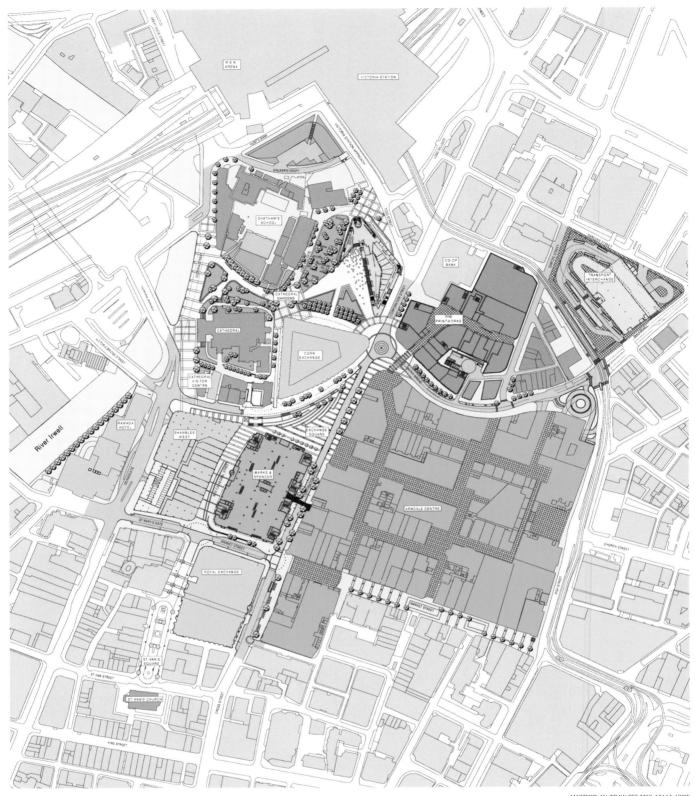

MASTERPLAN (EDAW REF M02-1811A 1999)

Retail
Leisure
Mixed Use
Cultural
Residential
Transport Interchange
Pedestrian Areas
Pedestrian/ Vehicles
Green Space/Parks

The new route, New Cathedral Street, now links the Cathedral with St. Ann's Church and Square. This necessitated the demolition of Shambles Square and resulted in the reconnection of the medieval core (the Millennium Quarter) to the Georgian heart of the city. A wholly new public park, Cathedral Gardens, now forms an appropriate setting for the historic area and buildings, and the new and dramatically contemporary Urbis develpoment. The space liberated by the closure of the four-lane Cannon Street/Cateaton Street vehicle route between Deansgate and High Street facilitated the formation of the second of the new civic spaces, Exchange Square, which also formed a major component in the improvement of the rediscovered Corporation Street route. Along this route and throughout the area new development, including the refurbishment of existing buildings and the restructuring of the Arndale Centre, has generated new destinations and active ground-floor street frontages where none existed previously, contributing to an expanded retail core and the significant increase in the pedestrian desire to use these routes and areas throughout the week and 24 hours a day.

The re-engagement with the medieval core was intended to open up the opportunity for northward expansion of retailing and for a significant increase in the scale, density and quality within this area, and the Masterplan identified significant opportunities for new development and activity.

The new urban blocks created to the east and west of New Cathedral Street reflect the successful Georgian and Victorian scale to the south and have become the major focus of new high quality development in the retail core. The prominent, raking, glazed residential tower on the Deansgate frontage of these urban blocks gives a new landmark on the Manchester skyline.

The formation of New Cathedral Street required the relocation of the Shambles public houses which now enhance and reinforce the character of the medieval core and are in sharp contrast to the nearby Urbis building. Such a dramatic juxtaposition of old and new, and of changes in scale, are characteristic throughout the city centre.

The potential for a major new leisure destination was identified behind the retained façade of a long-time redundant former printing works. The 'Printworks' has now significantly increased the diversity and density of use as part of the northward push of the retail core. Still more activity has been brought to this area by the refurbishment for high-quality retail and office use of the adjacent former Corn Exchange because of the opportunities opened up by the Masterplan. This increasing level of activity will be further enhanced by the completion of the ongoing restructuring of the Arndale Centre where it faces Exchange Square and the Printworks, which will include a new internal shopping mall on the approximate line of the closed Cannon Street, as sought by the Masterplan.

The Masterplan was supported by proposals for an integrated transport network, with the primary objective being to strike the appropriate balance between good car access and encouraging people to use public transport and enabling appropriate service and emergency access. In parallel with the physical rebuilding and environmental works the use of routes within and adjacent to the Masterplan area were reconsidered – with some routes being closed completely to vehicles, and private traffic being removed from others including, by day, from Corporation Street. This, and restrictions on servicing hours, has dramatically altered the manner in which the area functions and has contributed to the provision of a safe and pleasant environment for pedestrians and cyclists.

Project sign-off

The Masterplan process was designed to provide opportunities to actively recreate and reinforce the relationship of the retail core with surrounding areas. The soon-to-be-completed transport interchange (with combined Metrolink, bus and car parking facilities) adjacent to the Printworks will provide immediate accessibility to the retail core and will deliver new patterns of footfall that will enliven areas of the city centre and further extend regeneration

PHOTO: EDAW/PHOTOGRAPHY BY DIXI CARRILLO

PHOTO: MANCHESTER CITY COUNCIL

benefits. The implementation of the Masterplan and the resultant new city structure has acted as a catalyst for the regeneration and improvement of a much wider area – a principal example being the refurbishment of Piccadilly Gardens. The Masterplan structure reinforced the value of public spaces, permeability and a high-quality public realm to a successful city centre. It also reinforced the very real and positive benefits of all the city-centre stakeholders working in partnership to continue to deliver this ongoing city-centre-wide regeneration process.

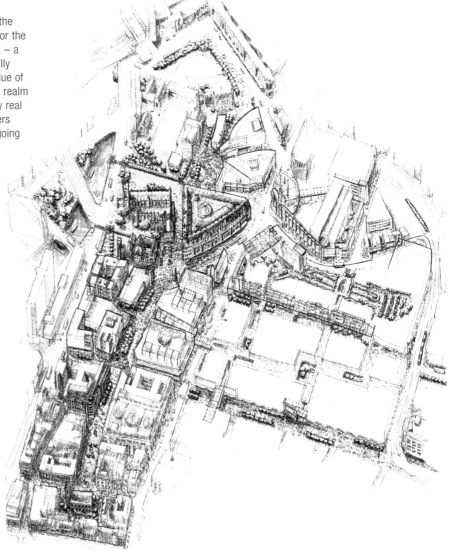

PHOTO: EDAW/PHOTOGRAPHY
BY DIXI CARRILLO

CITY CENTRE MASTERPLAN

PROJECT TEAM

Lead Masterplanners, Design Coordination and Public Realm:
EDAW

Transportation Consultant: **Oscar Faber**

Masterplan Consultant: **Ian Simpson Architects**

Retail Strategy: **Benoy**

Infrastructure: **Alan Baxter & Associates**

Masterplan Consultant: **Building Design Partnership**

Program Management: **MACE**

Quantity Survey: **Davis Langdon**

143

The flagship Manchester store, located at the heart of the
regenerated city centre, covers six levels, and represents a major
statement of M&S's aspirations and image for the future.

MARKS & SPENCER
BUILDING DESIGN PARTNERSHIP

7 Market Street, Manchester

Construction Value: £85 million
Completion Date: November 1999

Description

A new flagship store, whose design concept delivers long-term
flexibility for Marks & Spencer through a functional clarity that
divorces the building's 'servant functions', located on the east
and west flanks, from the sales area on the north/south axis.
This is further expressed through the building's external
envelope, where the fully glazed north and south façades offer
dramatic views into the store through the biggest shop windows
in Europe.

History

Proposals were formulated as a result of the international Urban
Design Competition held in the Autumn of 1996 as part of the
rebuilding of the city centre. The new development was a
catalyst among the rebuilding initiatives, and the spearhead of
the reconstruction programme.

Client's brief

The design-and-build brief for the Marks & Spencer project was
to design an appropriate, forward-looking, memorable and
durable external image for the store and to marry this with the
best possible working, trading and servicing arrangements for
the future.

Design process

BDP worked closely with the City Centre Masterplan team to
help evolve and inform the formation of the public realm around
the perimeter of the store. The building footprint has a significant
impact on the city with all four elevations fronting onto important
city routes.

The design concept proposed large-span, rectangular floorplates
repeated over six levels. Sub-basement car parking feeds
customers into feature lifts which rise through a spectacular
atrium connecting at all levels. Principal trading is at basement
(food hall), ground and first floors. Customer café-bar, sales and
fallow space (for future expansion) are located at second floor,
with staff facilities and offices plus further fallow space at third.
Major plant is at rooftop level. All the service functions – escape
stairs, service riser, goods lifts and the like – have been

positioned along the long sides of the plan, leaving the central
spaces clear and flexible for trading.

This large building integrates well into the grain of the city,
respecting the grid pattern streetscape and supporting
permeability. This is reinforced by the high-level bridge across
Corporation Street which connects directly into the Arndale
Centre.

Externally, the building is fully clad, with full-height glazing giving
maximum transparency to the end walls. This is partly as a
display device – activity within the space being the best possible
advertising – and partly to help orientation within such a large
footprint by capitalising on excellent views out – south to the
Royal Exchange, north to the Corn Exchange. The cornice level of
the Royal Exchange has been used as a datum for the new
building, which steps back in response. The importance of the
appearance of the building at night has been recognised by the
design team, who have designed the artificial lighting to
complement the architecture of the scheme.

The Marks & Spencer store uses large areas of glazing to assist
the orientation of customers and to make a strong urban-design
statement in the context of its prominent city-centre site. The
extensive areas of glazing exhibit a number of unique features
for a retail store, including a south-facing ventilated 'double wall'
construction with motorised blinds and roof panels, the use of
low-iron glass to provide maximum transparency, and 4m-high
fritted 'super graphic' lettering.

Stone was used as cladding to the core elements. The curtain
walling for the project was specially developed in collaboration
with Focchi Spa (the Italian curtain walling company) to an
exacting specification.

In early 2001, Marks & Spencer determined that their
operational requirements had changed. BDP was instructed to
prepare a design for subdivision of the building to produce two
stores, each of 11,000m² retail area with one being for Marks &
Spencer and the other for Selfridges. The flexibility of the original
concept was to be tested at an early stage as it was clearly
important that the resultant building should have the appearance

of having initially been designed in this way and not look like a subsequent conversion. The resultant scheme opened in June 2002 with Selfridges occupying the northern side of the building overlooking Exchange Square, whilst Marks & Spencer was at the southern end with views towards the Royal Exchange building. Between the two stores, and lying adjacent to the elevator cores, is a new internal street. This connects New Cathedral Street to Corporation Street and also to the high-level pedestrian bridge into the Arndale Centre.

Project sign-off

The flagship Manchester store, located at the heart of the regenerated city centre, covers six levels, and represents a major statement of M&S's aspirations and image for the future.

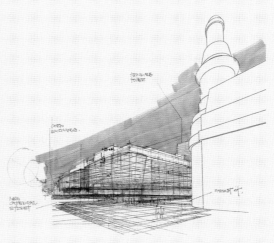

MARKS & SPENCER

PROJECT TEAM

Client/Owner: **Marks & Spencer**
Architect: **BDP**
Interior Design: **BDP**
Lighting Design: **BDP**
Structural Engineer: **WSP**
Services Engineer: **ACD**
Quantity Surveyor: **Cyril Sweett & Partners**
Main Contractor: **Bovis**

PHOTOS: CHARLOTTE WOOD

A symbol of Manchester's recovery after the bomb, Corporation Street Footbridge is a cutting-edge symbol of modernity and captures the optimism of the city's growth and future.

CORPORATION STREET FOOTBRIDGE
HODDER ASSOCIATES

Corporation Street, Manchester

Construction Value: £650 thousand
Completion Date: November 1999

Description
This new footbridge replaced the original which was demolished following the bombing on 15 June 1996.

History
The explosion shattered the footbridge which connected the Arndale Centre with Marks & Spencer across Corporation Street.

Client's brief
The footbridge is a pedestrian route which connects the Hallé Mall West, of the Arndale Centre, and the central atrium of the new Marks & Spencer store. The design challenge was to link the two public areas of the buildings and to facilitate clear and unobstructed pedestrian flows between the M&S store and the Arndale Centre, while contributing to the character of Corporation Street.

Design process
Contextually Corporation Street is canyon-like, and is a significant, linear north-south route through the city linking the new Exchange Square with the civic space of Albert Square. The initial sketch proposed a highly transparent tube of regular cross section through which would pass a delicate oak boardwalk, spanning across the structure and inclined to redress the existing change in level between the two shopping centres. The intention was for a minimal intervention within the street scene. The structure was a curving di-grid of steelwork. Early computer modelling demonstrated a tendency for the structure to deflect excessively at mid span. By twisting the structure along its horizontal axis the deflection was eliminated and collectively we recognised the advantages of the resultant hyperbolic paraboloid arrangement, in that the footbridge could be constructed from straight members and flat facets or planes. Additionally and poetically the resultant form presented an object of tension, seemingly stretched across the street, tying one side to the other.

The developed footbridge is a pure geometrical structure of eighteen 25mm-diameter steel rods pre-stressed against eighteen compression members of 110mm-diameter circular hollow-steel section via compression rings at each end. It is 'self-contained' in terms of pre-stressing loads and does not rely on adjacent buildings for anchorage (a further requirement of the brief). Indeed this assisted construction, being fabricated off-site and craned into position in once piece – an operation that took only 40 minutes. The glazing system comprises purpose-made elliptical stainless-steel castings, each clamping six triangular sheets of silicon-jointed laminated glass panels. The expressed steel structure is intended to impart a grain of city scale externally, whereas the silicon-jointed glass membrane, presents a smooth, tactile, finer grain to pedestrians using the footbridge.

Once on site the two openings within the respective shopping centres were discovered to have a 4° misalignment. This was re-dressed by a truncated conical collar clad in perforated metal at each interface. The collars not only manage the visual transition from bridge to building but also have an environmental function. The void beneath the boardwalk acts as a plenum. Air is admitted via the collars at each end and heated in winter, the warm air rising at the edges of the boardwalk and venting, once again through the collars, at high level. Ventilation in summer is by similar means and thus the profile of the bridge also optimises the pattern of natural ventilation. Access to the void for maintenance is via two access hatches within the boardwalk.

Project sign-off
The reinstatement of the Corporation Street footbridge was intended as a symbol of the city's recovery after the bomb. More than this, it is hoped that the footbridge has generated a landmark necessary in a successful urban framework and, additionally, a cutting-edge symbol of modernity and the city's culture. In fusing architecture, innovative structural design, and the latest glass technology we have sought to create a piece of public art and a structure which captures the optimism of the city's growth and future.

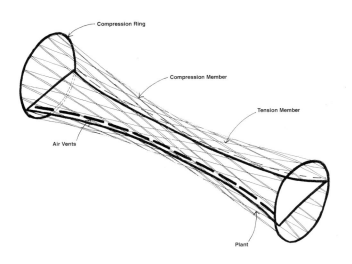

Compression Ring

Compression Member

Tension Member

Air Vents

Plant

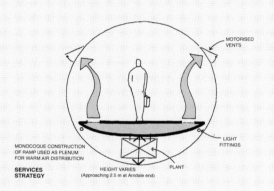

MOTORISED VENTS

LIGHT FITTINGS

MONOCOQUE CONSTRUCTION
OF RAMP USED AS PLENUM
FOR WARM AIR DISTRIBUTION

**SERVICES
STRATEGY**

HEIGHT VARIES
(Approaching 2.5 m at Arndale end)

PLANT

CORPORATION STREET FOOTBRIDGE

PROJECT TEAM

Client: **Manchester City Council**

Architect: **Hodder Associates**

Structural Engineer: **Arup**

Façade Engineer: **Arup Façades**

Construction Manager: **Bovis Construction Ltd**

Sub-Contractors:

Steelwork: **Watson Steel Ltd**

Glazing System: **Dane Architectural Systems Ltd**

Finishes: **J. W. Taylor Ltd**

Mechanical & Electrical: **Farebrother Group Ltd**

151

Exchange Square has become the focus for many city
events and continues to evolve in line with the
challenges of an active city centre.

EXCHANGE SQUARE

URBAN SOLUTIONS

City Centre, Manchester

Construction Value: £3.4 million
Completion Date: December 1999

Description
Exchange Square is bounded by the former Corn Exchange
Building, now the Triangle, Corporation Street and the new Marks
& Spencer and Selfridges stores.

History
The site had been a heavily trafficked junction of inner-city
streets and was dominated by buses, cutting off the Cathedral,
Chethams School of Music and Victoria Station from the retail
and commercial core of the city. The City Centre Masterplan
created a setting for the three major new retail spaces facing
onto the square, reconnecting the Cathedral to the city centre,
relocating two listed buildings – The Old Wellington Inn and
Sinclair's Oyster Bar – and promoting the opportunity to create a
pedestrian space at the heart of the city.

Client's brief.
The Square was to be a major civic space, resolving a series of
complex movements and cross-falls across the site. It had to be
instrumental in linking the historic buildings to the new retail
activity, maintain the good public transport linkages and improve
connections to the existing main rail, Metrolink stations and the
proposed new transport interchange at Shudehill. The Square
had to be dynamic: the focus for New Cathedral Street, a street
created to link retail activity and open up vistas to the Cathedral.
Exchange Square had to be fully accessible and be a memorable
space.

Design process
The fundamental concept of the design by Martin Schwartz,
winner of the international design competition was to generate a
vibrant focus for the city and resolve the disconnections between
a historic quarter, including the Cathedral, and the heart of the
city. The selected proposal reinforced the urban form of the
square and proposed to 're-invent' the historic line of Hanging
Ditch, a medieval watercourse which follows the line of the face
of the Corn Exchange, a landmark listed building.

The proposal identified two primary planes on site. The lower
level follow the existing grade of Hanging Ditch and would
contain a moving watercourse. This plane was connected to the
upper level, the largest area of the square, by a series of ramps
and stairs which would also support seating. This level is a large
stone plane delineated by coloured lights and 'rail-tracks' which
take reference from both historic and contemporary Manchester.
The upper level maintains the level of New Cathedral Street
which terminates at a belvedere enjoying views of the square,
and the two relocated listed pubs.

The paving has been designed to articulate the scheme and
stone is the dominant material throughout. There is a change of
material at the river's edge differentiating between the old and
new. The lower square, ramps and the stairs are primarily York
stone, respecting the existing natural colour of the cathedral, the
upper plaza is in granite and contains the 'rail-tracks'

Gentle stone ramps which slope at 5 per cent and stone steps
connect the two levels. The lengths of the ramps and steps
gradually shorten as the slopes of the two planes meet to the
west of the Corn Exchange. These ramps and stairs are the most
exuberant feature of the square and articulate the three
dimensional form of the space. They allow a range of movement
and provide casual seating, thus providing pleasure in moving
through the plaza as well as in stopping within it.

Planting is used as a landscape highlight in the scheme.
River Birch trees mark the line of the water feature at Hanging
Ditch giving a soft quality to the area. The canopies of the trees
are transparent enough to allow dappled sunlight to fall in front
of the shops and the seating areas at low level.

The historic line of Hanging Ditch is brought to life through an
abstract river. A line of stones within the water sit level with the
York stone paving and flush-mounted water heads that spray in
arcing jets down the stream. The water element is such that it is
low enough to see over, and the base of the fountain is texturally
rich enough to be visually interesting when switched off.

There are two major lighting strategies within the area. At the
lower level, lights are installed within the river and emphasise
the line of Hanging Ditch. At the upper level, bands of light are
inserted between the railway tracks. The curved walls to the
ramps are articulated by individual lamps set within the wall
surface.

In The Interest Of Safety
Please Refrain From Climbing
On The Water Feature.
Do Not Drink The Water

SELFRIDGES&C°

153

PHOTO: LEN GRANT

Seating is provided throughout on the ramp walls and at the base of the ramps adjacent to the fountain. Movable seats are available on the rails at the upper level.

The 'Windmills' – a major vertical element in front of Marks & Spencer, facing into the square – were designed by John Hyatt and installed at the end of the contract.

Project sign-off
Exchange Square is a successful location for many city events. The square continues to evolve, meeting the challenges of an active city centre and responding to further development at its edges.

PHOTO: IAN LAWSON

EXCHANGE SQUARE

PROJECT TEAM

Client: **Manchester City Council**

Concept and Landscape Architect: **Martha Schwartz**

Implementation Architects and Engineers: **Urban Solutions (Chapman Robinson Architects and Manchester Engineering Design Consultancy)**

Quantity Surveyor: **Davis Langdon**

Artist for the 'Windmills': **John Hyatt**

No 1 Deansgate's crystalline prismatic form, delicately supported on a series of dramatic inclined steel columns, has created an iconic and instantly recognisable building.

NO 1 DEANSGATE

IAN SIMPSON ARCHITECTS

Deansgate, Manchester

Construction Value: £20 million
Completion Date: April 2002

Description

A new-build residential and mixed-use development that formed a key component of the Masterplan which was adopted following the terrorist bomb of 1996, and the creation of New Cathedral Street.

History

This important site has a prominent frontage onto Deansgate and provides an opportunity to create a focal point from all directions. The tall, slender, simple form of the residential tower relates in scale to other tall buildings in the vicinity, including the Ramada Renaissance Hotel on the opposite side of Deansgate. This relationship strengthens the dramatic long views down this major route through the city and frames the view of the Cathedral further north along Deansgate. The height of the residential tower steps down from its highest point on St Mary's Gate to relate to the Cathedral and to acknowledge and respect the variety of the building heights in the surrounding context.

Client's brief

The City Council as landowner, and Crosby Homes North West Ltd as developer, entered into a commercial agreement and became development partners for the project. They required a dynamic landmark building on this important city centre site.

Design process

No 1 Deansgate comprises two distinct elements, a fully glazed residential tower 'lifted' 9m above a retail podium by a raking transfer structure. The simple, elegant 7m-high two-storey fully glazed podium, which sits above a 74-space basement car park, provides animated façades and an active frontage at street level and wraps around the corner to form a coherent whole with the overall city block.

The dramatic raking steel columns articulate the retail and residential components and form a triple-height sky lobby for the residents. This allows the building to cantilever over the street and facilitates a change in the structural grid between retail/car parking and residential. The generous height between the podium and the underside of the apartment 'tower' accentuates the visual separation of the retail and the residential. This gives the residential element its own identity while the strength of the transfer structure, which can be read through glazed façades, anchors the residential element to the podium and unifies the whole building.

A storey-high steel transfer truss which supports the frame to the upper 14 floors is in turn supported by the inclined tubular steel columns and is accommodated within the first residential floor level.

The building has 84 apartments within the upper 14 floors. One and two-bedroom homes combine with triplex and duplex penthouses.

The apartment building has a twin-skin envelope, each apartment has access to a semi-external space formed between the inner and outer skins of the glazed cladding. The inner skin is double-glazed and the outer skin comprises fully openable single-glazed louvres. The double-skin system provides a habitable and flexible outdoor space to each apartment at all times of the year and an extension to the living accommodation. It also assists with acoustic, thermal and solar-gain issues, and creates a constantly changing, animated and shimmering façade as occupants individually adjust their louvres. The sloping roof incorporates open terraces to the eight penthouse duplex and triplex apartments.

Project sign-off

No 1 Deansgate's crystalline prismatic form, delicately supported on a series of dramatic inclined steel columns, has created an iconic and instantly recognisable building within the city.

It reflects the determination of the City Council to renew and enhance the city centre and a desire by the developer to build a beautiful building that would be widely regarded as a symbol of excellence. These aspirations have been achieved by a combination of vision, creative and ground-breaking design and innovative construction management and techniques, critically delivered through a unique partnership between the city, the client, the architect and the construction manager.

157

PHOTOS: CROSBY HOMES NORTH WEST LTD

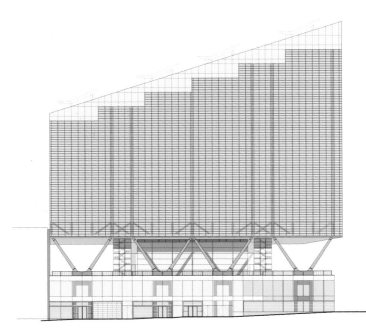

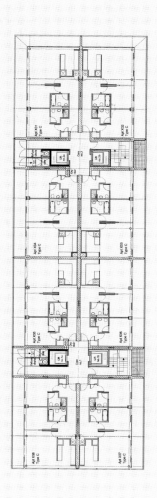

NUMBER ONE DEANSGATE

PROJECT TEAM

Development Partners: **Manchester City Council and Crosby Homes North West Ltd**

Architect: **Ian Simpson Architects**

Structural Engineer: **Martin Stockley Associates**

Services Engineer: **Roberts and Partners**

Quantity Surveyor: **Davis Langdon**

Construction Manager: **Mace**

159

Cathedral Gardens offers a spectacular green oasis in
the centre of the city and celebrates the unique
character of the medieval heart of Manchester.

CATHEDRAL GARDENS
BUILDING DESIGN PARTNERSHIP

Cathedral Gardens, Manchester

Construction Value: £4.4 million
Completion Date: June 2002

Description

The Gardens sit within the Millennium Quarter area of the public
realm between Victoria Station approach, Chetham's School of
Music, the Cathedral, the refurbished Triangle shopping centre
and the new Urbis building. Extending out onto the edge of
Victoria Street, they include a new garden area in front of the
ancient monument of Hanging Bridge and the Cathedral Visitor
Centre.

History

Improving the quality and attractiveness of the city-centre
environment and creating new safe public spaces were the two
key priorities asked for during public consultation following the
1996 terrorist bombing.

The people of Manchester asked for more trees, greenery and
open space. The site for Cathedral Gardens had become a
congested, unattractive area which had fallen out of favour.
Manchester City Council commissioned the scheme that would
seek to revive the character of this historically significant site.

Client's brief

Cathedral Gardens will 'present the opportunity to create a major
open space within the city centre largely derived from roads and
a car park'. An area within the Millennium Quarter which
completes the programme for the pedestrianisation of the
city centre.

The design of the park 'must reflect the budget available', and
'must be distinctive, a uniquely Manchester place, reflecting the
significance of its location within the historic core of the city and
adjacent to a major cultural building for the new millennium'.

The park had to respond to the existing and proposed needs of
the main built elements within its boundaries Urbis: the
Cathedral, the Corn Exchange and Chetham's School of Music.

Design process

The scheme consists of a series of themed lawns, trees, water
features, artworks and hard-landscape areas to create the new
green space in this part of the city. The lawns consist of four
areas:

> The 'Cathedral botanical lawns' sweep down the length of the
  old Fennel Street between the Cathedral and Chetham's
  School. These follow the contours in the form of flowing
  plateaux edged by stepped walls with integrated layered glass
  blocks which are lit at night.

> The 'Podium lawns' form an arena of grass terraces in front
  of Urbis and the Triangle. Glass blocks, which are illuminated
  at night, have been integrated within the steps consisting of
  artworks elements referring to the archaeological context of
  the Millennium Quarter.

> The 'Pillow lawns' form the main feature of the gardens.
  These lawns create a playful mix of sculptural illuminated
  walls and soft rolling mounds. The walls make reference to
  the old cellars of the houses which once stood on this site.

> A majestic Cedar sits within a formal lawn at the gateway
  from Victoria Station to welcome visitors to the city, in front of
  the new Urbis.

The artworks have been the subject of a limited competition and are
integrated into the landscape using the theme of 'The Seasons' with
emphasis on them being elements of a 'Trail of Discovery' within the
gardens. Four artists worked with the designers to create these
discovery elements in the gardens.

The water feature links all these elements together. A source
pool with cascading bronze leaves runs into a rill channel along
the entire length of Long Millgate with more bronze seasonal
inlays. The watercourse tumbles into the final pool amongst a
series of water jets which reach up to seven metres in the air
between four vertical majestic sculptural gateway poles.
To achieve the objective of minimising the through passage of
pedestrians and traffic in this area, the first phase of
construction included the closure of Fennel Street and diversion
of traffic around the site. In this way it was possible to replace
and install utilities without disruption to surrounding highways.
The second phase of construction was largely dictated by the
interface with the construction of Urbis. It was necessary to work
closely with the Urbis project team as their works largely
dictated when Cathedral Gardens could be completed.

Project sign-off

Cathedral Gardens has provided a high-quality new public space which enhances the setting of existing buildings. The Gardens offer a spectacular green oasis in the centre of the city that celebrates the unique character of the medieval heart of Manchester. They create a relaxing space for office workers, shoppers, tourists and Manchester residents alike. The Gardens are attractive all year round and perfectly complement both the medieval and modern buildings that surround them. The green lawns are arranged to respond to the geometry of Urbis and the surrounding buildings, to create areas of play, to sit and contemplate or watch events in front of Urbis.

CATHEDRAL GARDENS

PROJECT TEAM

Client: **Manchester City Council**

Landscape Architect and Engineer: **BDP**

Artists: **Chris Brammall, Stephen Broadbent, Oblique Ltd and Lauren Sagar**

Quantity Surveyor: **Davis Langdon**

Programme Manager: **MACE**

Contractor: **Manchester Contracts**

163

Urbis is a beautiful, powerful and inspirational landmark building for the enjoyment and visual delight of the citizens of Manchester.

URBIS

IAN SIMPSON ARCHITECTS

Cathedral Gardens, Manchester

Construction Value: £30 million
Completion Date: June 2002

Description
The £30m development of Urbis (including exhibition costs) was funded as part of the £42m Manchester Millennium Quarter.

History
The solution to the island site follows the street edge, drops down a subtle incline, turns the corner, and begins the journey back on itself, defining the entrance and forming a sheltering backdrop to a new public landscaped space. The sculptural form of Urbis was placed to the edge of the site to maximise the area for Cathedral Gardens and respond to the strong context, allowing the prominent and listed façades of the Corn Exchange and Chetham's School of Music to be equally expressed.

Client's brief
The client had aspirations for a landmark cultural building, and launched an international design competition in 1998 to find a unique concept for this key component in the City Council's strategy for regenerating the city.

Design process
The building envelope consists of a curving, sandblasted glass skin of varying transparency, offering glimpses in and out of the building, a textured and constantly changing surface made up of 2,500 glass tiles which are combined with an internal double-glazed unit to provide a passive low-energy envelope. The glass creates a sense of openness internally which maximises the use of daylight, whilst allowing attention to be focused on the exhibits. The triple-glazed skin provides a buffer zone, which is ventilated at high and low levels and allows solar gain to be dissipated. It also encloses further layers of louvres and blinds which control glare and capture solar gains in winter.

The dominant roof slopes and cants towards the city. Pre-patinated copper tiles on a diagonal grid cover the roof surface, and seek to blend with the soft green hue of the sandblasted glass, reinforcing the strong, sculptural form. An angular rooflight cuts through the centre of the roof and forms an emphatic spine to the building. The spine extends above the building and is expressed as the mast, a contemporary finial.

The building accommodates a variety of interactive displays and exhibits that seek to describe the experience of world cities. The building was conceived and designed to be totally flexible. The exhibits, by their nature, are transient and changeable. The building, in response, provides open-plan floorplates. Services and escape circulation are located within the east buffer zone; public circulation and movement are positioned adjacent to the west elevation overlooking Cathedral Gardens.

On entry, the interior reveals the whole building volume, as the four exhibition floors slide away above each other. A glazed inclined elevator connects the entrance foyer with the uppermost gallery space. Each floorplate is open and visible from above and below, and every visitor to Urbis is able to enjoy the people-watching that this open interior invites. Above the exhibition are two floors providing a restaurant with views across the city. The restaurant is accessed separately to allow independent control and varied opening hours to that of the museum.

Legibility of parts, articulation of components, order, simplicity and clarity are key themes explored within the programme, organisation and materiality of the building.

Project sign-off
Urbis is the culmination of our endeavours to produce a beautiful, powerful and inspirational landmark building for the enjoyment and visual delight of the citizens of Manchester. There is no national or international precedent for Urbis, either the building or its contents. The success of the project is a result of the close working partnership that developed between the architect and the client, through the evolution and interpretation of the brief. For those who have contributed to the scheme, the combination of risk-taking and problem-solving has resulted in a building that has become an icon for the city.

PHOTOS: SHAW + SHAW

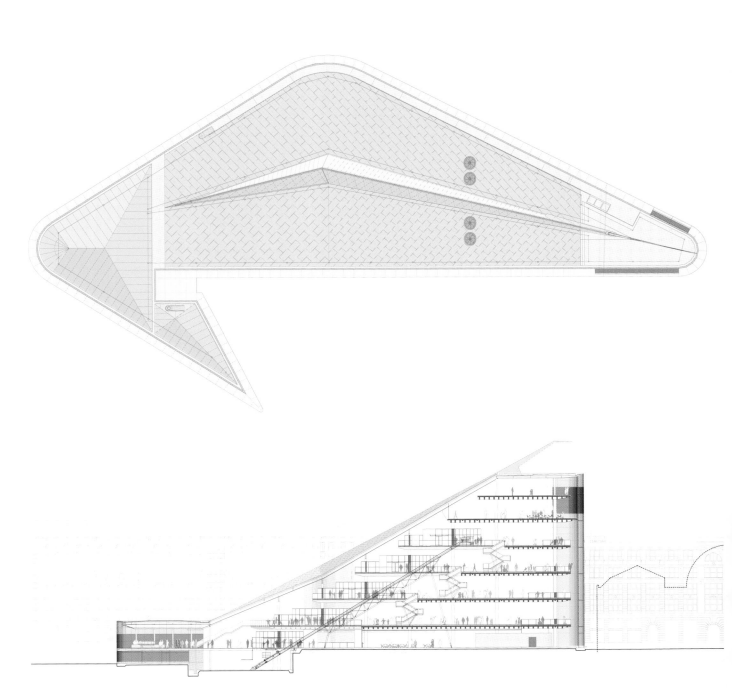

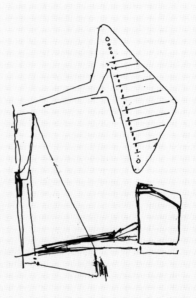

URBIS

PROJECT TEAM

Client: **Manchester City Council**
Architect: **Ian Simpson Architects**
Structural Engineer: **Martin Stockley Associates/Halcrow**
Services Engineer: **Farley Consulting**
Cost Manager: **Davis Langdon**
Construction Manager: **Laing O'Rourke**
Project Manager: **Capita Projects**

A major contribution to the ongoing improvement to Manchester's integrated transport system.

MANCHESTER TRANSPORT INTERCHANGE
IAN SIMPSON ARCHITECTS

Shudehill, Manchester

Construction Value: £25 million
Completion Date: Autumn 2005

Description
A single cohesive entity to be known as the Manchester Transport Interchange comprising three primary components: the bus concourse and passenger stops, a new Metrolink Tram stop and a multi-storey car park.

History
The Transport Interchange forms a key component of the Manchester City Centre rebuilding strategy following the IRA bomb in 1996, allowing the relocation of the bus station from within the Arndale Centre and hence the creation of a new winter garden on the site of Cannon Street.

Client's brief
Ian Simpson Architects was appointed to propose a new concept for the Transport Interchange and design a unified development that will be a high quality and recognisable landmark for the city, and improve the environment for the travelling public, maximising user comfort, safety and security.

Design process
The design of the Transport Interchange has been carefully considered in relation to its setting within the Shudehill conservation area and its proximity to a number of listed buildings. In order to identify the primary elevation and entrance to the concourse the form of the building is orientated so as to present a narrow frontage to Shudehill. The bulk of the building extends into the depth of the site so as to relate to the larger buildings associated with the CIS and the Printworks development.

Bus entrance and egress is from Shudehill. Bus circulation is single direction anti-clockwise around a central concourse.

The concourse has a gently sloping floor following the contours of the site and varies in height from 3m to over 6m. The perimeter of the concourse is primarily clear glazed with waiting areas situated around the perimeter immediately adjacent to the bus stands. Within the body of the concourse are two metal and glass pod structures containing the support accommodation, comprising offices, travel centre, shops and café.

A secondary finger island is positioned to the south of the main concourse, utilising similar materials and forms to the primary concourse and providing additional passenger capacity.

The perimeter of the site is bounded by a new feature wall to back of pavement, which changes in colour, texture and articulation in response to its adjacent context, the activity behind the wall and the historical street pattern. The primary corners are emphasised by raised canopies, over the staff accommodation on Shudehill and to the Dantzic Street/Hanover Street corner.

The wall steps down and follows the contours of the site and leads to the north platform of the metrolink stop. A high level steel and glass aerofoil shaped canopy provides shelter to the tram stop and defines the primary pedestrian entrance to the concourse along Shudehill. The canopy will also announce the entrance to the Interchange from the retail section of the city and strongly define/reinforce the corner.

The multi-storey car park is accommodated within a very spatially efficient concrete framed structure. Vertical circulation within the car park is achieved by an arrangement of tilting floor plates, commencing at approximately 6m above the ground floor level. Access to and egress from the car park is from Hanover Street, via a dedicated concrete and steel ramp. The bulk of the ramp is shielded by the staff accommodation on the corner of Hanover Street and Shudehill.

The structure of the car park has a vertical emphasis in response to the surrounding context, this verticality is further reinforced by the lift and stair towers.

The envelope to the car park consists of an arrangement of fritted glass panels, heavily articulated within the horizontal plane and varying in width. The intention is to achieve the required natural ventilation, whilst presenting an animated and varied façade; the translucency of the glass will achieve visual order but allow movement and structure to be subtly expressed.

169

Project sign-off

The design of the Interchange reflects the client's desire to create a high quality built form with facilities akin to airport standard which seeks to promote public transport as a quality alternative to the car. The design carefully reconciles the needs of operators and passengers to create a vibrant, animated and beautiful building.

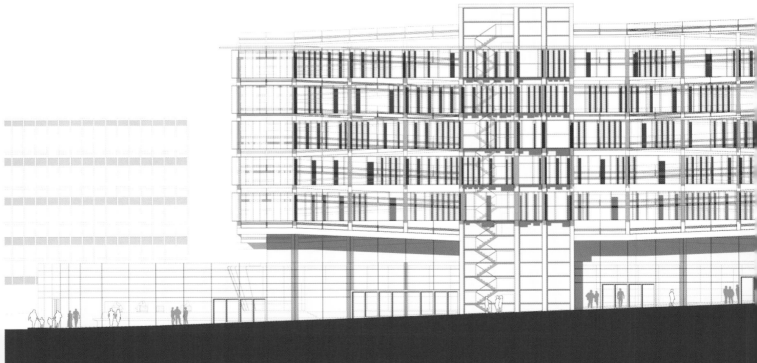

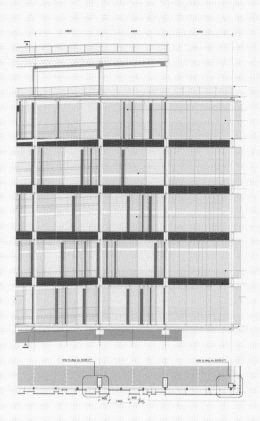

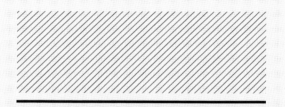

MANCHESTER TRANSPORT INTERCHANGE

PROJECT TEAM

Client: **GMPTE** (in partnership with MCC, NWRA and Richardsons)
Architect: **Ian Simpson Architects**
Associate Architect: **Jefferson Sheard Architects**
Project Manager: **GVA Grimley**
Structural Engineer: **Faber Maunsell**
Services Engineer: **Hoare Lea**
Quantity Surveyor: **Gleeds**
Contractor: **Costain**

Arndale North will be transformed into outward-looking contemporary buildings bringing architectural variety and active frontages to the surrounding streets.

ARNDALE NORTH
CHAPMAN TAYLOR ARCHITECTS

Market Street, Manchester

Construction Value: £150 million
Completion Date: Autumn 2006

Description

Manchester Arndale is a covered shopping centre containing 110,000m² of retail space with a 20,000m² prominent 20-storey office tower sitting above a podium deck at roof level. The site owner, Prudential, is currently redeveloping the northern part of the centre to provide 50,000m² of new and replacement retail and catering space, bringing the total for the centre as a whole to 140,000m², together with a new single-level market hall and improved access from an adjoining 1,475-space multi-storey car park.

History

Originally designed in the late 1960s, Manchester Arndale was constructed in a number of phases in the early to mid-1970s and was at the time the largest city-centre shopping centre in the UK. Prudential purchased the controlling interest in Manchester Arndale in March 1998 and immediately appointed a design team to explore redevelopment opportunities for the ailing northern part of the centre.

Client's brief

The brief was to produce a scheme for redeveloping and extending the northern part of the Manchester Arndale that would meet the aspirations of the masterplan. The scheme needed to create a viable and attractive long-term retail solution by providing shop units of modern dimensions in a new and vibrant environment. It also needed to fully intergrate the northern with the southern part of the centre, as well as the surrounding developing areas of the city.

Design process

Whilst the southern part of Manchester Arndale was successful and well connected to the city centre, the northern part was isolated by Cannon Street and had been in relative decline for some years, with poor retail units, a dark and unwelcoming market hall, a disused bus station and confused circulation to the southern part. Externally the building was introverted, with little or no life at street level along its Corporation Street, Canon Street, Withy Grove and High Street frontages.

The masterplan provided for diverting Canon Street and closing it as a public highway, as well as the removal of the bus station and

car park ramps. It also allowed for the building frontages to the northern part to be extended outwards from their existing line.

The scheme currently under construction builds over the former public highway area, necessitating major services diversions, and provides a new alternative east-west pedestrian route through 'New Canon Street', together with a new pedestrian entrance opposite Dantzic Street to the north that will link to the new Transport Interchange at Shudehill. The scheme redevelops some 50 per cent of the existing Manchester Arndale site and creates two clear and easily understandable shopping circuits within the Centre that, because of level changes across the site, link both mall levels comfortably with the surrounding streets. These new fully-glazed malls incorporate the two new feature spaces of Exchange Court and the Wintergarden, creating much improved orientation within the Centre itself.

From the outset, the City Council was keen to see the old monolithic appearance of the Manchester Arndale building broken down, bringing a variety of architecture to the street scene and providing, wherever possible, active frontages at ground level. Thus the new extended frontages have been designed as a sequence of individual buildings that relate to the separate uses within, and which are interrupted at intervals by new branded entrances emphasising the scale and importance of the centre.

A new stand-alone department store for Next completes the enclosure to the eastern side of Exchange Square and incorporates a prominent curved glass wall on the corner of Withy Grove facing Urbis and The Printworks. Glass and metal cladding is used on an individual shop immediately south of the major new entrance to Arndale North from Exchange Square. The retail/restaurant façades to Withy Grove follow the curved line of the road and change form to respond to the smaller scale, width and character of the street. A fully glazed ground-level frontage is introduced to the new single-level market hall that sits below the retained car park on the High Street. Materials for the new 'buildings' are drawn from the traditional and modern Manchester vernaculars (limestone, granite plinths, metal, glass, glass blocks and traditional red brick), are high-quality and have contemporary detailing.

The project has not only had to overcome the usual challenges presented by a constrained city-centre site – access, site logistics, environmental, and health and safety issues – but also has the added complication that uninterrupted trading had to be maintained at all times in the adjoining southern part, which is serviced through the site via a retained basement service road. The complexities of the part-retained/part-new structure, programme commitments and many site logistics issues have led the team to adopt a structural steel solution together with, wherever possible, prefabricated cladding assemblies and minimal use of 'wet trades'.

Project sign-off

Arndale North will be transformed into outward-looking contemporary buildings bringing architectural variety and active frontages to the surrounding streets. Interior planning will meet the needs and aspirations of both retailers and shoppers into the future and provide clear easily-understood shopping circuits that fully integrate into the city centre.

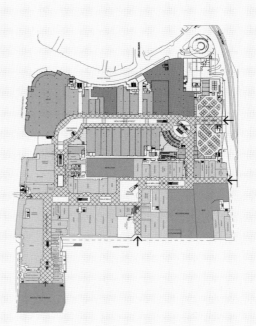

ARNDALE NORTH

PROJECT TEAM

Building Owner: **Prudential Assurance Company Ltd**
Client: **Prudential Property Investment Managers Ltd**
Architect: **Chapman Taylor Architects**
Consulting Engineer: **Connell Mott MacDonald**
Services Engineer: **Roberts and Partners**
Cost Consultant: **Cyril Sweett Limited**
Access Consultant: **CS2**
Highways Consultant: **Symonds Group Ltd**
Planning Supervisor: **Cyril Sweett Limited**
Façade Engineer: **Arup Façade Engineering**
Acoustic Consultant: **Arup Acoustics**
Lighting Consultant: **Kondos Roberts**
Main Contractor: **Bovis Lend Lease**

Century Buildings was among the first commercial-to-residential conversions in central Manchester and brings the best out of this historic city's existing fabric.

CENTURY BUILDINGS

ASSAEL ARCHITECTURE

St Mary's Parsonage, Manchester

Construction Value: £17 million
Completion Date: September 2001

Description
The building is a combination of a Grade II listed building and an adjoining, glass-fronted 1960s office block, converted for residential use.

History
Century Buildings is located in the former National Boiler and General Insurance Company Headquarters which fronts St Mary's Parsonage and backs onto the River Irwell. The buildings are located in the Parsonage Gardens Conservation Area and were originally designed by Harry S. Fairhurst between 1905 and 1909. The attic storey was added in 1929 and the glass extension building in the late 1960s.

Client's brief
The focus was on converting existing buildings in inner-cities into private residential apartments of the highest quality.

The client's brief was to convert the two parts into a single residential building of 121 apartments, adding new accommodation at the top, and with restaurant uses on the lower floors. The key question was how to retain something of the characteristics of the two existing buildings while creating a unified whole. In addition, the dramatic change of level across the site meant that ground floor on the street side was two storeys above the River Irwell at the rear.

Design process
The existing plan form of the listed building seemed unpromising for residential conversion; an ornate, tiled central staircase, with some of the first lifts to be installed in Manchester, led onto open-plan floorplates arranged around two lightwells. The key aspect of the design, agreed through extensive consultation with Manchester City Council and English Heritage, was the use of the lightwells for circulation, thereby altering as little of the listed fabric as possible. This also avoided the unsatisfactory long corridors which are often associated with conversions from office to residential use.

Stacks of lightweight glass-and-steel bridges, suspended from central supports that continue down to sub-basement level, were inserted into each lightwell, creating a circulation route that links the two lightwells but also creates a route through to the 1960s building. The bridges ramp up and deliver residents to their apartment at window-sill level, meaning that interesting changes of level could be created within each apartment, and that the need to punch through areas of existing glazed white bricks below each window was avoided.

Each lightwell, asymmetrical in plan, was covered with a 'loose-fit' glass roof to make it watertight but not airtight. New steel-framed penthouses were added to both buildings – two stories on the listed building and four on the 1960s block. The roof beams in the new penthouses on the listed building cantilever beyond the face of the building and support aluminium-decked balconies over the river, hung from the roof beams on steel wires. Similarly to the access bridges, the balconies are accessed at window-sill level to leave as much of the original fabric intact as possible.

Externally, the terracotta or faience on the listed building was cleaned and repaired. Existing steel-framed windows were retained. However, the glass and stainless-steel cladding on the 1960s building was not suitable for residential use and had corroded; it was completely replaced with a new curtain-walling system that takes its cue from the original cladding (using the same relation between the proportions of the cladding module and the building as a whole) but which re-provides floor-to-ceiling glass elevations in all the flats. The new cladding system also incorporates balconies and sections of rainscreen timber cladding to soften the elevations. Sustainably-sourced iroko hardwood was selected for its durability and because its reddish-grey hue linked well with the terracotta of the listed building.

Restaurant and bar uses have been included on the ground floor of the 1960s building and in the basement of the listed building. The change in level across the site is such that the latter has access onto the riverside walkway at the rear, two full stories above river level. This walkway has been designed so that it can, in the future, be connected via adjoining schemes along the river to Calatrava's landmark Trinity Bridge and the new developments across the river in Salford.

Project sign-off

Century Buildings was among the first commercial-to-residential conversions in central Manchester. Like Smithfield Buildings before, it showed how a creative approach to residential living, together with an open-minded attitude on the part of the planners, could bring the best out of this historic city's existing fabric and bring vitality to the city centre.

LIGHTWELL 2

LIGHTWELL 1

PHOTO: IAN ATKINSON

PHOTO: © NICK GUTTERIDGE

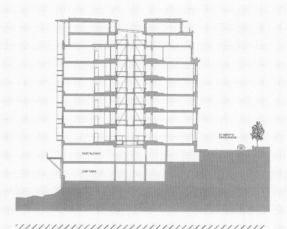

CENTURY BUILDINGS

PROJECT TEAM

Client: **Crest Nicholson plc**
Architect: **Assael Architecture**
Quantity Surveyor, Project Manager: **GTMS**
Structural and Services Engineer: **WSP**
Fire Engineering: **Fire Check Consultants**
Acoustic Consultant: **Hann Tucker**
Cladding Consultant: **Wintech**
Lighting Consultant: **Isometrix**
Planning Comsultant: **Drivers Jonas**
Interior Designer: **Mary Fox Linton, Tegerdine Associates, Marren**
Main Contractor: **C. H. Pearce**

PICCADILLY INITIATIVE

3.21

Piccadilly is a key gateway into the city centre for many thousands of people arriving by road and rail. In addition to Piccadilly Station, which serves intercity regional routes and Manchester Airport, the area benefits from direct links to a regional road network and Metrolink.

Piccadilly was a thriving district during the 1800s and early 1900s with its success based on the cotton industry, but the area suffered from years of decline and under-investment. The City Council – working in partnership with the private sector, the European Commission and others – has recently delivered hundreds of millions of pounds of investment into the area's transport facilities, public realm and buildings. This has attracted new uses to the area, repositioning Piccadilly in the economic and social life of the city.

Piccadilly Station is one of the area's key assets. Built in 1842 as the Store Street Station, it was renamed London Road and then Piccadilly Station. This was one of four railway terminals constructed in Victorian times and it was immensely popular with traders and producers delivering their goods to the main Smithfield Market situated in the Northern Quarter. The station was the terminus of the Manchester and Birmingham railway line, with direct rail links to London in a travel time, then, of nine-and-a-half hours, as compared with a 24-hour journey by stagecoach. The Manchester Royal Infirmary stood on the present site of Piccadilly Gardens, and the nearby department stores and shops along Oldham Street made the district one of popular fashion in the late 1890s.

The character and appearance of the area changed during the 20th century, as the whole city suffered from the loss of traditional manufacturing industries. The 1945 *Manchester City Centre Plan* identified Piccadilly as 'the people's place', with Piccadilly Gardens as 'the most

fig 3.21
Piccadilly
Gardens

fig 3.22
Malmasion Hotel

3.22

attractive feature of the city centre and one whose popularity was limited only by its restricted size'.

The area then suffered a period of decline and change, in spite of key investments, during the 1960s, in Piccadilly Station and the Piccadilly Plaza retail, office and hotel complex. The station was rebuilt in 1969 with a new approach area landscaping. The serpentine glass-and-steel structure of Gateway House followed the curve of the approach to the station, behind which a ten-storey office block dominated the station's front entrance. However, Piccadilly Gardens, the largest area of open space in the city centre, began to suffer from an image problem as it became associated with crime – a situation not helped by its being somewhat inaccessible.

Picking up on the 1984 *City Centre Local Plan* which had identified Piccadilly and London Road as a major gateway in need of development, the Central Manchester Development Corporation (CMDC), aimed to carry out regeneration initiatives in the area. These were not achieved in the lifetime of the Development Corporation but CMDC, in partnership with the City Council, did play a key role in improving the Ashton Canal. With grants for environmental improvements, they were able to repair towpaths and provide new lighting, seating and mooring facilities. These improvements, in turn, levered-in private funding for Piccadilly Village, an attractive waterside housing project which contributed to the Council's aim of increasing the population of the city centre.

Piccadilly, however, was continuing to underperform and was unable to attract significant private investors, so, in order to create the required momentum for change, the City Council set out a new regeneration strategy for the area in 1997. This strategy established a number of key projects that were required in order to deliver the step change in Piccadilly necessary to ensure the area contributed as much as possible to the wider city centre. These key projects included the refurbishment of Piccadilly Gardens and Piccadilly Plaza, the Rochdale and Ashton Canal basins and the total refurbishment of Piccadilly Station – as well as providing improved linkages through the area.

181

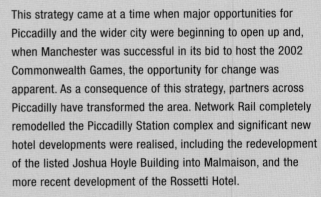

3.23

This strategy came at a time when major opportunities for Piccadilly and the wider city were beginning to open up and, when Manchester was successful in its bid to host the 2002 Commonwealth Games, the opportunity for change was apparent. As a consequence of this strategy, partners across Piccadilly have transformed the area. Network Rail completely remodelled the Piccadilly Station complex and significant new hotel developments were realised, including the redevelopment of the listed Joshua Hoyle Building into Malmaison, and the more recent development of the Rossetti Hotel.

The remodelling of Piccadilly Gardens to re-create a modern, high-quality open space was a key element in this overall strategy. This was achieved through a unique partnership between the Council, the private sector, the European Union and other public-sector agencies, whose funding would deliver a scale of change that would have a catalytic effect on the whole Piccadilly area. In a unique deal, the City Council disposed of part of the Gardens for the construction of a quality commercial building, in return for which the resources generated were used to completely transform the Gardens. The team – led by the City Council, and made up of EDAW, Ove Arup, the acclaimed Japanese architect Tadao Ando, Chapman Robinson Architects and Peter Fink Lighting Specialists – created the high-quality, contemporary urban space that is Piccadilly Gardens today. The associated office block, One Piccadilly Gardens, was developed following an international design competition and provides a unique commercial environment with a strong and positive relationship to the landscape.

fig 3.23
Tadao Ando
Pavilion

fig 3.24
One Piccadilly
Gardens

3.24

Another key objective of the scheme was a dramatic upgrade of the bus interchange and pedestrian area and the resulting comprehensive redesign improved links between Piccadilly Station, Chinatown and the Northern Quarter of the city. The Gardens are popular with local people and provide Manchester with a new public space of international standing.

With such significant public-space improvements, the private sector's confidence in the area grew. A new development, Piccadilly Place, will see Argent Group Plc bring forward a major scheme on the vacant and under-used land opposite Piccadilly Station. This area will be transformed over the next ten years into a busy, mixed-use area comprising new offices, apartments, a hotel and retail space – all set out around new public spaces. The area to the south and east of the station, which currently feels relatively remote and isolated from the city centre, but which is highly accessible, is a key focus for future regeneration activity. This 'Eastern Gateway' will be redeveloped to create new jobs, and will build upon the direct rail links to Manchester Airport as well as its proximity to the city's higher education institutions.

The regeneration of Piccadilly complements and reinforces other regeneration activities throughout Manchester and it is the renewed confidence in the city centre – along with the City Council's objectives and the projects delivered in partnerships – that has created a buoyant climate for investment.

To illustrate the important developments in this city gateway district, case studies include Malmaison Hotel, Piccadilly Gardens and One Piccadilly Gardens.

The construction of the hotel and its subsequent success has acted as a catalyst for a large number of developments within the immediate area.

MALMAISON HOTEL
DARBY ASSOCIATES

London Road, Manchester

Construction Value: £9 million
Completion Date: June 1999

Description
The Conversion and extension of a listed textile warehouse, the Joshua Hoyle Building, into a four-star hotel with conferencing and leisure facilities.

History
The site is at the corner of London Road and Auburn Street in a prominent location near the Piccadilly Station approach. The Rochdale Canal passes below the building. The Joshua Hoyle Building was designed by J. W. Beaumont and constructed in 1904 and is a Grade II listed building. The main façade is clad in elaborate glazed terracotta panels in browns, cream and green.

Client's brief
The requirement was to provide a luxury hotel at a budget price, consisting of approximately 120 stylish rooms, a bar and restaurant that would become a destination in its own right, a leisure facility that offered spas and beauty therapy in addition to a gym, and full conferencing facilities. The brief for the appearance of the hotel was to provide a building that raised curiosity in the passer-by as to its use.

Design process
In order to meet the brief's requirement for guest rooms it was apparent that an extension would be required, and that this should match the existing storey heights which were much greater than in those required for a new-build hotel. The existing entrance to the building, whilst on the corner, was not sufficiently grand in scale for a hotel, nor in a convenient location for a taxi drop-off, so the main entrance was located in the new extension on the Piccadilly elevation. In order to echo the French motif used by the Malmaison group a large glazed entrance canopy was provided in an interpretation of the Art Nouveau Metropolitan style. The entrance area was located at the intersection of old and new and was designed as a double-storey-height attachment to both buildings.

The extension was planned to occupy the rear of the site, extending one of the two guestroom corridors which open from the lift lobby, as this was perceived as quieter than the main road frontage. Elevationally the extension contained the main lifts expressed behind vertical-channel glazing at the meeting point with the existing building. Guest rooms are fenestrated with small openings in a shallow curved façade which terminates in a glazed corner-tower feature which acts as an end stop. The extension is constructed in grey-green granite aggregate block, polished and split face to tone with the existing glazed terracotta but also to add a dark contrasting element. A legal requirement was that the extension must be no higher than the existing building. The method of construction used was steel frame with concrete-plank floors. Internal walls were concrete block for durability and to prevent sound transfer, external walls were concrete inner and outer leaves with cavity insulation to achieve thermal mass in the construction.

Project sign-off
Since opening, the hotel has been extremely successful often being at 100 per cent occupancy. The building was designed not to occupy the full site, both because of a covenant on the site and to allow for a later extension. Leach Rhodes Walker carried out a 60-bed extension with further conferencing facilities in 2002. In the period since completion of the hotel the local area has improved greatly with Piccadilly Station being extensively refurbished and listed buildings on Piccadilly being refurbished and brought back into use. In the longer term a major development is planned for the triangular open space facing the Malmaison on Auburn Street straddling the Metrolink tracks. The construction of the hotel and its subsequent success has acted as a catalyst for a large number of developments within the immediate area.

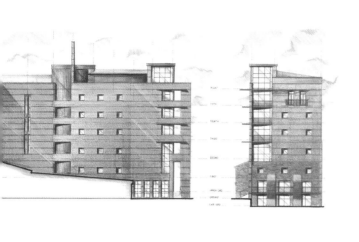

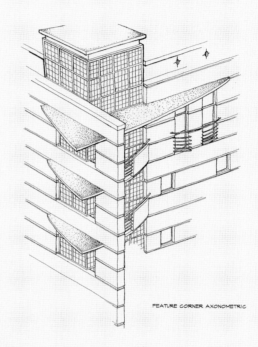

FEATURE CORNER AXONOMETRIC

MALMAISON HOTEL

PROJECT TEAM

Client: **Malmaison Hotels Limited**
Architect: **Darby Associates**
Structural Engineer: **Shepherd Gilmour**
Services Engineer: **RSP**
Quantity Surveyor: **Baker Hollingworth**
Project Manager: **E. C. Harris**

Piccadilly Gardens has been transformed into a bright, open, safe and enjoyable space.

PICCADILLY GARDENS

ARUP

City Centre, Manchester

Construction Value: £10 million
Completion Date: May 2002

Description

The refurbishment of Piccadilly Gardens into an international quality public space was the centrepiece of a much wider regeneration strategy for the infrastructure of the surrounding area.

History

Piccadilly Gardens is one of few green public spaces in Manchester city centre. The Gardens are surrounded by major transport corridors and facilities including a bus station, Metrolink, taxi ranks and servicing to the adjacent businesses. The old site consisted of a sunken garden with shrubbery and flowerbeds and was perceived as an unsafe area, particularly at night.

Client's brief

The challenge was set to create a new public space of international standing. The principal design objectives set out in the brief were:

> Redefine Manchester's principal public space

> Create a major green open space

> Provide a contemporary design

> Reconfigure and expand the size of the Gardens

> Create strategic links to adjacent areas

> Provide a gathering place – day and night

> Ensure a safe place

> Look at incorporating a significant water feature and a boundary feature to the Parker Street Bus Station

Design process

The first task for the team was to develop a masterplan for Piccadilly Gardens. The masterplan pulled together the various transportation and public-realm issues to create an integrated solution. Over the years Piccadilly Gardens has grown in importance as a key public-transport interchange providing the point of arrival for thousands of people daily. Construction work for the transport corridor therefore required very careful planning to ensure that the work could be phased for minimum disruption to the city centre. The first phase of the works was named the

'Corridor Works' and comprised remodelling and resurfacing of the roads and pedestrian areas in the vicinity of Piccadilly Gardens. A series of road diversions and closures, and bus-station closures, was required to undertake these works. The resulting development incorporates remodelling of the surrounding transportation systems to create a balance of separation and integration linking Manchester Piccadilly railway station with Piccadilly Gardens. Disabled access has been considered at all times and there was very close liaison with all the necessary authorities and public throughout the entire design process.

The second phase was that of the regeneration of the existing central gardens, this was named the 'Garden Works'. A 90m-long curved concrete-structure pavilion was positioned at the southern boundary of the site. It has an exposed concrete finish forming an elegant structure as well as being functional. It forms the physical barrier between the gardens and the busy bus station/Metrolink route along Parker Street.

The site also houses a large computer-controlled water feature set into extensive landscaping. This fountain is elliptical in shape with 180 water jets capable of firing water 2m high with four central jets capable of firing water 10m into the air. Operation of the water jets is sequenced with individual fibre-optic lights, which illuminate each jet and have the capability to change to many different colours. Water is collected by means of a channel around the perimeter of the plaza which is uplit with submersible lights. Within the water channel there are over 250 fogging jets which are capable of spraying a ring of mist around the plaza. The plaza is constructed of Chinese black granite, cinza antas white granite and acid-etched white precast concrete. The fountain plaza is one of the largest fountains in Europe.

A 5m-wide pedestrian catwalk access running north to south through the site is constructed in Welsh slate planks. The catwalk crosses over the water feature giving the impression of a bridge. Specially designed balustrades with integral lighting provide an interesting and safe passage for pedestrians across the water feature, which is also fully accessible for the enjoyment and fun of everyone.

The lighting for the Gardens has been designed to create a

189

PHOTO: EDAW/PHOTOGRAPHY BY DIXI CARRILLO

contemporary lighting scheme and a safe environment at night with feature lighting to the pavilion, benches, trees, catwalk, pathways and water feature forming an integral part of the scheme.

The Gardens have been transformed into one area (4ha) by bringing the site to one level and taking landscape design across the areas from building face to building face to incorporate the Gardens and surrounding footpaths using low-maintenance materials.

Project sign-off

The objectives of the Client's brief had to be achieved with minimum disruption to the city centre, by careful planning design and phasing of construction work which comprised the following elements:-

> Safety was a critical issue as much of the work involved working close to main pedestrian routes or on busy public highways.

> The concrete pavilion provides an important link and transition between the transport interchange and the gardens.

> The surrounding roads have been remodelled to reduce the traffic on the north side of the Gardens and create a bus island on the south with simplified access and egress routes for buses.

> The Tadao Ando-designed pavilion provides a meeting place for people.

> Entrances to the Gardens are provided at all four corners and north and south walkways link radially across.

> The water feature provides a sound and visual attraction of cascading and dancing water.

> The soft landscaping has provided the Gardens with large lawn areas where, during the summer, people can relax in the sun or read under the shade of the large trees.

> The listed statues of Queen Victoria, Peel, Wellington, Adrift and Watt have been restored.

> The contemporary lighting design has provided a safer environment, highlighting the features that make up the Gardens.

The Gardens have been transformed into a bright, open, safe and enjoyable place which is used by the people of Manchester and visitor alike and provided a central space for the Commonwealth Games.

PICCADILLY GARDENS

PROJECT TEAM

Client: **Manchester City Council Civil**

Lead Consultant: **Arup**

Civil Transport and Building Engineer: **Arup**

Masterplanning and Landscape Design: **EDAW**

Pavilion Architecture: **Tadao Ando and Associates and Chapman Robinson Architects**

Lighting: **Art2Architecture / Peter Fink**

Quantity Surveyor: **Davis Langdon**

Planning Supervisor: **Shepherd Gilmour**

Main Contractor: **Balfour Beatty Civil Engineering Ltd**

This building provides an excellent backdrop to Piccadilly Gardens and is an exciting, efficient and well-conceived office building.

ONE PICCADILLY GARDENS
ALLIES AND MORRISON

One Piccadilly Gardens, Manchester

Construction Value: £23 million
Completion Date: September 2003

Description
One Piccadilly Gardens provides a dramatic portal to link with the surrounding city and closes the northwestern end of the formal gardens within the larger square formed by the existing historic city fabric.

History
Piccadilly Gardens was a landmark public open space in need of revitalisation. The immediate area, despite its location, had become underused and needed to fulfil its potential.

Client's brief
Having established a new public square, the City of Manchester wanted a landmark building for the proposed, revitalised public realm.

Design process
The building sits within a site parcel in a rectangular plan form extended to the maximum permissible area within constraints set by the below-ground services, giving an overall structural footprint with a width of 36m and a length of 82.5m. The elevations that face onto the Gardens and onto Portland Street are subdivided into eleven 7.5m bays. The end elevations are subdivided to suit the most efficient structural layout for the car-parking levels below ground. Cut through this regular rectilinear form is a diagonal slot, part void, part filled with accommodation.

The entrance to the offices is via a double-height diagonal mall cut through the footprint of the building at the angle of the surface grain of the hard landscape in the Gardens, and at an angle to the main façade of the Ando pavilion. This feature reinforces the bond with the topography and extends it upwards as a three-dimensional volume that resonates at each of the upper floors and in the roofscape of the new building. Setbacks at each of the upper floors, within the two long elevations, extend the feature to the top of the building and draw daylight into the plan.

The floors are serviced via three passenger lifts accessed from the double-height reception within the main core, positioned on the central axes of the plan. A dual-purpose goods/passenger lift is also provided within the main core with access from Portland Street. An accommodation staircase rises from here into an

atrium, 9m by 15m. At the upper floors the plan provides depths of 13.5m from the external windows to the atrium glazing. A fire stair and fire-fighting lift are located within satellite cores at each end of the floorplate.

The building is constructed of brickwork in stretcher bond placed in front of, and restrained by, a reinforced concrete frame.

Large window bays with a splayed reveal to one side face onto the Gardens and Portland Street. The reveals provide accents to the garden elevation as a whole, and are intended to lead the eye towards the mall from both sides. On Portland Street additional brickwork panels have been introduced to reduce the scale of the window openings in order to form a more responsive interface with the existing city context, comprising warehouses and finer-scale Victorian façades opposite.

The windows on all the elevations are set at the back of the brickwork frame within a metal cladding layer. At the mall and setbacks to the upper floors this metalwork layer folds back through the interior elevations, emphasising the linkage between the main façades and allowing the opportunity to modify the scale and precision of component parts and the size of glass panels. On both sides the building façade is set back from the structure at ground level and in of the areas first floor, to form a colonnade. This provides a covered pedestrian route and accentuates the flow of space around the lower two floors from one side to the other via the diagonal mall.

At the top two floors the largely glass external envelope is set back behind the brickwork frame to provide a continuous terrace and allow access for window cleaning for the fenestration of the office floors below. The frame itself forms a large, expressed series of portals.

Project sign-off

The new building provides a significant backdrop to the hugely successful Piccadilly Gardens. The elevation facing the public space combines with the geometry of Tadao Ando's pavilion, set at 90 degrees, to produce a sense of containment and a strong corner in contrast to the open, more informal arrangement.

While the size and scale of the composition perform the duties of a civic building in such a setting – completing the street frontage on Portland Street and contributing to the sense of place in Piccadilly Gardens – the use of red brick, the inclusion of public uses at ground-floor level and the extension of a public route under the building between the gardens and Portland Street temper this, resulting in a building that contributes to the living city.

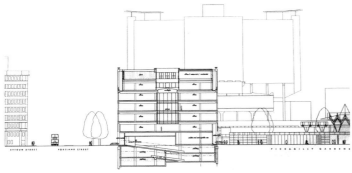

ONE PICCADILLY GARDENS

PROJECT TEAM

Client: **Argent Group plc**
Architect: **Allies and Morrison**
Detailing Architect: **Weedon Partnership**
Structural Engineer: **Arup**
Services Engineer: **Arup**
Quanity Surveyor: **Faithful and Gould**
Contractor: **Carillion Building**

195

NEW EAST
MANCHESTER

3.25

The East Manchester Initiative is one of the largest, most challenging and comprehensive regeneration programmes in the country. A wide range of physical, social and economic improvements – delivered over 10 to 15 years – will reverse decades of decline and deliver an area that is an attractive place in which to live, work and do business.

East Manchester was once the bustling and thriving economic powerhouse of the city. It grew and developed in the 19th and early decades of the 20th century as a home to the traditional manufacturing industries of coal, textiles, chemicals, steel and engineering. This brought jobs, housing and employment to the large workforces required to create the wealth on which the city was founded. Its economic success floundered during the recessions of the 1960s and subsequent two decades. Between 1970 and 1985, 60 per cent of its economic base was lost, with a consequential decline in jobs, skills, population and demand for housing. The decline continued and the area became a shadow of its former self, with high unemployment, poor housing and health, low education attainment and high rates of crime. East Manchester was identified as one of the country's poorest and most disadvantaged areas, although it has been the focus of regeneration activities by Manchester City Council since the mid-1980s.

The opportunity to fully address the complex and interrelated problems of East Manchester came through the city's vision to use sport as a driver for change. The potential for regeneration improvements, benefits to the local community and global profile for the city from staging a world-class sporting event was recognised and pursued. Manchester's Velodrome, which is the National Cycling Centre, was built in East Manchester as a joint venture between the English Sports Council, Manchester City Council and the British Cycling Federation and is one of only two facilities in the country to be awarded British Olympic Association Accreditation. Since the centre opened in September 1994, World Track Cycling Championships records were broken and then broken again. While Manchester was unsuccessful in its bid for the 2000 Olympics, it was host city

fig 3.25
National Cycling
Centre

fig 3.26
Sportcity

3.26

for the 2002 Commonwealth Games, the largest multi-sport event ever to be held in the UK.

The 2002 Games provided the unique stimulus for the regeneration of a much wider area. The purposeful creation of Sportcity, developed with its own masterplan, became the catalyst and symbol of the rebirth of this inner-city area. Although built for the Games, it was essential for all venues to have a sustainable and economically successful after-life. Sportcity today is a centre for elite athletes, a world-class sports hub for the community and is linked to a commercial development. It is a dramatic example of how a quality public initiative can influence wider physical transformation. The City of Manchester Stadium, now home to Manchester City Football Club, is the jewel of Sportcity, where the Northwest regional home for the English Institute for Sport (EIS) is located. The sport facilities for the EIS are, for the majority, located within Sportcity but they also include the Manchester Aquatics Centre which is only 20 minutes away. This complex, with two Olympic-size pools, was built as a result of a partnership between Manchester City Council and the city's three universities, and serves both elite and community swimmers.

The plans for East Manchester, a vast area of 1,100 hectares stretching from the fringe of the city centre to the boundary of Manchester, are underpinned by a regeneration framework delivered through the New East Manchester Urban Regeneration Company (NEM), one of the first of three designated urban regeneration companies in the UK. Established in 1999, NEM is a partnership between Manchester City Council, the North West Development Agency, English Partnerships and the communities of East Manchester. The company provides the strategic direction to the proposed regeneration, secures the required public and private funding and takes a lead on the specific major development projects.

Local residents are very much a part of the delivery of the regeneration programme and the wide range of initiatives in the area today are introduced and implemented with extensive community consultation. The framework is holistic in nature, addressing housing, economic development, employment, education, transport and social and environmental issues in an integrated manner. It will deliver up to 12,000 new homes, improvements to 7,000 existing homes and a doubling of the population to 60,000. With new businesses and investors now attracted to the area, the drive to create 15,000 new jobs, with local people receiving local training, is on track. It is estimated that public and private-sector resources to deliver this comprehensive long-term programme will be in the region of £2 billion.

3.27

One of the key employment initiatives is the development of a new business park that will occupy 180 hectares. Fujitsu will relocate to its new purpose-built headquarters on the site, and a partnership between Manchester's universities and Manchester College of Arts and Technology will operate and manage One Central Park, a facility for knowledge-based activities.

To capitalise on the area's proximity to the city centre, an integrated public transport system is being developed to improve accessibility. Central Park will have a dedicated transport interchange, with the government providing funding for a transport gateway to link the site into the national road network and allow interchange between heavy rail and bus services and the proposed Metrolink stop. With Manchester Airport only 20 minutes away, the completion of the orbital M60 motorway ring-road, and the expansion of the Metrolink system, East Manchester will be linked to the city centre; the university district; and regional, national and European markets – vital components to the success of the area.

East Manchester's heritage, in terms of its canals and open spaces, is a positive force for regeneration providing a unique sense of place. Environmental improvements have included the regeneration of the Ashton Canal Corridor, a key strategic link from Manchester city centre to Sportcity and the City of Manchester Stadium. With funding from the North West Development Agency, European Regional Development Fund and other sources, the rejuvenation of the Ashton Canal Corridor has introduced a pedestrian and cycle route from Manchester Piccadilly to Sportcity, which was the most popular route during the successful Commonwealth Games. The revitalised canal has opened up development opportunities for Victoria Works, Albion Works and Ancoats Hospital with design work focusing on the reuse of existing structures.

fig 3.27
New Islington will
replace the old
Cardroom Estate

fig 3.28
Residents
consultation on
the plans for
New Islington

3.28

Ancoats in East Manchester was the world's first industrial suburb and a cradle of the textile industry. Its buildings include former cotton-spinning mills, housing, and community and commercial buildings of every period from the 1790s. So rich is its history, Ancoats is a short-listed World Heritage Site. 'Little Italy', as it was once known, is being brought back to life as an urban village, and significant redevelopments are underway. These include the Grade II* Royal Mill and Murray's Mill; the Grade II listed Victorian church of St Peter's and the Manchester Millennium Community which is emerging from the Cardroom Estate and is being renamed New Islington.

East Manchester remains one of the region's major concentrations of industry and employment and with a significant number of Government initiatives focused in the area, the education and skills attainments among local people is resulting in a workforce prepared to meet new challenges. The blend of initiatives specifically designed to tackle the worst problems of inner-city deprivation are reaping rewards. There has been a 30 per cent reduction in crime in the area, unemployment is showing a downward trend and improvements have been recorded in educational attainment. 2,500 new homes have been built, more than 37,000 m^2 of new business space is under construction, Sportcity's venues were completed with the opening of the Athletics Arena, environmental improvements have been achieved and public art commissioned for key spaces – the change is clearly visible.

While so much has been achieved in such a short time, the size and complexity of the task ahead means that complete regeneration is a 10–15 year commitment. However, the strategic vision to make East Manchester a stable and successful part of the city, providing a high quality of life for residents; where businesses choose to locate; where people want to live, work and learn; is being fulfilled, and the area is once again contributing to the economic and social success of Manchester.

To illustrate the regeneration initiative, case studies include Sportcity Framework, City of Manchester Stadium (English Institute of Sport), Manchester Acquatics Centre (English Institute of Sport), Gateway Interchange - Central Park, Fujitsu - Central Park, New Islington and St Peters Church.

Revitalising an older part of the city, Sportcity Framework provides
a fresh and dynamic regeneration programme that will improve
the lives of people living and working in the area.

SPORTCITY FRAMEWORK

EDAW

East Manchester

Description

The development of a framework to consolidate the Sportcity site as a major sport, leisure and commercial destination, and to connect the site to the city centre along a corridor based on the routes of the Ashton Canal and the River Medlock.

History

Sportcity was initially developed as a centre of sporting excellence to provide facilities for the 2002 Commonwealth Games which would, in turn, spearhead the regeneration of East Manchester. The site for these sports facilities was located immediately to the west of the intermediate ring road, but it was always intended that Sportcity would embrace adjoining land to the east of the ring road, to create additional and complementary activities; this, however, needed to be established within a coherent development framework. Whilst being less than 2 kilometres from the city centre, a pedestrian-friendly and environmentally attractive route from the city centre to Sportcity did not exist. Also, the site itself was divided by the Ashton Canal, and bordered by major road and rail infrastructure. To add to the complexity, a new Metrolink route was proposed, cutting through the site along the line of the canal. Accessibility was therefore a key ingredient to making Sportcity work for pedestrians, both in getting to the site and moving around it on arrival.

The framework evolved to include not only linkages with the area surrounding the Sportcity site but also the primary link to the city centre along the Ashton Canal and Medlock River Valley. Ultimately, these strategies would come under the remit of New East Manchester Limited as part of their delivery of the regeneration east of the city centre.

Client's brief

Manchester City Council and New East Manchester envisaged the development of the area as supporting a range of regeneration objectives:

> to create world-class sporting facilities to host the Commonwealth Games and to be accessible and affordable to local communities in perpetuity

> to build Sportcity as a visitor destination to support the economic restructuring of the area

> to secure complementary facilities – particularly retail, leisure and residential development – which would make Sportcity into the commercial heart of the new East Manchester

> to provide a high-quality public realm commensurate with the area's role in attracting visitors and complementary to the planned investment in new transport infrastructure

> to reconnect East Manchester with the city centre and the wider conurbation through the improvement of the canal corridor and river valley as a safe, accessible and attractive pedestrian route

> to open up the development potential of historic buildings and key development sites within the corridor to create a new mixed-use district within the city

Design process

The framework fell into two distinct areas: the Sportcity site and the linking of Sportcity to the city centre.

The stadium was to be the centrepiece of the Sportcity proposals; augmented by wider national and regional facilities as part of the sporting centre of excellence.

Design development ultimately placed the stadium at the centre of a huge circular public space contained by sport buildings, leisure and recreation development. Adjacent sites were identified for further leisure, commercial and residential development, and a strategy was developed to ensure quality linkages within the Sportcity site and to the immediate surrounding areas, overcoming the issues of severance caused by substantial transportation infrastructure on the site and around it.

The Ashton Canal and Medlock Valley link to the city centre formed the second part of the Sportcity framework. Using the city centre, Piccadilly Station, the stadium and Phillips Park as anchors, the framework envisioned the opening up of the canal and river corridor as a high-quality environment linking the city centre to East Manchester and providing the route of the proposed Metrolink extension.

The route was planned to combine the retention and reuse of listed mill buildings and the introduction of new residential, commercial and leisure space. Neighbourhoods would take their character from the canal and riverside setting, as well as the

PHOTO: LEN GRANT

201

PHOTOS: EDAW/PHOTOGRAPHY BY DIXI CARRILLO

existing and adjacent urban form. The linear regeneration plan would 'touch' many areas of the adjacent city, acting as a catalyst for wider regeneration.

The environmental improvement works were initiated as part of the Commonwealth Games and further detailed work. Public spaces were carefully designed both to serve the existing community and to promote pedestrian activity between the city centre and Sportcity. Car breakers and other dirty industries were removed to create riverside spaces and a new pedestrian route along the River Medlock. New housing and commercial space is being introduced into existing mill buildings as regeneration stretches out from the city centre.

Project sign-off

The framework successfully consolidated Sportcity as a centre of sporting excellence, with commercial and other activities highly accessible to surrounding areas. In particular, the framework was instrumental in providing a vision for a direct route from the city centre along the Ashton Canal and Medlock River. Environmental improvements to the corridor have been dramatic, and new buildings and refurbishments are underway.

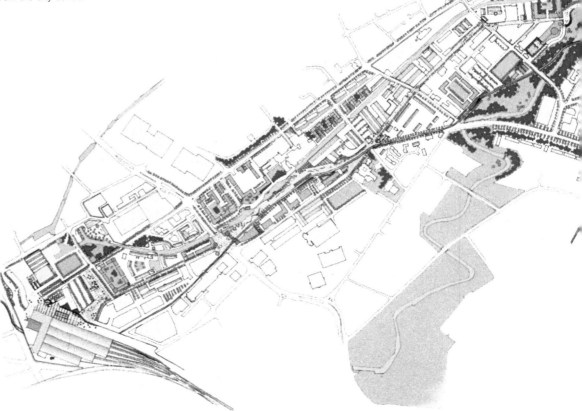

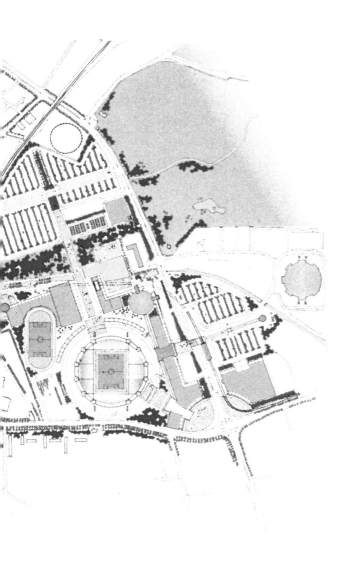

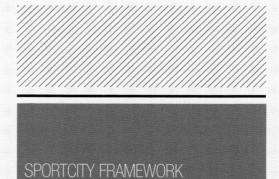

PROJECT TEAM

Client: **Manchester City Council & New East Manchester Ltd**

Masterplanner: **EDAW**

A high-class sustainable stadium that
has been carefully designed with form,
structure and circulation in mind.

CITY OF MANCHESTER STADIUM
ARUP ASSOCIATES WITH ARUPSPORT

Sportcity, Eastlands, Manchester

Construction Value: £90 million
Completion Date: July 2002

Description
This iconic stadium was used as the 2002 Commonwealth
Games venue, and is now the new 48,000-seat home for
Manchester City Football Club. The low, curving stadium roof
and a mast-and-cable structure, in metal with transparent
panels, enhances the skyline.

History
The stadium was built on a contaminated brownfield site as part
of a wider regeneration programme providing sport and leisure
facilities for the community. The 50ha site was formerly occupied
by mining, residential and industrial uses. The stadium's
development stimulated the city's regeneration and affirmed its
growing association with sporting excellence.

Client's brief
Manchester City Council had three fundamental principles:

> Manchester deserved a new high-profile sports venue
  reflecting its status as a major sporting centre
> The venue should be both a central component of urban
  regeneration and a catalyst for further renewal
> The project needed a long-term and sustainable future

Design process
From Arup's original 1992 design for an athletics-only stadium,
the concept for a stadium to accommodate national soccer
games was developed. Certain basic features like the swooping
'saddleback' roof and the spiral access ramps remained in the
design. When the City Council came to its agreement with
Manchester City FC, the design intention was that the stadium
would be ready to stage athletics for the Commonwealth Games
and then be converted for football. The capacity was increased
by the removal of the athletics track and the addition of extra
seating. This was made possible by excavating down one level.
Almost 90,000m^2 of fill would be removed, the pitch laid, and
the temporary north stand for the Games replaced with a
permanent structure in time for the 2003–4 football season.

Manchester City Council's vision for the stadium was that it

should have a viable long-term future after the Games. Its role
as a new home for Manchester City FC not only aided the project
financially but also meant that it would become a permanent and
momentous part of the city's civic infrastructure.

From the outset the objective was to approach the City of
Manchester stadium as a key civic building. Every element is
designed to fulfil as many functions as possible, making the
design very clear and maximising use of the available funds. This
stadium was carefully designed with form, structure, and
circulation in mind.

The first internal experience addresses spectator comfort. The
space is akin to airport concourses, unlike other stadia where
spectators make do with 'left-over space'. An innovative fire
strategy allowed the creation of continuous concourses –
deliberately large, clean, uncluttered, and calm spaces designed to
minimise the typical half-time scramble for refreshment and relief.

A key element of the design is the cable-net roof. The cable net
itself was already erected in time for the Games and the
temporary north stand was fitted around the permanent masts
and tie-down cables.

An inherent problem in designing large stadia is creating a roof
that not only shelters (with 'drip-line' cover to all spectators) but
also ventilates the pitch. Daylight, sunlight, and air movement
over the pitch are essential for healthy grass growth, but a wind-
free and comfortable arena is also needed. To maximize the
amount of sunlight falling onto the playing surface, a 10m-wide
strip of translucent polycarbonate is provided in the roof on all four
sides of the pitch. The cable-net structure only intrudes minimally
into this band, thus creating very little shadow on the grass.

The dramatic roof form and corresponding stand configuration
allowed movable louvre vents in the high-level corner voids.
These vents can be adjusted to increase or decrease air flow
through the stadium, benefiting both air movement over the pitch
and the spectator environment.

Project sign-off

The City of Manchester Stadium is not only an architectural landmark building for Manchester and the UK, but also a pioneer in the integration of technology and architecture. Its story evolved over more than a decade of commitment and co-operation between the public and private sectors.

The client's aspiration for the City of Manchester Stadium was for a high-class sustainable facility that would be economically reliable and a catalyst for regeneration. These aspirations have been met in full and often exceeded, and the City of Manchester Stadium is now considered to be one of the best in Europe.

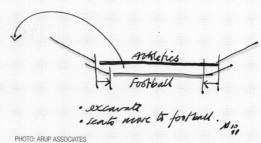

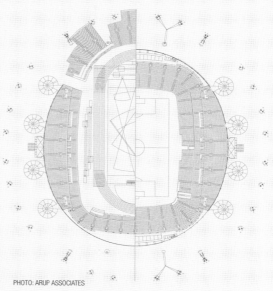

CITY OF MANCHESTER STADIUM

PROJECT TEAM

Client: **Manchester City Council**

Operator: **Manchester City Football Club Ltd**

Architect: **Arup Associates**

Lead Consultant: **ArupSport**

Architect (fit-out): **KSS Architects Ltd**

Civil and Structural Engineer: **Arup**

Building Services Engineer: **Arup**

Acoustic Engineer: **Arup**

Communications: **Arup**

Quantity Surveyor: **Davis Langdon**

Project Manager: **Arup**

Main Contractor: **Laing O'Rourke**

Steel Fabricator: **Watson Steel Ltd**

This important building, sensitive to
its context, brings a new dynamic
form to the city.

MANCHESTER AQUATICS CENTRE
FAULKNERBROWNS ARCHITECTS

2 Booth Street East/Oxford Road, Manchester

Construction Value: £22.6 million
Completion Date: July 2000

Description
This is a new aquatics complex with superb high-performance
training and international competition facilities. It is also a highly
successful public sports centre for Manchester and its
universities.

History
The site was part of the UMIST campus at the point where it
touched both Manchester Victoria University and Manchester
Metropolitan University. It lies adjacent to a new business school
on the arterial Oxford Road and therefore has a prominent
central location.

Client's brief
Facilities were to include: two 50m swimming pools with divider
booms and movable pool floors; an international-size diving pool
with a movable pool floor and diving stages at 10m, 7.5m, 5m,
3m and 1m; a leisure lagoon for children; sports science and
sports medicine facilities and a specialist conditioning room for
swimmers; a 700m^2 dry fitness suite and steam rooms; a
cafeteria; changing and plant rooms. The main pool should have
1,000–1,200 permanent spectator seats with the ability to
extend to 2,500 capacity using temporary seating.

Design process
Flexibility of use was the key criterion. A competition-pool
complex was required for the 2002 Commonwealth Games, but
revenue economics dictated that the pool could be afforded only
if it enjoyed wide public community usage. The water areas have
subdivider booms and movable floors to create shallower water.
The main 50m pool can be subdivided into three separate areas.
The diving pool has a movable floor to transform it into a 25m
recreational or lane swimming pool. The greatest challenge was
the resolution of spectator seat numbers. The Commonwealth
Games required 2,500 seat spaces but 1,200 would be
sufficient for all other occasions. The pools have been laid out in
a way that allows the *ad hoc* installation of 900 temporary seats
on the top of the leisure waters and 900 temporary seats on top
of the diving pool.

The placing of the aquatics centre in a prominent and central
location was an important objective. Such sites are difficult to
find or create in the densely built-up areas of inner cities. A
small site was enlarged (by the relocation of student residences)
to create an ideal location for public and university use. The
building shape and the choice of external materials had to be
sensitive to the urban context, and a building section was
required which respected its neighbours. From the south the
19m-high pool-hall arched roof pivots on a stone-clad ancillary
block which matches the height and material of the adjacent
business school. To the north this roof angles down to the
ground to create a wedge of airspace for the adjacent
residences. To the east the gable wall of the aquatics centre
transforms the existing residential horseshoe into a delightful
quadrangle. The southern concourse to the main entrance
provides a landscaped threshold alongside the gardens of the
business school.

The available site area was extremely limited and this led to the
accommodation being developed on three levels. The main pool
hall is at ground level and contains a 50m x 21m x 2m deep
pool, a 25m x 16.5m x 5m deep diving pool and 300m^2 of
shallow children's leisure waters. At the level above this are the
spectator seats and generous fitness suite. The basement level
accommodates the second 50m pool, the sports science suite
and the technical plant rooms. Laterally, the plan layout has a
classical simplicity: the four staircases required for means of
access and escape divide the complex into three zones. The
middle zone contains the main entrance, which has views
through the café area to the pool. The overall building form is
very compact, with 30 per cent below ground level. The envelope
area is, therefore, exceptionally low for a building of this nature
and high levels of insulation ensure the minimum need for
artificial mechanical systems.

The 110m-long, 55m-wide building is contained under a simple
steel superstructure. At the apex, over the 10m diving board, the
roof is almost 20m above ground level, while the basements and
foundations are 7m below ground level. An *in situ* concrete
frame and thrust blocks support and stabilise the steel

superstructure. This concrete frame carries the changing areas, spectator seating, upper-level fitness facilities and the leisure pool, which is partly suspended. There are no movement joints within the steel and concrete structures. The one-piece concrete pool tanks were cast on slip membranes to a specific constructional sequence to avoid early thermal-shrinkage cracking. What shrinkage there will be is accommodated with carefully designed control junctions.

Pool halls have a long reverberation time because of the innate hardness of their surfaces. In this aquatics centre, the sound absorbance of the perforated soffit sheet of the roof decking has been supplemented with 'clouds' of additional absorbers in the form of sinuously profiled high-performance panels. The combined effect produces a remarkable acoustic environment.

The construction budget of £22.6m was established through work undertaken at feasibility stage. To reduce the risk of costs escalating, a procurement method was evolved whereby the main contractor was brought into the team during the detailed design stage. This enabled the contractor to contribute to the selection of materials and to produce the critical-path construction programme. The project was completed in July 2000 on budget and
ten weeks ahead of programme.

Project sign-off

This is an important building, sensitive to its context yet bringing a new dynamic form to Oxford Road. The innovative mix of activity areas, coupled with the flexibility of wet and dry activity spaces, has allowed a programme of varied use which has included the highly successful 2002 Commonwealth Games and an annual public attendance of over 700,000. A legacy of the Games has been the attraction of national and international organisations to view the facility and study its construction and operation.

In 2003, Manchester Aquatics Centre won a prestigious International Olympic Committee/IAKS Award for its exemplary design and operation.

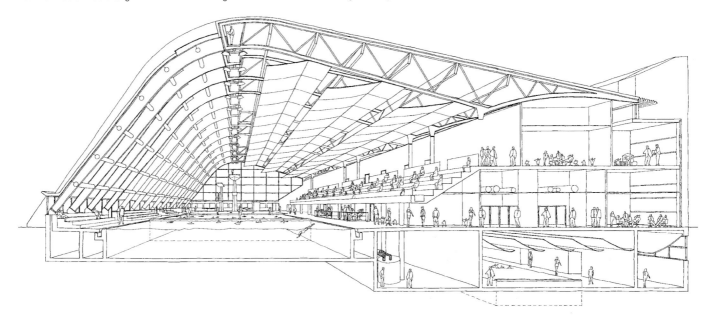

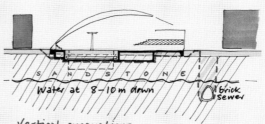

Water at 8-10m down

brick sewer

S A N D S T O N E

Vertical excavations

MANCHESTER AQUATICS CENTRE

PROJECT TEAM

Client: **Manchester City Council**

Architect: **FaulknerBrowns**

Water Treatment Engineer: **FaulknerBrowns Engineering Services**

Structural and Services Engineer: **Arup**

Landscape Architect: **Landscape Projects**

Quantity Surveyor (pre-contract): **Tozer Capita**

Contractor: **Laing O'Rourke**

211

A multi-modal transport interchange and world class
business park.

GATEWAY INTERCHANGE – CENTRAL PARK

AUKETT LTD

Central Park, Manchester

Construction Value: £36 million
Completion Date: November 2005

Details of the building

The Gateway Interchange project links Oldham Road with
Northampton Road, creating the frontage for phase 1 of Central
Park and forming the first part of a longer north-south link
connecting Central Park and Sportcity.

Description of the building

The gateway consists of a dual carriageway road passing under
an existing heavy-rail line with associated public landscaped
works and the formation of a new multi-modal transport
interchange. The interchange includes a bus station, a vehicle
drop-off serving phase 1 of Central Park, and a proposed
Metrolink tram station.

History of the site

The site has two parts, the parcel of land north of the heavy-rail
line and the land located to its south. The northern plot was
formerly a railway sidings and carriage works which ceased
operation in 1999. The land to the south is currently vacant and
was occupied by a number of industrial premises in the location
of Wellock Street and Cramer Street.

Client's Brief

New East Manchester (NEM) and the Greater Manchester
Passenger Transport Executive's (GMPTE) brief was to provide a
new gateway access road into phase 1 of Central Park, creating
a frontage for the park on Oldham Road and releasing the
development potential of the first 92 acres of land. A multi-
modal transport interchange was required to marry together the
proposed phase 3 Metrolink extension and the public transport
requirements for Central Park.

Design Process

A transport strategy was required that connected Central Park to
Manchester city centre and to key regional and national networks,
in order to encourage businesses to the area. A corridor running
north-south through the regeneration area was identified as a key
element in linking the park to the primary radial routes that serve
the city centre and provide access to the M62/M60 and beyond.
The GMPTE, as part of the proposed phase 3 Metrolink extension,
had located two stations either side of the park and, as plans for

the business park developed, Central Park was identified as a
further station location. This then identified an opportunity to
create a multi-modal transport interchange.

At a similar time New East Manchester, as development
facilitator, identified the multi-modal transport interchange and
the associated civil structures as an opportunity to create a
landmark structure that would firmly locate Central Park as a
world-class business park able to compete on a regional,
national and international basis.

Architecturally a number of key aspirations were identified as
fundamental to the success of the scheme:

> The need to create a frontage for Central Park on Oldham
  Road, facilitated by the formation of a high-quality landscaped
  pedestrian access adjacent to the gateway road

> The creation of a visual link with the heart of the park,
  facilitated by an architecturally clad retaining wall of constant
  height above the eastern side of the road.

> The creation of an underpass of appropriate proportions
  under the heavy-rail line, in order that an open, pedestrian-
  friendly environment could be maintained and a tunnel effect,
  both on plaza and roadway, avoided.

> The opportunity to create a landmark structure: a 45m-wide
  canopy over the Metrolink station acting as a symbol of the
  area's regeneration and identifying Central Park as a key
  business location.

> The need to create a formal square at the termination of the
  gateway road in the heart of the business park.

> The intention to include high-quality finishes throughout the
  development, and to use these to establish quality standards
  for the park.

The design for the Metrolink bridge was progressed to create a
profiled bridge deck and station with a side-platform
configuration. The three-span bridge tapers across its cross-
section to reduce the apparent depth of the structure.

In line with the developing aesthetic, a cable-stay canopy was
designed to provide coverage to the station platforms and link
the bus stand/vehicle drop-off, thereby forming a multi-modal

transport interchange. The canopy, supported by a steel tapering mast, creates the landmark element of the scheme and provides an unmistakable identity to Central Park. Circular in plan, it reflects the form of the plaza below it.

Landscaping and lighting were developed in line with the overall design concept. High-quality materials were selected throughout: granite aggregate paving, used to reflect light into the scheme interspersed with bands of colour to add structure and scale to the plaza. A formal square terminates the gateway road and uses a centrally located water feature/sculpture to signify arrival within the heart of Central Park. Lighting was identified as a key element in celebrating the architectural quantity of the scheme and enhancing the drama of the created space. Throughout the development, specialist lighting was designed in tandem with the architectural and civil structures to ensure an integrated design.

Project sign-off

This project is under construction.

214

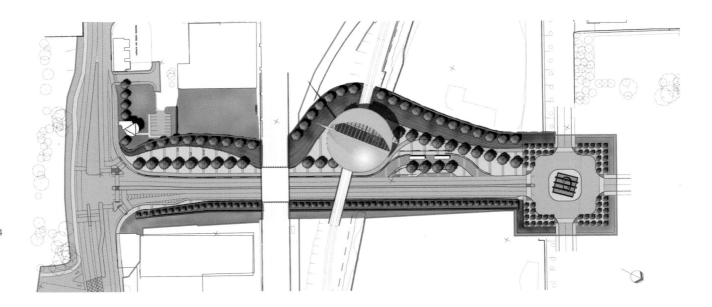

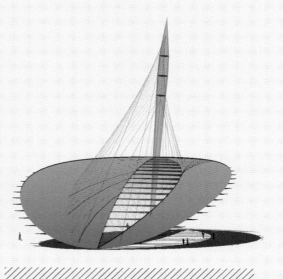

GATEWAY INTERCHANGE – CENTRAL PARK

PROJECT TEAM

Client: **New East Manchester Ltd and Manchester City Council, GMPTE**

Conceptual Engineer: **Arup**

Project Manager: **C2C Project Management Ltd**

Client's Consulting Engineer: **Sinclair Knight Merz**

Main Contractor: **Balfour Beatty Civil Engineering Ltd/Bilfinger Berger**

Architect/Landscape: **Aukett Ltd**

Civil/Structural Engineer: **Gifford Consulting Engineers**

Traffic Engineer: **MEDC**

Specialist Lighting Consultant: **Indigo Light Planning**

A state-of-the-art business environment with first-rate infrastructure and communication networks.

FUJITSU – CENTRAL PARK
AUKETT LTD

Central Park, Manchester

Construction Value: £17 million
Completion Date: Spring 2005

Description
Located at the heart of phase 1 of Central Park – being developed by Ask Akeler Developments – the Fujitsu office development comprises three buildings, each three storeys in height, arranged within a landscaped environment on a site of approximately 5 hectares.

History
The site, formerly Moston Brook High School, was identified as a key element of the wider regeneration of northeast Manchester by the development facilitator (New East Manchester) in 1999. Following purchase of the site, the land was remediated and prepared for future development.

Client's brief
Fujitsu identified a requirement for a regional office headquarters of approximately 14,000m² net area. The potential was identified to accommodate this requirement within three, separate, identical buildings on a prime site fronting the gateway to Central Park.

Design process
The concept for the scheme was to create a landscaped public frontage behind which the three buildings would be arranged in a crescent formation. Each building is designed with an overhanging canopy supported by a colonnade creating a visual link that unifies the development. Particular attention was paid to the landscape design, the frontage of the development and its relationship to the proposed Gateway Road and Metrolink Station.

Each building is formed of two splayed office wings linked by two, three-storey atria The atria are split by the building core, circulation areas and by a 'bridge' of office space that creates a contiguous office floorplate. The circulation space adjacent to the core maintains a visual link between the two atria and accommodates a 'floating' staircase within the three-storey void, adding a vertical dynamic to the space. Each building has been designed to allow maximum flexibility for single or multiple occupancy.

The steel-frame structure of each building is formed on a 7.5 x 7.5m grid and consists of downstand beams at the building perimeter and asymmetrical beams in the centre of the 15m-wide floorplate. These beams support precast concrete planks to form a slim floor construction. At roof level, steel I-section rafters form the structures supporting an aluminium standing-seam roof. Steel flat cross-bracing is used within the core and stair zones to add further rigidity to the structure.

Externally, each office wing has been expressed as a solid element linked by the transparent and public areas of the building. The external finishes of the elevations reinforce this concept. The office wings are predominantly faced in a warm brick which makes reference to the traditional Manchester red brick, whilst the atria are enclosed by glazed curtain-wall façades.

New East Manchester's aspirations for Central Park were to create a state-of-the-art business environment with first-rate infrastructure and communication networks. The park, as part of the wider regeneration of East Manchester, is expected to attract key employers to the area resulting in external investment and job creation. Fujitsu, who have an established presence in the city of Manchester were looking for an office facility that would suit their future business needs whilst retaining their knowledge-based workforce. Central Park has provided the solution.

Project sign-off
This project is under construction.

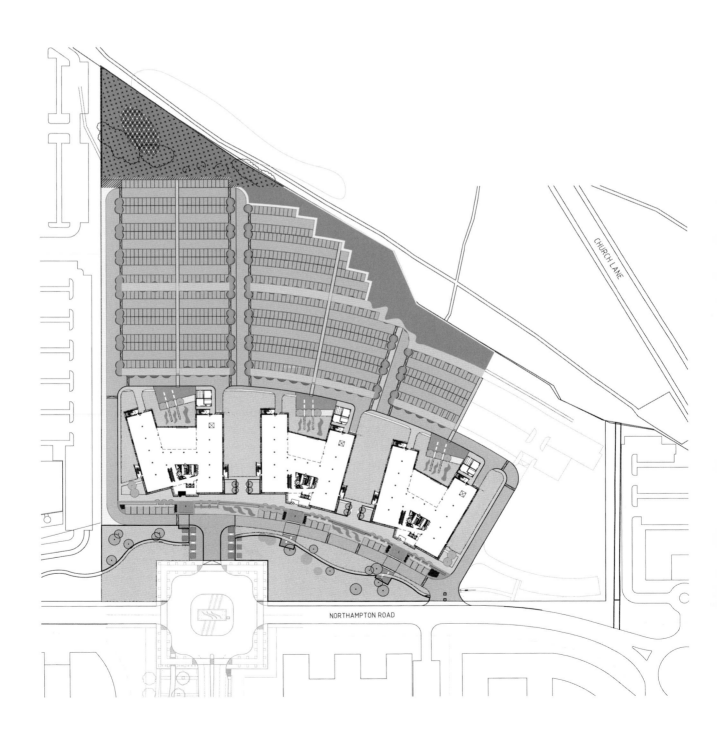

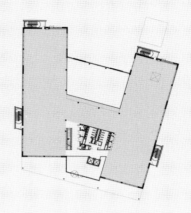

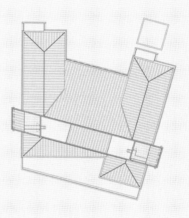

FUJITSU – CENTRAL PARK

PROJECT TEAM

Development Facilitator: **New East Manchester Ltd,
Manchester City Council, North West Development Agency
and English Partnerships**

Client: **Ask Akeler Developments Ltd**

Architect, Landscape Architect and Interior Designer:
Aukett Ltd

Structural Engineer: **Arup**

Services Engineer: **Rybka**

Planning Supervisor: **Norder**

Main Contractor: **Bowmer & Kirkland Ltd**

Project Manager: **C2C Project Management Ltd**

Services Sub-Contractor: **N. G. Bailey Ltd**

Manchester Millennium Village forms a
vital component of the diverse parts of
the city's undervalued eastern flank.

NEW ISLINGTON
ALSOP ARCHITECTS

New East Manchester

Construction Value: £240 million
Completion Date: 2014

Description

The plan envisages a rich mix of housing, distinct architectures, and multiple activities that will promote a sustainable and varied community and an urban development as a destination for visitors and a home for its residents.

History

The site lies between the Rochdale Canal to the north, the Ashton Canal to the south, the Central Retail Park/Great Ancoats Street to the west, and interlocks with a tighter grain of existing residential streets to the east. Currently the site is occupied by Cardroom Estate, characterised by suburban housing on a low-density, curvilinear pattern of streets.

Client's brief

The proposals for the Manchester Millennium Village were based on a premise of increased residential densities and a demand for high-quality residential and commercial accommodation close to the city centre. There was a desire to avoid any tendency to social exclusion, with the promotion of mixed and seamless tenure types.

Design process

Proposals had to accommodate a small group of households which would be displaced from the existing housing estate by the new development. A number of workshops were held with members of Cardroom households at which a sacrificial scheme was presented for discussion and revised according to the needs and hopes of this core population. Additionally, all 74 of the existing households were visited by the design-team leaders to gather community views. The greatest challenge to the project was to promote and foster positive support for the shift to higher-density living upon which the success of the project depends. Apartment building will support the shared facilities – shops, public transport and high-quality public realm – that the area needs, but existing residents feared that these would be the high-rise, low-quality solutions of the 1960s with which they were familiar.

The second main challenge for the scheme was to achieve a form which matched the principles of seamless tenure with a variety of households and income groups co-existing.

Captialising on the presence of the revived canals, and working closely with British Waterways, the framework scheme incorporates new waterways, linking the historic navigations and giving the new quarter an identity of waterside parkland. Hard and soft banking to the water, including narrowboat mooring, creates opportunities for leisure activities and wildlife havens. The main residential buildings radiate spoke-like from the curve of the new canal, each afforded an individual character by a dynamic range of architectural firms who have been subsequently appointed to develop the framework scheme. Provision of local shops, a pub, restaurant and commercial office space will coalesce a community heart for what will be an entirely new and vital district of Manchester. New public facilities include a primary school and play areas, a health centre, a crèche, a shared community hall and community green.

The scheme identifies several housing types. Urban barns and terraced houses suitable for young and growing families, lofts suitable for single occupation or couples, apartments of different sizes suitable for a broad demographic including families and older people wanting to move back to the city centre.

A central concern for the design team has been the delivery of a scheme which meets exacting standards for environmental sustainability and promotes innovative low-consumption energy systems. The provision of an innovative energy engineering programme has been based on the following principles:

> Residents should not have to make a conscious effort to reduce energy consumption, the building and service infrastructure should do that for them

> The developer becomes part of the supply chain, with additional capital costs of energy-efficient buildings which can be justified in long-term cost returns

> The homes built should cost less to run and thus have a competitive advantage in the Manchester housing market

> A flat-rate service charge, and local provision of principal utilities – heat, electricity, water and waste treatments – means that there is no financial incentive to provide more of any given utility, and hence no waste

Project sign-off

Manchester's Millennium Village will be delivered over a ten year period and Its successful delivery will also be an exemplar of public-private partnership. It forms a vital component of the diverse parts of the city's undervalued eastern flank, sitting between Piccadilly Basin, the Ancoats Mills heritage quarter and Sportcity, and also radically enhances – and expands – the housing on offer within a mile of the city centre itself. It is upon such developments that Manchester's long-term emergence as a city of world-class standards and high expectations of its own urban provision will rest.

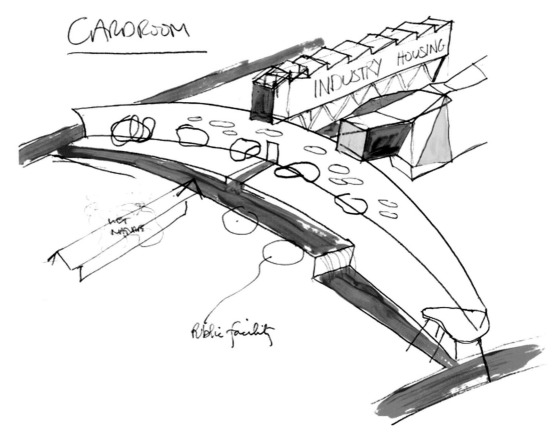

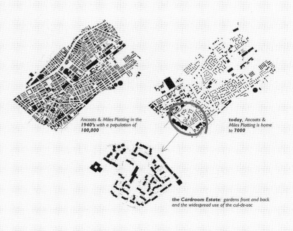

Ancoats & Miles Platting in the *1940's* with a population of *100,000*

today, Ancoats & Miles Platting is home to *7000*

the Cardroom Estate: gardens front and back and the widespread use of the cul-de-sac

NEW ISLINGTON

PROJECT TEAM

Client: **Manchester City Council**
Developer: **Urban Splash**
Lead Architect: **Alsop Architects**
Energy Engineer: **Martin Stockley Associates**

The legacy of St Peter's Church and Ancoats, in addition to becoming a thriving and liveable area again, is that, together with Worsley and Castlefield, it forms part of a potential World Heritage Site.

ST PETER'S CHURCH

IAN FINLAY ARCHITECTS

Blossom Street, Manchester

Construction Value: £425 thousand
Completion Date: March 2000

Description

Intervention and conservation works to save a key heritage landmark building at risk of total loss, prior to redevelopment for a future sustainable use.

History

St Peter's Church, designed by Isaac Holden and Son in 1859, is a Grade II listed building in the Ancoats Conservation Area. Repeated arson attacks and systematic vandalism had by 1996 reduced this fine Romanesque-style church to a condition close to total dereliction. Built to serve the needs of the working population of Ancoats, the world's first industrial suburb, it nonetheless remained a landmark building in the heart of the proposed Ancoats Urban Village, lying within a five-minute walk of the city-centre.

Client's brief

Manchester City Council acquired St. Peter's Church in 1998 and entered into a 125-year lease with the Ancoats Buildings Preservation Trust.

The Trust developed a brief to save the building by immediate intervention. This was followed by detailed design of conservation works to stabilise and retain the fabric of the building, whilst renewing worn-out and decayed elements and putting back key features, like the tower, which had been destroyed.

Design process

The key issues and complexities were the condition of the building, its status as a listed building, the requirements of English Heritage in terms of the high quality materials to be used and the ever-present constraints of funding.

The original intention of the scheme was to carry out temporary protection works to the building under the Conservation Area Partnership Scheme operated between Manchester City Council and English Heritage. This was the basis of a successful CAP application to English Heritage for £50,000. At that stage, the roof was to be covered by tarpaulin sheeting and given temporary guttering to provide the building with protection for a two-year period whilst the major capital monies were sought and

obtained from the Heritage Lottery Fund.

In January 1998 English Heritage offered £145,000 to enable the main roof of the church to be re-slated. The building was also cleaned and pointed, taking advantage of the external scaffolding that was in place for the temporary works.

During the course of the works, from the vantage point of the internal scaffolding to the full height of the church, a more comprehensive and detailed understanding was reached of the full extent of repairs and renewals required to the building.

The extent of deterioration made conservation issues more complex and required ongoing discussions with the Trust as client and English Heritage as the primary funder.

In July 1998 the Deputy Prime Minister, John Prescott, announced outside St Peter's Church that English Heritage had approved further grant funding of £230,000.

In consultation with the Trust and advised by the quantity surveyor, expenditure of the new budget was prioritised from the tower down, to ensure that works were finished to full standard to the areas of building unlikely to be re-scaffolded again.

This 'top down' expenditure approach resulted in the tower being fully refurbished. The main roof was completely overhauled structurally and re-slated, the dry rot in the building eradicated, and the external envelope to the building made structurally sound. The building was 100 per cent cleaned and 75 per cent repointed, with cast-iron guttering and cast-iron down pipes installed to serve the main church roof.

Due to funding limitations, the remaining, lower areas of the church aisle roofs, were re-roofed in profiled metal decking with PVC guttering and down-pipes fixed, on the basis that these areas, being first-storey, would be cost effective to re-scaffold and finish to full standard at a later date. This more relaxed approach to the lower materials meant that the building could be made properly watertight within the budget.

Completion of the works took two years, a lengthy period for a complex project with many stop-starts. However the combined determination of the City Council, the Trust, English Heritage and

225

the project team, meant that St Peter's was successfully saved and retained, to await a future conversion scheme for a new long-term use.

Project sign-off

The works to St Peter's have ensured that this landmark building will now be saved for future generations to enjoy.

This is as a direct result of intervention by Manchester City Council, who stepped in to ensure (with the supporting role of the Ancoats Buildings Preservation Trust) that St Peter's acted as a catalyst for the regeneration of Ancoats, giving encouragement for other development and investors to follow.

There are now tangible results that show the City's vision of an urban village in Ancoats is becoming a reality. A number of conversion and new-build residential schemes now front Great Ancoats Street and Oldham Road and, perhaps most tellingly,

Manchester Millennium Village is planned adjacent to Ancoats, overlooked by the famous Royal Mill Complex, now itself the subject of a major residential conversion into apartments.

The legacy of St Peter's and Ancoats, in addition to becoming a thriving and liveable area again, is that, together with Worsley and Castlefield, it forms part of a potential World Heritage Site.

226

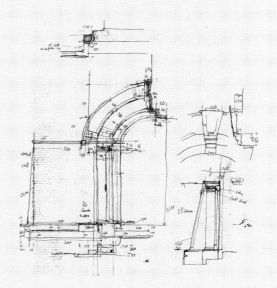

ST PETER'S CHURCH

PROJECT TEAM

Building Owner/Client: **Manchester City Council and The Ancoats Buildings Preservation Trust**

Architect: **Ian Finlay Architects**

Structural Engineer: **G.C. McDonald and Partners**

Quantity Surveyor: **Simon Fenton Partnership**

Building Contractor: **DLC (Manchester) Ltd**

SPINNINGFIELDS

3.29

The largest and most ambitious regeneration project in Manchester's city centre is Spinningfields, a nine-hectare site off Deansgate. The area is bounded by Deansgate, Quay Street, Bridge Street and the River Irwell. Originally, a 1960s office development was added to the Magistrates' Courts, the Crown Court, Cumberland House and Manchester College of Arts and Technology (MANCAT) estate, making the site relatively impermeable to pedestrians and hostile to those who worked in its buildings.

The opportunity to introduce change in this area was based on three key events: MANCAT's decision to rationalise its occupation of the site, the award of private finance initiative funding to build a new Magistrates' Court, and Allied London Properties' acquisition of land and property there.

The City Council formed a partnership with Allied London Properties to deliver wide-ranging change to the area. A regeneration strategy was prepared and a masterplan framework and planning guidance was approved by the City Council to underpin and ensure the successful delivery of change. As a result, one of the most exciting regeneration projects in the Northwest is transforming the western side of Manchester city-centre, and the regeneration process is well underway.

Allied London Properties, working in partnership with the council, are providing more than 325,000 m^2 of high-quality commercial, civic, residential, retail and open space, integrated into the thriving city centre. The size, scale, quality and location of Spinningfields will realise the largest single urban development scheme in the Northwest – and one of the largest new city-centre business quarters in Europe.

Spinningfields has been designed to deliver a dynamic new business quarter, combining stunning architecture with high-quality urban design to create a mixed-use, modern and distinctive area. It will provide a focus for significant new investment and employment, and – by securing major development projects, including modern large-floorplate office

fig 3.29
New Court
facilities

fig 3.30
Leftbank
apartments
construction
site

3.30

buildings – the city will improve its competitive advantage both on a national and international level. The new business district will meet the demands of world-class companies and major office users.

The development, with a total project value of £650 million, will open up an area that had seen scant investment for 25 years, and which was inward looking and unfriendly in appearance. Despite its proximity to the busy city centre and access to the River Irwell, it was a concrete complex that was cold and uninviting. In its place will be a bustling commercial district and judicial complex.

The Spinningfields development represents a private and public-sector initiative that has seen the successful pooling of land and resources for the benefit of a major regeneration project. The initiative is underpinned by a comprehensive masterplan, adopted after public consultation. The plan is supported by the Council's regeneration strategy and planning guidance. Once completed, the site will be fully integrated into the rest of the city and the new, office-led, mixed-use quarter will increase Manchester's overall competitive edge, create new job opportunities, enhance the regional capital and improve its status as a vibrant European city.

The creation of an entire new city quarter is reliant on critical mass, and the opportunity to bring about change in this area was based on a proactive and dynamic partnership, principally between the Council and Allied London Properties, but one which also includes the Royal Bank of Scotland, National Car Parks Manchester Limited, the Department of Constitutional Affairs and the Guardian Media Group. The partnership is fundamental in both developing the concept of Spinningfields, and in delivering its key components.

Crown Square, Gartside Street and Hardman Street are being revitalised with new public squares with distinctive landscaping and walkways. Four major new, or reconfigured, public squares, a tree-lined boulevard and enhancements to existing streets and riverside walkways will deliver 2.84 hectares of new public realm. The education building, Cumberland House, and the Magistrates' Courts that overlooked a barren concrete enclave are being replaced with high-

229

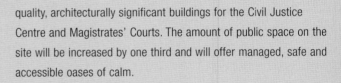

3.31

quality, architecturally significant buildings for the Civil Justice Centre and Magistrates' Courts. The amount of public space on the site will be increased by one third and will offer managed, safe and accessible oases of calm.

Over the five-year phased development, the four new public squares – Spinningfields Square, Hardman Square, Crown Square and Irwell Square – will encourage outdoor activities within the area. Under the scheme, the River Irwell will become more accessible, a pedestrian bridge will link Manchester and Salford and there will be better provision for public transport, pedestrians and motorists. A Metroshuttle bus will provide fast, free and frequent links from Spinningfields to the main transport hubs in the city centre and to car parks.

The expansion of the central business district – with modern, high-quality – large office floorplates – will add 300,000 m² of new office space in fourteen signature commercial buildings, and address the need for large-scale office space in the city centre. The Royal Bank of Scotland will move its administrative headquarters into two of the signature buildings. This represents the biggest letting to a single commercial user, and the largest post-war leasing, deal the city has seen.

Shops, restaurants and bars will offer leisure opportunities to those working, studying and visiting Spinningfields. Residential accommodation will be located in the Left Bank development with its 391 luxury apartments situated on the bank of the River Irwell. Two new luxury hotels will be built to serve the commercial district and visitors.

fig 3.31
Manchester
Magistrates' and
Coroners' Court

fig 3.32
Mixed use
development

3.32

The Spinningfields Partnership will deliver a holistic residential, commercial, leisure, legal, education and public-space development. The new district within the city centre will deliver radical economic and physical change. Spinningfields is fundamental to the continued economic success of the city, which has helped to create the strongest-performing regional centre in the UK. It will become a major city-centre destination providing life and activity throughout the day. It will build upon the success of, and provide linkages to, the city centre renewal area, Castlefield and the Great Northern Initiative.

To illustrate the emerging new European business quarter, case studies include the Spinningfields Masterplan, the Magistrates' Court, No.1 Spinningfields Square and the Civil Justice Centre.

The Spinningfields Masterplan provides for a rich and diverse range of activities, where people will be able to live, work and enjoy themselves.

SPINNINGFIELDS MASTERPLAN
BUILDING DESIGN PARTNERSHIP

Spinningfields, Manchester

Description

Due to be completed by 2010, Spinningfields is a multi-million-pound development which covers an area of 9 hectares extending from Deansgate to the River Irwell between Bridge Street and Quay Street. It is projected to become a new office-led mixed-used quarter, fully integrated functionally and physically with the rest of the city centre.

History

The name 'Spinningfields' dates to the early 18th century, when the area was in transition from agricultural to industrial use based on home textile manufacture. Following the decline of the textile industry during the 20th century, the area was developed in the 1950s and 1960s. The new primary users were civil justice (Crown Courts, Magistrates' Courts and County Court) and MANCAT (Manchester College of Art and Technology), with each being disconnected from the other and laid out so that they were either uninviting or positively discouraged movement from surrounding parts of the city.

Client's brief

The client's brief for the Spinningfields masterplan was to create a new European business destination with 418,000m² of development that will help consolidate Manchester's standing as a modern, dynamic international city and as a centre for major investment. It will offer:

> 255,475m² of quality office space
> 400 residential apartments
> A five-star hotel (leisure and business use)
> 30,500m² of retail, restaurant and bars
> 49,361m² of civic and educational buildings
> A series of new public squares and open spaces

Design process

The primary objective for Spinningfields is the creation of a distinctive, high-quality and well-integrated city quarter that will naturally support a wide variety of activity at all times of the day.

Within a hitherto inaccessible and uninviting area of the city,

connections are forged along a series of well-defined new streets punctuated by several new public spaces. As well as a series of shorter north-south routes including the re-aligned Gartside Street, a major new desire line is established on the east-west axis from the bustling action of Deansgate to the banks of the River Irwell.

There are four primary new or reshaped public squares. Each of these has an individual character by virtue of their shape, the buildings and functions which define them, and their degree of activity or calmness.

Commencing to the east alongside Deansgate, Spinningfields Square is an uncluttered space allowing maximum appreciation of the adjacent Grade I listed John Rylands Library. This part of the site lies within the Deansgate/Peter Street Conservation Area. Spinningfields Square acts as an entry point to the pedestrian sequence which connects through to Crown Square. Formerly the product of sterile 1950s planning, this space has been re-orientated through 90°. This results in the Crown Court building only occupying a short side of the square, which is important because of the deadening effect this structure has had on its surroundings due to its lack of interaction. By contrast, the new Magistrates' Courts situated on the longer, north elevation of Crown Square will have active ground-floor uses as will the office buildings opposite. These include bars and restaurants which will spill out into Crown Square on sunny days.

From Crown Square, the pedestrian moves through to Hardman Square, situated on the site of the former 1960s-designed Magistrates' Court which effectively blocked movement to the west. This is the most dominant of the four major public spaces within Spinningfields. It lies at the intersection of Hardman Street and Hardman Boulevard, defining the point where the city grid is influenced by the line of the river. It is within Hardman Square that the commercial heart of Spinningfields beats most strongly, with both major approaches to it also being predominantly lined with offices. This sense is to be reinforced by a new tower, 35 storeys tall with a presence onto Quay Street, which will become a major new city landmark and a symbol for the revitalised Spinningfields.

Progressing westwards along Hardman Boulevard, Irwell Square

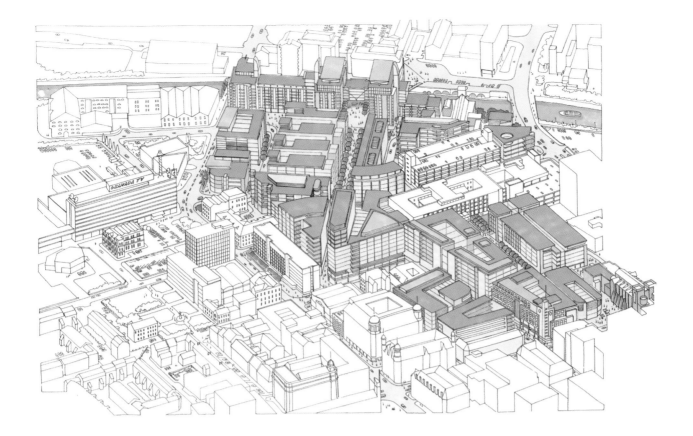

is the final space in the urban sequence. Lying alongside the Irwell over which a new pedestrian bridge gives access to Salford (and particularly Salford Station), Irwell Square gives on to Left Bank and the River Walk. Here there is a residential and cultural focus. 400 apartments overlook the river in a line of buildings which rise up to a peak of 14 storeys above ground-floor restaurants, bars and galleries alongside the existing Pump House Museum. This is a gateway site, denoting the edge of the City of Manchester as it addresses its neighbour, Salford, across the river.

Servicing and vehicular access into Spinningfields is provided via a series of four loops, one in each corner of the site with only the re-directed Gartside Street providing a through route. Car parking is provided both below ground and in new above-ground structures to the west of the River Irwell. Good public transport is available, with both Salford Central and Deansgate Stations lying within a five-minute walk of the site. In addition, three city-centre shuttle buses connect Spinningfields to all main destinations within the city centre.

Project sign-off

The Spinningfields masterplan provides for a rich and diverse range of activities where people will be able to live, work and enjoy themselves. A variety of well-defined public streets and spaces which are permeable to the surrounding city are being produced. A carefully conceived balance between pedestrian and vehicular dominated space is being delivered. A sense of continuity comes from the best of the existing building stock being retained, alongside which new architecture of outstanding quality is to be introduced.

For these reasons we are confident that Spinningfields will become a major European business destination. It will not only regenerate its immediate environs but also strengthen the entire city centre, helping to consolidate Manchester's standing as a modern, dynamic, industrial city and as a centre for investment.

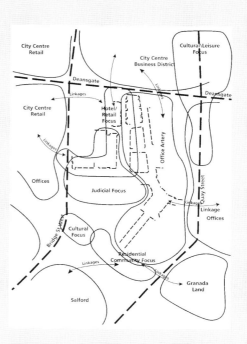

SPINNINGFIELDS MASTERPLAN

PROJECT TEAM

Client: **Allied London Properties Ltd in partnership with Manchester City Council**

Masterplanner: **Building Design Partnership**

Transparency, openness and clarity of concept define the spatial organisation of the Magistrates Court, reflecting the Lord Chancellor's vision for the future of the criminal-justice system.

MAGISTRATES' COURT

CARILLION PLC

Spinningfields, Manchester

Construction Value: £31 million
Completion Date: March 2004

Description

The courthouse is both a new civic building, accommodating the needs of a modern court, and an integral part of a thriving metropolitan environment. It includes 18 magistrates' courts, one coroners' court, staff accommodation, underground parking and retail.

History

The courthouse is located on a site of redundant office space adjacent to the Grade I listed John Rylands Library, just off Deansgate. It is at the heart of the city's administrative centre and forms an integral part of the City of Manchester's masterplan, which aims to revitalise and connect underused public spaces.

Client's brief

The brief called for a new courthouse that would replace an existing facility which no longer meets modern needs, and would incorporate functional, commercial, and planning requirements.

The Department for Constitutional Affairs and the City of Manchester's brief aimed for a courthouse which would both challenge conventional procedures and become an vital part of the city's fabric.

Design process

The design of the courthouse is almost entirely an exercise in masterplanning, from an urban context to the various discrete functions of the court building itself. This approach enriches and supports the functions of the court building and surrounding spaces.

Historical research into the development of Manchester revealed several proposed masterplans for Spinningfields. The 1945 and 1960 plans both identified a processional route linking the Town Hall and Albert Memorial with the River Irwell.

Maintaining a direct visual link between Crown Square and the Town Hall became a primary concept driver. The architecture of the new courthouse is designed to relate sympathetically to the existing Crown Court buildings and emphasise the former processional route, which is reconceived to extend into the court building.

The glazed street in the atrium orients the users and delivers the public to the heart of the building on the second floor. The street becomes a clear extension of the public realm, with the public entrance located at the end of the pedestrianised Spinningfields Square.

A new pedestrian path runs to the south of the site, linking the processional route to Crown Square. The mix of uses, and inclusion of retail within the ground floor of the building along this path, contributes to the overall aim of the Spinningfields masterplan and will help to revitalise the area. Courts and offices will run independently of the retail space.

Fundamental to the design concept was the clear differentiation of three functions: the courthouse and associated security facilities; office accommodation and car parking; retail and delivery spaces. Expressing the separation of functions in the architecture of the building increased the efficiency of the structure and services and provided appropriate civic and contextual responses to the surrounding buildings, which vary in age and architectural style. This separation of function also exposes the inner life of the building, the core of which is the practice of justice.

The site is bounded by the John Rylands Library to the east, Wood Street to the north and Crown Square and the Crown Courts to the west. Materials were selected in conjunction with Manchester Planning Authority to respond to the local context. This was achieved through the use of red sandstone for the court building, tempered by the fully glazed ends to the atrium and the lighter metal-and-glass finish to the offices.

The separation of functions allowed two discrete servicing strategies. The court facilities needed to support knowledge and procedural functions, often in stressful conditions. The strategy for these facilities consisted of displacement ventilation with local perimeter heating and ventilation controls governed by the court clerks. Natural ventilation was considered for the courtrooms but was impossible to achieve due to restrictions of privacy, noise and air quality.

The office accommodation needed to support a healthy and comfortable environment with user control. Because of the

relatively narrow floorplate, natural ventilation was achieved, complemented by mechanical ventilation for internal spaces. External brise soleil to the south elevation and louvres to the east and west elevations completed the strategy.

The glazed internal street was key to the delivery of natural light to courts, office and magistrates' areas. It was thermally modelled to ensure that summer peak temperatures at the highest walkways were not excessive.

The scheme, which included a three-month demolition of existing properties and the construction of basement car parking, was constructed in 128 weeks, and used a labour force which included 50 per cent local labour.

Project sign-off

Manchester Magistrates' Court exemplifies Gensler's rigorous and innovative approach to public buildings. The 14,000m² complex balances the need for a secure, flexible, efficient courthouse with a building of welcoming atmosphere and distinctive civic presence that responds to its surroundings.

Transparency, openness and clarity of concept define the spatial organisation of the scheme, reflecting the Lord Chancellor's vision for the future of the criminal-justice system.

The design concept splits the two main functions of the building. A fully glazed atrium street and link-bridges both separate and connect courthouse accommodation to the north, to office accommodation to the south. Locating the secure court function within the offices and retail in a single building is revolutionary in terms of courthouse design. The bridge links expose to the public a part of the process of the administration of justice, thus celebrating it rather than shrouding it in mystery.

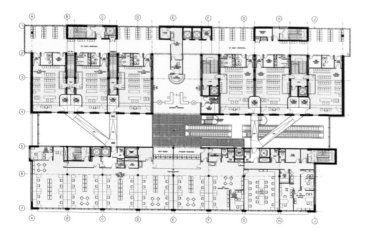

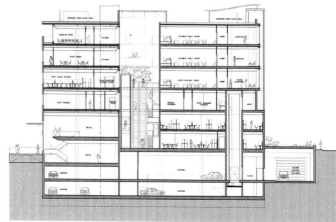

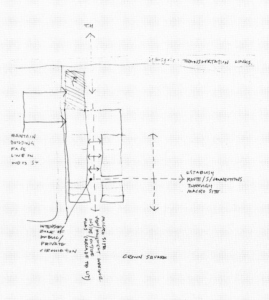

MAGISTRATES' COURT

PROJECT TEAM

Client: **Lord Chancellor's department and Manchester City Council**

Developer: **Carillion plc**

Design Architect: **Gensler**

Executive Architect, Civil Engineering, Structural Engineering, Security: **TPS Consult**

Services Engineer: **Crown House Engineering**

Planning Supervisor: **Schal**

Acoustic Consultant: **Han Tucker**

The new public space of Spinningfields Square
provides a unique opportunity to create a tension and
dialogue between old and new.

NO.1 SPINNINGFIELDS SQUARE
SHEPPARD ROBSON

Spinningfields Square, Manchester
Construction Value: £13 million
Completion Date: 2004

Description
This new building was developed by Allied London Properties as the headquarters for the Royal Bank of Scotland, to create an entry marker for the wider aspirations for the regeneration of the whole 9 hectare masterplan area known as Spinningfields.

History
The new building for the Royal Bank of Scotland sits on the site of Northcliffe House – which itself was built in several phases, incorporating elements of earlier buildings, and completed in 1932. The building was used as a newspaper editorial and printing facility until the printing business vacated the building in December 1989. The site is within the Deansgate/Peter Street Conservation Area, facing the Grade I listed John Rylands Library, which opened in 1900.

The location is of significant prominence: a major pedestrian and vehicular thoroughfare through the western side of the city. It is close to all the major business and leisure attractions, and within five minutes' walk of the cultural, retail and administrative districts of the city centre. The setting – opposite John Rylands Library, across the new public space of Spinningfields Square – provides a unique opportunity to create a tension and dialogue between the old and the new. The relationship between the proposed new building and the library is fundamental to the overall success of
the Spinningfields masterplan.

Client's brief
The brief was very simple: to create an efficient, flexible, office building of 12,000m² that met institutional standards yet created a dramatic presence in the Manchester cityscape. The building should reflect RBS brand aspirations, including those of a responsive and responsible environmental strategy.

Design process
The intention was to re-interpret issues of context, scale and rhythm which had been set by the historical built form. It was to replace the 'spire' of Northcliffe House with a dramatic vertical component and to provide a calm, non-competitive façade to form a backdrop for the John Rylands Library.

The building was conceived as three distinct components:

1. The dramatic 'curvilinear' prow form to Hardman Street and Deansgate, which provides the entry signifier for the entire Spinningfields development, its active façade promoting environmental and contextual responsiveness.

2. The 'floating box' facing the John Rylands Library across Spinningfields Square creates an unashamedly modern, yet calm and restful foil to the ornate richness of one of Manchester's historic architectural icons.

3. The connecting 'slot' allows a visual separation of these two primary components, reducing the mass of the building and creating a central and internal focus.

Architecturally the building is minimalist in its application of elevational features. There is a play of planes working with a limited palette of materials and fitness of detail to give a consistency to each of the elevations.

The overall integration of the elevation design with the environmental system for the building informs the function and appearance of the façade. A light, open building has been created which reduces the requirement for artificial lighting. In order to enable the building to function to the level of comfort required, passive and active façades have been developed and employed. These use static or dynamic elements such as louvres, perforated screens and light-shelves, designed to reduce the impact of solar gain and minimise energy demand on the building's cooling systems. These elements have been further refined to add details and interest to the façades without disrupting to the quality of views in or out of the building. The predominant use of glass and aluminium further enhances the image of a modern, light, functional building with a high degree of visibility inside and out.

Project sign-off
The aim was to reinforce the idea of the building as three
distinct constituent parts, The external fabric is used to define
three-dimensional forms which respond to differing contextual
and climatic circumstances.

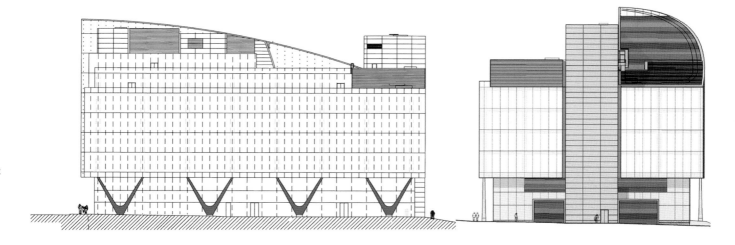

NO.1 SPINNINGFIELDS SQUARE

PROJECT TEAM

Client: **Allied London Properties**
Tenant: **Royal Bank of Scotland**
Architect: **Sheppard Robson**
Contractor: **Sir Robert McAlpine**
Project Manager: **Capita Symonds**
Structural Engineer: **FaberMaunsell**
Services Engineer: **Troup Bywaters & Anders**

The Civil Justice Centre will create a powerful
sculptural form and visual impact but will maintain a
sense of seriousness, dignity and calm.

CIVIL JUSTICE CENTRE
DENTON CORKER MARSHALL

Bridge Street, Manchester

Construction Value: £100 million (approx)
Completion Date: Early 2007

Description
The Manchester Civil Justice Centre is the result of an open
OJEC *(Official Journal to the European Communities)* designer
selection process followed by a design competition. The
competition was promoted to create a new major public building
to act as both a symbol and a focus for civil justice in the
Northwest.

History
The site is located adjacent to the existing Manchester Crown
Court at the north eastern boundary of Spinningfields precinct, a
major city-centre development located in the northwestern
sector of the city. The triangular site is bounded by Gartside
Street to the east, Left Bank to the west, and a new road to the
south.

Client's brief
The requirement for was for a new Civil Justice Centre which
would accommodate 47 modern, purpose-built courts, together
with a variety of facilities for the smaller hearing rooms required
by the variety of civil-justice functions. Public facilities for access
and meetings and staff office accommodation were also
required. All of the accommodation incorporates state-of-the-art
technology including videoconferencing facilities.

Design process
'*The design of public buildings carries with it a responsibility to
understand the significance of the institution which the building
will embody, and to ensure that this is translated into built
form.*'

A court building is, for the public, both symbol and workplace of
the judicial system. The courts are seen as public at one level,
but very private on another. If we do not wish the justice system
to been seen as remote, inaccessible or intimidating, it is
imperative to provide not only an atmosphere within the courts
which works to eliminate these characteristics, but to ensure
that the external imagery of the building carries the same
message.

The Manchester Civil Justice Centre building, in specific design
terms, aims to be:

> Unintimidating
The building should not be monumental, heavy, overpowering.
It should convey a sense of human scale in its form and
massing.

> Context Respectful
The building aims to respond and relate in scale to its
surroundings, yet without having is character determined by them.

> Visually Accessible
The building expresses a sense of openness and transparency.

> Contemporary and Innovative
The building aims to convey a sense of 'looking forward' in its
architectural expression, whilst still serving to 'remind' us of
tradition and sense of the enduring strength of the judicial
process.

> Environmentally Appropriate
The design includes for the use of groundwater cooling with
natural ventilation in the majority of courtrooms and public
spaces. A bespoke BREEAM (Building Research
Establishment's Environmental Assessment Method)
assessment is being prepared and it is anticipated that the
design will satisfy the 'very good' criteria.

These elements of design are brought together to create a Civil
Justice Centre building that not only creates a powerful
sculptural form and visual impact but which maintains a sense
of seriousness, dignity and calm.

The building is broken into three elements, essentially the long
rectangular plates. The westernmost plate is a glazed public
atrium, 11 levels tall. The central plate is a tall, narrow
'anchoring' spine element containing lifts, services and rooftop
plant. The eastern plate is a glazed/solid element containing all
courts, hearing rooms etc as well as offices.

Long rectangular forms (fingers) – containing the courts and
associated offices – project and cantilever well beyond each end
of the façades, providing a striking and irregular profile. The
visual expression of the fingers aims to convey not only a sense
of openness and accessibility of the courts to the public through
the use of physical transparency (the outer glass facing) but in
so doing 'reveal' the interior volumes as though they were

objects captured within the external container.

On the eastern façade, a filtering screen overlays these rectangular forms. The screen is a metal veil, revealing and concealing the functions behind. It incorporates openable windows for judges' suites and office areas, varied requirements for glazed and solid external skin, natural ventilation grilles and openings, sunlight controls and privacy. From a distance the veil is a single clear element. Close to, it reveals itself as subdivided into a series of smaller plates; closer still it becomes an array of individual panels with a complex arrangement of void, solid and mass.

A fully glazed atrium runs the length of the western façade of the building. This is the public face of the building providing visual accessibility and a clear sense of the scale and levels of the building; all parts are visible, but the overall form allows ready understanding, with a minimum need for assisted direction-finding.

Project sign-off

As a major public building the design seeks to act at city scale as a civic marker with a strikingly memorable presence, yet retain the openness and transparency appropriate to a centre for civil justice.

The building is designed to address the established road network, and hence to reinforce the existing structure, while acting as a gateway to central Manchester and the Spinningfields precinct.

At a local level the composition of linear vertical forms residing in a public open space provides for a formal plaza at the building's entrance and a less formal 'pocket park' linking Bridge Street with Hardman Boulevard, which is the central access of the new precinct.

The building provides efficient and comfortable working space for the court service, its staff, and the public who will visit and use the new facility.

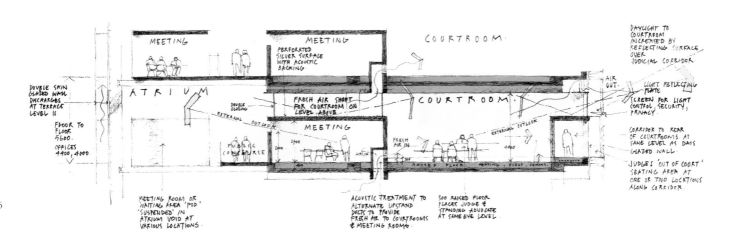

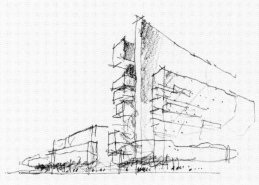

CIVIL JUSTICE CENTRE

PROJECT TEAM

User: **Department for Constitutional Affairs**
User's Technical Advisor: **Mouchel Parkman, JYM Partnership and Feilden & Mawson**
Developer: **Allied London Properties**
Architect: **Denton Corker Marshall**
Engineer: **Connell Mott MacDonald**
Landscape Architect: **Hyland Edgar Driver**
Access Consultant: **Drivas Jonas**
Acoustic Engineer: **Sandy Brown Associates**
Developer's Quantity Surveyor: **Gardiner & Theobald**
Project Manager: **Second London Wall Project Management**
Building Contractor: **Bovis Lend Lease**

04
CONNECTIONS

A city must have a high level of accessibility to ensure a successful economy. As the transport hub for the Northwest, Manchester recognises people's right to choose the way in which they travel and it aims to make all transport safe, convenient, affordable and as sustainable as possible.

fig **4.1**
Piccadilly Station
concourse

04

4.1

The regional capital has developed an improved transport system that supports its development as a cosmopolitan and international city, one that attracts investment, activity and visitors from around the world. Manchester works within a much broader city-region economy and is the transport hub of five core cities (Manchester, Liverpool, Leeds, Newcastle and Birmingham) identified as critical to the delivery of a 'Northern Way' (see Chapter 5). This new government initiative draws on the natural strengths of the northern counties and looks to them becoming competitive regions. Manchester occupies a central position in 'The Northern Growth Corridor', which takes in major cities from Liverpool in the west, Hull in the east, and Newcastle and Sunderland in the north. With its international airport and superior location in the nation's transport system, the city is well positioned to play a key role in development plans for the North. Providing access to jobs outside the city is as important as the provision of jobs within it, and an effective and high-quality public transport system, both within Manchester and across the wider conurbation, acts as an incentive to investors with an eye for a large labour force. A good transport system also significantly improves Manchester's ability to act as a focal point for wider regional cultural, tourism and recreational activity, and maintains the momentum behind the idea of Manchester as a place to visit.

As a regional communications hub, a range of transport systems drives an infrastructure that supports the economy and activity of Manchester. The city has gateways to the world through Manchester Airport and the two inter-regional rail stations, Piccadilly and Victoria. It is served by an orbital motorway which gives easy access to London and other major cities, and its recently completed circular Inner Relief Route alleviates traffic congestion in the city centre. Public transport is provided by Metrolink, the light rapid transport system that connects Manchester city centre to its surrounding districts and suburbs; an extensive local heavy-rail network; and a bus system, which is integrated with the heavy and light rail modes in the city centre. In a city where only about 60 per cent of households have access to a car, and where the centre needs to remain competitive, a good public-transport service is essential. A free service within the city centre is provided by Metroshuttle bus, which operates two circular routes connecting rail stations, car parks and key business districts. People also need to be able to walk safely and comfortably around the city centre and pedestrianised streets, bridges and walkways linking public spaces have greatly improved circulation for those on foot or who cycle. The City Council has a policy that aims to make public transport and the city's streets as accessible as possible to those who are disabled or who have young families. Historically, the rivers and canals provided Manchester with the opportunity to compete economically on a global scale. Today they support regeneration and leisure initiatives and have played a vital part in the renaissance of the city. Achieving an integrated service that

fig **4.2**
Manchester
Airport

fig **4.3**
Manchester's
Transport
Sysytem

4.2

4.3

incorporates many of these transport systems is a challenge and is only possible through concerted partnership action involving the City Council, the Greater Manchester Passenger Authority/Executive (GMPTA/E), transport providers, Government and others.

If the Manchester Ship Canal linked the region 100 years ago with the commerce and industry of the world, Manchester Airport fulfils that role today. The airport is the key international gateway to the city and a vital asset to the economic growth of the region. As a major contributor to the economy, the airport generates almost £600 million a year for the Northwest region, and £1.7 billion nationally. In 15 years' time, these figures are projected to rise to £1.6 billion income for the Northwest and nearly £4 billion nationally. The airport handled just under 20 million passengers in 2003 and by 2015 that number is expected to rise to 42 million. Its two biggest freight markets are the Far East and North America and the services that supply these markets provide a vital economic link for UK industry. Around 125,000 tonnes of freight and mail are moved across the world to and from the airport each year and, currently, goods to the value of £7.5 billion pass through the World Freight Terminal annually.

The superlatives continue; travel agents from across Britain voted Manchester 'Best UK Airport' in 2003; it was voted 'Best Leisure Airport' by a trade journal in the previous year and passengers in the International Air Transport Association's Airport Monitor Survey, declared it the 'World's Best Airport' in 1996. Manchester Airport is part of the Manchester Airports Group (MAG), Britain's second largest airport operating-company. MAG also owns and operates Nottingham East Midlands, Humberside and Bournemouth Airports and, uniquely, the group is owned by the ten local authorities of Greater Manchester, with Manchester City Council owning 55 per cent and the other nine authorities each holding five per cent.

With two parallel runways and three modern terminals and its own rail station, the airport's convenience, accessibility and comfort to all those who use it is legendary. To further improve services to passengers Britain's largest ground-transport interchange has recently opened. The £60 million complex is a flagship project for the Government's integrated transport policy. It will provide seamless travel into the heart of the airport by bus, coach and rail, and, by locating additional check-in desks inside the interchange, passengers will be able to get to their destinations even more quickly. The airport is also included in the Metrolink's long-term programme of expansion in South Manchester. The aim is to encourage a quarter of those travelling to and from the airport to use public transport by the year 2005, including many of the 18,000 people who work at the airport.

fig **4.4**
The Mancunian
Way is part of
the inner ring
road

fig **4.5**
Piccadilly Station
approach

04

4.4   4.5

Rail in Manchester was the revolutionary new transport of the 19th century. Since it opened as the London Road Station in 1842, Manchester Piccadilly has been a major gateway to the Northwest. It is one of two main stations in Manchester and it handles more than 55,000 passengers every day. It provides vital links to other major UK cities including London, Glasgow, Edinburgh, Birmingham and Cardiff. With the upgrading of the West Coast Main Line, which has a dedicated link to Piccadilly Station, Manchester's links to the rest of the UK have been maintained. The station was in need of upgrade, especially as it was to be a principal entry point for visitors arriving by rail for the 2002 Commonwealth Games. Network Rail ploughed millions into the project and in doing so, they created an award-winning passenger transport hub.

Manchester Victoria is the second of the city's mainline railway stations. Originally, it was a single-platform building, designed by George Stephenson in 1844 to serve the Manchester and Leeds Railway, and the building still carries an iron-and-glass canopy bearing the names of its original destinations. The station serves destinations north and east of Manchester and some trains to Liverpool. It is the main terminus for the adjacent Manchester Evening News Arena, opened in 1996, and joined onto the original station, which now has its own Metrolink stop. Generally, however, the local rail network badly needs investment in more, and better, trains, track and signalling. New links are also needed, especially to Piccadilly, to increase the capacity of the network. Much of this work is long term, but the city continues to work with the Network Rail and others at a national level, including train operators, to deliver a network that supports the local economy as well as providing more effective inter-urban, and inter-regional, links.

As with many urban centres, Manchester has to deal with increasing volumes of road traffic. The 1945 City of Manchester Plan predicted the burst of growth in private vehicle ownership and noted that most of the traffic congestion appeared to be caused by all routes converging on the city centre. To address this, the Plan proposed four major ring roads, 'offering rapid transit to long-distance and inter-suburban traffic which has no occasion to pass through the city centre'. One of which was an inner ring road linking the Hyde and Chester Roads with Trinity Way and Great Ancoats Street. The necessary link, it stated, 'would reduce congestion in the Deansgate area of the city centre'. Reducing unnecessary traffic travelling through the city centre has concerned the City Council for more than five decades. The Inner Relief Road, built in stages, was temporarily completed in July 2002, in time for the Commonwealth Games, and work is now underway to deliver a more permanent completion of the route under the rail line running into Victoria Station. The loop around the city had to accommodate the needs of Metrolink and the waterways, and to

fig 4.6-4.8
Transport choices

4.6   4.7   4.8

achieve that, a number of engineering feats were accomplished. The River Irwell was crossed by constructing the 80m-long Castlefield Bridge. As the scheme passes north, the road has been threaded under the site of a future development of the rail network, and over the soon-to-be-reinstated Manchester, Bolton and Bury Canal.

The other two ring roads mentioned in the 1945 Plan, and again in the City Council's 1961 Development Plan, related to the intermediate ring road, which was partially achieved with the building of the Alan Turing Way, and an outer ring road, the M60. The former is an important route that takes in the Velodrome, City of Manchester Stadium and other venues at Sportcity, while the latter is the main Manchester orbital route developed by connecting and consolidating the existing sections of the M63, M62 and an extended M66.

As Manchester continues with innovative ways to link transport comfortably with the city's activities, and to improve existing car parks, a joint venture between the City Council and National Car Parks Ltd was forged, and again it was the first of its kind in the country. NCP Manchester Ltd (NML) has helped deliver improved car park management through the installation of security measures within its car parks and variable message signage on arterial routes and the inner relief route. The illuminated signs clearly indicate the amount of car parking available to incoming motorists.

The Council encourages people to cut down on non-essential and short car journeys by helping to develop practical, attractive alternatives using public transport, cycling or walking. One of the most innovative methods was GMPTE's proposal in 1982 to create a light rapid transit (LRT) system based on a number of existing local railway lines. The new tram system was Britain's first on-street light rapid transport system. Metrolink trams today have replaced up to 3.5 million car journeys a year which would have been made on the roads of Greater Manchester. The trams are environmentally friendly, helping to reduce air pollution. With trams running every six minutes for the main part of the day, with eight stops in the city centre, the scheme has proved popular and efficient.

Metrolink was built in phases, the first of which was the 31km of track running through Manchester to Bury in the north and Altrincham in the southwest at a cost of £145 million. GMPTE involved the private sector in a funding partnership contract, the first of its kind – introducing a principle which has since been copied many times in transport schemes. The public sector's role was to define the primary features of the system, while the private sector carried out the detailed design and construction, and subsequently the operation and maintenance of the system. By March 1990, the construction of the Metrolink system in the city centre began, and by 1992 trams were running all

253

4.9

the way from Bury to Altrincham. Today this service carries more than 15 million passengers a year as compared with seven million on the trains Metrolink replaced along the Bury to Manchester and Manchester to Altrincham routes. Phase Two was the Metrolink extension to Eccles via Salford Quays where it integrated with the regeneration of the Quays. By July 2000, trams were running all the way to Eccles for the first time in nearly 60 years.

Today, the tram service carries 18 million journeys each year, and Manchester is determined that further expansions will boost the city's regeneration. The 'Metrolink Extensions Strategy' Phase Three proposals were submitted to Government in July 1998 and in March, 2000 the Deputy Prime Minister John Prescott announced government funding to build further extensions to deliver, on a phased basis, proposals for Oldham and Rochdale; East Manchester and Ashton-under-Lyne; and South Manchester, including Didsbury, Stockport and the airport. These plans hit a hitch when, in 2004, Transport Secretary Alastair Darling announced he could not approve funding proposals. The city has questioned his decision and, in true Manchester style, remains committed to delivering the expansion.

The City Council is working in partnership with the Passenger Transport Executive, local businesses, communities and MPs to ensure that the Greater Manchester Metrolink system will, over time, double in size and become the largest light-rail network in the UK, and one of the largest in Europe. It would then carry around 40–45 million passengers a year, boosting Greater Manchester's economy by an estimated £170 million per annum. The expanded Metrolink would have a dramatic influence in serving people using the third-busiest airport in the UK, the communities of New East Manchester and their business and education initiatives located in Central Park. The success of Metrolink demonstrates that a significant modal shift can be achieved if public transport is perceived to be reliable, comfortable, accessible, safe, convenient and quick.

fig **4.9**
Manchester
Airport provides a
vital link for the
North of England
with global
destinations

fig **4.10**
Market Street,
the cities busiest
pedestrianised
route

4.10

In common with the wider regeneration programme, transport decisions are increasingly made in line with the particular and individual needs of an area. A transport network integrated with land-use planning ensures that local transport can support new developments and contribute to regeneration initiatives. Local communities need to be able to use and enjoy local transport and the Manchester Community Strategy sets out a corporate vision for all service deliveries, including public transport, that promote social inclusion. Bus travel also needs to be quick and reliable and to that end GMPTA, together with bus operators and local authorities in Greater Manchester, are introducing Quality Bus Corridors covering more than 200 km of the main bus routes throughout Greater Manchester. On these corridors there will be bus priorities; timetable information at every stop; bus shelters at the majority of stops; modern, fully accessible buses; and frequent services. In addition, the objective of introducing more low-floor accessible vehicles, more environmentally efficient vehicles, real-time information and ticketing initiatives offering better value for money, continues. Some evening bus services are subsidised through the GMPTA, especially to those neighbourhoods where car ownership is low. Getting around comfortably and conveniently is important to a vibrant, active city centre and in September 2002 a free bus service was launched as a major expansion to the traditional central bus provision. The easy-access, low-floor, low-emission buses called Metroshuttle, operate two loops that connect rail stations, car parks and key business and retail areas. A third Metroshuttle route into the Spinningfields business area will follow from October 2004.

Access to and from the city centre will be even easier following the opening of the integrated transport interchange on Shudehill which is currently under construction. Located to the north side of the Arndale shopping centre, it is at the heart of the Council's transport strategy. High priority will be given to pedestrians and buses, with up to 2,000 buses expected to travel through the interchange each day, further encouraging the shift from cars to public transport. It will include a Metrolink stop and it also incorporates an 777-space multi-storey car park. The interchange has also been the key to unlocking Prudential's £100 million plan for regenerating Arndale North.

The City Council has established a hierarchy of road users and gives top priority to the needs of pedestrians, disabled people, cyclists and public transport. A planned comprehensive city-centre pedestrian network is being developed, and the Council is currently rolling out its Pedestrian Strategy – a long-term project to create pleasant, safe and convenient walking routes in all areas of the city, that takes into account the needs of all sectors of the public.

Within the city centre, the pedestrianised zones of Market Street and the south part of King Street, together with the pedestrianising of St Ann's Square, has significantly improved access to key retail

fig **4.11-4.13**
Retail therapy

04

4.11   4.12   4.13

areas. But it was the damage caused by the 1996 terrorist bomb that provided an opportunity to open up and to extend the retail core of the city centre. For many decades shops, offices and cafés were separated from the Cathedral area by a concrete barrier of offices and a bleak square known as Shambles. The plan created a new zone, around the Cathedral and Chetham's School of Music, now known as the Millennium Quarter. The new district is linked to St Ann's Square by a distinctive new curved pedestrian boulevard – New Cathedral Street. Pedestrianisation programmes are also being designed to complement local regeneration work, and the pedestrian-and-cycle route from Piccadilly to the City of Manchester Stadium has proved a major asset to those attending events at Sportcity, including the well-attended Manchester City football matches at the stadium.

The new Spinningfields business quarter under construction will have no less than four new squares linked by pedestrian routes that again extend the core of the city centre. Cyclists use safe cycle links to reach principal areas of employment, transport interchanges and the city centre. The most popular route is along the Wilmslow Road and Oxford Road cycle path, which is used enthusiastically by the students of Manchester's universities, and the partly completed 'Fallowfield Loop' encourages cyclists to enjoy a safe route along a pre-existing rail track that served the suburbs, and which will integrate with the pedestian route from Piccadilly to Sportcity in the near future. Cycle routes not only provide an affordable method of transport, they also promote healthier living and in support, cycle parking has been introduced, particularly within the city centre, to provide more security to bicycle owners.

The Council maintains its vision of making Manchester the most accessible city in Europe. This means it must be safe and convenient to those with physical and sensory disabilities as well as those with pushchairs and shopping trolleys. The Access 2000 Strategy is a key part of any plans for the built environment or open spaces, not only to architects, planners, leisure services and similar professionals, but also to those who manage buildings or who provide public-service access points such as libraries, markets and theatres. To achieve this there is ongoing consultation with disabled people's organisations through the Access Review Forum to ensure that particular consideration is given to the improvement and development of existing and future transport schemes. In the run up to the 2002 Commonwealth Games, key routes to each venue were made accessible by introducing dropped curbs, tactile street markings at traffic lights and at key road crossing points, and ramps to main buildings with public access. The 2002 Games made history as being the first fully integrated multi-sport event during which all medals won by both able-bodied and disabled athletes counted towards their team's overall success. In 2002, the first *Design for Access Manual* was launched by the City Counci,l providing a practical approach to inclusive

fig 4.14
Re-development
of public spaces
improves
connections

4.14

design. The manual, which was later updated to *Design for Access 2*, gives more detailed guidance to achieve exciting and creative accessible design. It is intended that standards in *Design for Access 2* should be used for all buildings and projects on which the City Council lead or are the client, for the maintenance and improvement of highways and to ensure that the standards are taken into account at the earliest possible stage in any design process.

In the past, the waterways of Manchester provided the city with a network of rivers and canals that contributed to it being an important transport hub in the 19th century. Today, the waterways are recognised as a major asset that can provide links to regeneration, the environment and leisure. The City Council commissioned a study in 2003 to examine the waterways and to evaluate how best they can serve the dramatic changes that the city has undergone over the past 15 years. The regeneration of Castlefield in the 1980s was dependent on clean canals and new pedestrian routes and bridges that provided links to the city centre. Today, the Ashton Canal Corridor project in East Manchester is another dramatic example of how a waterway has supported regeneration. Over a relatively short period of time, a new neighbourhood alongside the canal has been created, which now includes both residential and business accommodation in renovated mill buildings and new buildings that are easily accessible by public transport and the pedestrian walkway to Sportcity.

Manchester had a reputation across the globe for its pioneering transport strategies. It was the city that launched the canal era, built the first passenger rail station and delivered engineering feats to support methods of transport that have been copied around the world. As the city aims to become a leading European city, equally innovative ways of tackling transport and access are developed through partnerships. A multi-modal public transport system provides the alternative to private car journeys and offers a practical, attractive alternative which, in turn, develops a safer, more pleasant environment for pedestrians and cyclists.

But while good-quality public transport is critical to the life and vitality of a modern city like Manchester, road transport is also integrated in a way that supports businesses and personal needs. This is a holistic approach to transportation, which recognises the fundamental role that an effective transport system plays in the economic, social and environmental health of the city.

05
SHAPING THE FUTURE

The resilience, energy, determination and creativity that
drove Manchester through its industrial heyday of the
late 18th and 19th centuries, and again though its
renaissance from 1985 onwards, are the same drivers
pushing the city forward today. Manchester learns from
its past, it is self-critical and so its edge is always sharp.
It takes the best example of physical regeneration and
moulds it to fit new funding and partnership
opportunities. It capitalises on its successes to attract
recognition nationally and internationally – and it stays
aware of its social responsibilities, just as it did in the
late 19th century.

fig 5.1
Manchester
Metropolitan
University Library
building

05

5.1

The characteristics displayed in the mid-1800s by the first free-traders, the first trade unionists, and the first municipal masters – who introduced gas, water, trams and better housing for the people of Manchester – are still evident today. The radicalism of the risk-takers that influenced government, and secured the repeal of the Corn Laws in 1846, is replicated in the 21st century by those building an economically strong international city that makes its mark on the national agenda. The innovators who built canals and machines that revolutionised Manchester and influenced world history can be found today in the city's universities and science parks. Cultural masters, such as those who gained Manchester international recognition through the 1857 Art Treasures Exhibition and the Hallé orchestra, delivered the international popular music festival 'In The City' annually from 1995, the 'Cultureshock' Commonwealth Festival in 2002, and are planning the city's first International Festival for 2006.

The concept of partnerships forged between a local authority and private enterprise, which built the Manchester Ship Canal in 1894, has continued, and delivered revolutionary complex regeneration initiatives such as Hulme. Partnerships have driven many significant changes in Manchester and the city today is even more committed to the idea that joint working delivers results. Partnerships have moved forward and, recognising that key regional cities have a collective strength, the City Council believes that, by working together, key cities can significantly contribute to the national economy and ensure that all citizens benefit from regional and national growth. The 'Core Cities'[1] initiative was formed in 2000, to work with Government and others to make sure that regions get their share of resources and have an opportunity to play their part in creating a competitive nation. Sir Howard Bernstein, Chief Executive of Manchester City Council, firmly believes that 'A strong economy needs strong regions, and strong regions need to be driven by strong cities'. Manchester, as the Northwest's regional capital and leading economic driver, offers the single biggest opportunity to deliver an economic performance that will make it a productive city within a competitive nation.

The UK under-performs against major competitors in Europe, while London and the Southeast remain the most competitive regions in England. Professor Alan Gilbert, an Australian who has recently arrived in Manchester to take up his position as the first President and Vice-Chancellor of the new Manchester University, observes, 'The politicians who run Britain from Westminster ought to be embarrassed about the extent to which Britain is dominated in terms of wealth, influence and institutions from London and the South East.' He believes that this is not typical of 'most great societies which have a multiple foci of enterprise and energy.' Professor Gilbert feels that it is not typical of Britain at its most energetic. 'When Britain was the greatest economic power in the world, Manchester and Birmingham were the centres, not London, so this imbalance is not even true of Britain at its peak.' Richard Leese, Leader of Manchester City Council, went further to say, 'Manchester's future prospects should not rest solely on London's ability to drive forward the UK

1 The Core Cities are Birmingham, Bristol, Leeds, Liverpool, Manchester, Newcastle, Nottingham and Sheffield

fig 5.2
Students
celebrating
graduation

5.2

economy. We recognise the unique flagship position of the capital, but we question its perceived role as the only significant motor of growth in the country.' Creating a competitive region to counterbalance that of the Southeast is a long-term plan, and, as Professor Gilbert says, 'If it's going to work, it's going to work in Manchester.'

Government, under pressure from the Core Cities, now recognises their importance and has introduced 'The Northern Way', an initiative that sees the North of England as a place of great economic and social opportunity. Richard Leese is firmly behind the initiative which, in his opinion, is long overdue. 'Manchester has been arguing for almost as long as I can remember saying that Government should recognise the importance of cities and that, in doing so, there is no conflict with national agendas.' To realise the aim of creating this economically sustainable counterbalance, the Northwest, Northeast, Yorkshire and Humberside are developing a Northern Way Growth Strategy which will set out the ways in which the North can play its part in the country's economic growth.

Manchester in the 19th century was at the centre of national wealth and, even though it is unlikely that history will repeat itself in our lifetime, the city does generate nearly as much economic activity as Liverpool, Leeds and Sheffield combined. The city was once known as 'Cottonopolis', it took the opportunity that the raw material presented, combined it with innovation and entrepreneurialism and created a step change in history. Today, the key driver for change in Manchester is not cotton, iron or chemicals, it is knowledge-based industries. Manchester is a Knowledge Capital and many see this shift to an 'Ideopolis' as being equal in importance to that of the industrial revolution.

Manchester has a wealth of universities and further-education institutions and by using these as an opportunity for advancement, the determined city has created a launch pad for stronger economic performance and a distinctive external profile. By creatively exploiting the combination of its successful international airport, its world-class universities, high-growth businesses and knowledge-intensive industries, the Knowledge Capital has a strong foundation. Blend these elements together with a large skilled workforce, excellent traditional and high-quality well-designed new buildings, a vibrant city culture and strong civic leadership and therein lies a powerful mix of economic opportunity. Richard Leese says, 'the vision is bold, but Manchester is where bold ideas happen'. Knowledge Capital stands to create as many as 100,000 new jobs in the regional centre and airport environs. It will, in the 21st century, be the step change that Manchester is seeking in order to become a leading European city – one that has a quality of life that is enjoyed by all its residents.

Manchester's universities sit at the core of the knowledge economy, with a combined income of £670 million, 12,500 employees and a student body of 88,000. In addition, there are 26 further education colleges in the immediate vicinity; together, they provide a rich and diverse range of teaching and

261

fig **5.3**
Manchester's
universities form
the core of
Knowledge
Capital

05

5.3

research activities. This wealth of higher education links seamlessly into the city's growing service sector, which includes the largest financial and professional community outside London. The University of Manchester and UMIST [2] will cease to exist in 2004, but by joining their resources and strengths they will give rise to the new Manchester University. This consolidation, known as Project Unity, will deliver a world-class 'knowledge powerhouse', one that is capable of unlocking academic excellence and commercial 'spinouts'. Professor Gilbert is excited by the challenge. 'This is a once-in-a-lifetime chance to re-invent what Manchester University wants to be in the 21st century. It's an invitation to be imaginative and inventive.' An 11-year plan is in place and it aims to 'create a university akin to Oxford and Cambridge, one that will automatically appear on the list of the world's top 25 universities," says Professor Gilbert.

Knowledge-based achievements are not exclusive to the universities. Research and development is a critical part of creating academic excellence and these activities, in turn, create 'spinout' companies. 'Start up' businesses create local jobs, they provide training opportunities for local people and the work they produce improves the city's international profile as a place of innovation and creativity. The land on which industrial factories once stood is now the same ground on which the new breed of industrial clusters and business 'start ups' are flourishing.

One of the most recent is Number One Central Park, built on what used to be the industrial wasteland of East Manchester. This building is now a knowledge hub that is inextricably linked to the wide-scale regeneration of the area[3]. It is here that one of only five world centres offering the prestigious Executive MBA Programme conducted by the University of Pittsburgh's Joseph M. Katz Graduate School of Business is based and where the Manchester Science and Enterprise Centre (MSEC) – a research, technology and business-creation unit headed by Greater Manchester's four universities – is located. Here, also, is Manchester College of Arts and Technology (MANCAT), an academic and training base for the local workforce and on-site employees; and the regional headquarters of Fujitsu, which will offer job and training opportunities to local people. These centres of excellence support Manchester's reputation as a source of innovation and enterprise and they are an essential part of the city's drive to regenerate neglected areas, to create jobs and provide educational and skills opportunities to local residents.

Manchester has a long tradition of taking its social responsibilities seriously. The Corporation of the 1900s believed in providing clean water and sewerage facilities. The first free public library was opened in Manchester, the first municipal park, public bath houses and the first public bus service. The City Council today is driven by similar beliefs; wealth is not just for a few, it must create opportunity for all residents. Drivers of the city today know that although the city is enjoying its improved economic strength, there is a great deal of work yet to be done to redress social

[2] UMIST, University of
Manchester
Institute of Science and
Technology

[3] See Chapter Two

fig 5.4 & 5.5
Redevelopment
in East
Manchester

5.4   5.5

imbalances within Manchester.

4 See Chapter Three

The city leaders are aware that successful regional economies are driven by the health and vitality of those who work and live in the area, and those people need good quality homes. Creating a dynamic housing market and building up the city's population has been a key aim, but, as Sir Howard Bernstein says, 'we will never achieve our potential and maximise our productivity unless we create a housing market that meets the demands placed on it by the thriving economy.' In the past, much of the old housing stock in Manchester was built to provide homes for low-wage earners engaged in its traditional industries. Wage earners taking jobs in the new industries moved to the suburbs and adjoining regions, so parts of Manchester were left with the blight of abandoned housing. Those individuals and families left behind were faced with a degenerating environment, accelerating crime and neighbour nuisance. Manchester addressed this problem initially with the radical renewal of housing stock, firstly in Hulme and now in East Manchester,[4] where a range of private and social housing, apartments and family homes is part of recreating sustainable communities.

Even though the Council was improving houses in many parts of the city, a significant number were not being occupied. To understand this, the Council commissioned a study to provide insight into why investment failed to deliver a thriving community. Previously a needs-led approach had been applied to housing, of which Richard Leese says 'it assumed that by providing someone with a nice front door and sound roof, people would automatically want to live there. This approach ignored the housing market and the fact that people make choices, and if choices within an area are not provided, people go elsewhere.' Once the problem was identified, Manchester sought to find the solution. It joined with Salford and other northern cities and successfully lobbied and engaged Government in the need to target specific areas of poor housing and deprivation. The result of this effort was the introduction of the Housing Market Renewal Fund (HMRF), against which local authorities can bid for money. A bid submitted jointly by Manchester and Salford was successful, and will realise 12,000 new houses and rid the city of some of its worst properties. Once again, Manchester influenced the national agenda and effected social change.

Manchester is a strategic city. It used two Olympic bids to drive regeneration programmes and it used the Commonwealth Games in 2002 to further those regeneration plans and raise the city's profile internationally. A series of strategies exist today which will underpin the way the city moves forward through the next decade. *The Manchester Community Strategy 2002-2012* is a key road map that is addressing cross-cutting issues such as poverty, inequality, crime, the environment, health, education, and the impact of new technology – issues that affect many of the city's communities. The Strategy has identified the key mechanisms for delivering better public services in a co-ordinated way through Manchester Partnership, an influential group of public, private and community organisations working

fig 5.6
Manchester is
the latest city to
be visited by
CowParade
which showcases
community talent
and raises
money for
charitable
causes

05

5.6

5 See Chapter Two

together to create a better life in a better city. At a more local level, Strategic Regeneration Frameworks (SRF) will address specific areas and manage change over the next decade. This is a whole-city approach, and it moves away from the single-area-based regeneration initiatives such as that for Hulme.[5] Richard Leese expresses strong commitment to managing change in a holistic way across the whole city, 'We have initiated pioneering regeneration work in Manchester, these frameworks extend that innovative way of working. Agencies, community, investors, employers – everyone in a particular area will understand their specific framework, where it is going, why we are taking the actions we are, and how the radical change will be achieved.'

The frameworks provide clarity of purpose and identify clear methods of delivery. They are designed to manage the complex mechanisms delivering radical social and physical change. In the hierarchy of city plans they bridge the district-wide 1994 *City Pride Prospectus*, the citywide *Unitary Development Plan* (UDP) and the *Manchester Community Strategy* with ward or neighbourhood plans. Sir Howard Bernstein says, 'The economic and social well-being of residents is vital to the future success of our city. We are good at being competitive but we have a long way to go with our communities which have yet to access the economic benefits that have been generated over the past decade.' He believes that the future of the city is heavily dependent on the success of these strategies, but, if recent history is to be a guide, the city's residents can surely be optimistic about their future.

The first regeneration framework was for East Manchester and it created a new way of delivering physical, economic and social change within the city. The long-term plan crosses ward boundaries and combines a plethora of mainstream public-sector funding sources. The framework for the city centre is in place to ensure, among other aims, a continued regeneration investment and service improvement in the city centre. The framework for North Manchester was completed in June 2003, and the one for Wythenshawe will be in place by late 2004. South Manchester will have two frameworks and, once these are in place, the whole-city approach to regeneration will be effecting change.

This co-ordinated and partnership approach touches everything – including the city's drive to capitalise on its internationally heightened image, which resulted from the successful 2002 Commonwealth Games. Cities that are economically competitive also deliver other factors such as world-class sporting events or exhibitions, iconic buildings, unique spaces and cultural objects or experiences. Manchester has all those elements, but to develop its competitive edge, pride of place and unique identity, a marketing strategy has been developed in partnership with leading creative professionals and Northwest marketing and tourism agencies. Manchester, as the regional capital, is driving the strategy, part of which is to develop an internationally recognised brand. Through the partnership, a Creative Director has been appointed to encapsulate the essence of the Northwest,

fig 5.7
City Centre
renaissance

5.7

Manchester, and its people – and the person selected through open competition is Peter Saville, the man described as 'the Mancunian guru of modern design'.[6] The brand will provide a focus for the regional marketing and economic development strategies of the North West Development Agency and other key partners. It will also drive an events programme that will achieve international recognition for the city and surprise and delight all those who live in, work in and visit it.

In 2006, the first International Festival, based on the theme of innovation and ideas, and a celebration of 'Manchester Firsts', will be held. The festival will attract world-class performers and celebrated artists and, at the same time, stimulate community festivals and events. As Manchester's reputation as a centre for media and creative industries grows, the BBC's plan to make a major shift in focus, funding and jobs from London to Manchester is a powerful vote of confidence in the city from the world's most respected broadcaster, reversing the corporation's long-term trend of concentration on London and the Southeast.

Manchester can justly claim that it is a modern and original city, but there is no resting place for those who deliver change. Sir Howard Bernstein believes that 'changes over the last decade have indeed been dramatic – but we must keep that momentum going and further develop the distinctiveness of Manchester as a centre of fine buildings and public spaces.' The desire to push the boundary, be trendsetters and creators of something unique never diminishes. Manchester thrives on challenge, it is tenacious and opportunistic. It likes to be recognised for its achievements, though every new accolade merely propels it forward with new determination. Richard Leese and Sir Howard Bernstein's offices groan with accolades and tributes placed on every wall, desk and shelf. In 2003, RIBA presented Manchester with awards for eight schemes in the city in addition to making it the only local authority to be acclaimed as RIBA Client of the Year.[7] In The Civic Trust Awards of 2004, Manchester walked away with 11 successes,[8] the highest number of top awards ever given by that organisation to a local authority area.[9]

The recognition of Manchester's many achievements is there, but Richard Leese is resolute and focused,

> *If we continue to drive the city forward, if we continue to be self critical regarding our strengths and weaknesses, recognise what we have done well and what we have done not so well, we will succeed in our aims. It would be very easy to slip back, to become complacent, to become lazy, we will not do that. We have to go up a gear again to become a world class regional capital. I believe that with the strength of our partnerships, Manchester Airport, Knowledge Capital, the strong City Centre, competitive commercial and research centres and outstanding new buildings we can do this and, most importantly, everyone in the city will benefit.*

6 Jonathan Schofield, *21st Century Manchester*, supplement published in *The Observer*, May 2004

7 The schemes awarded were: Boxworks, Manchester – Arkheion; Chorlton Park Housing, Manchester – Stephenson Bell; Number One Deansgate, Manchester – Ian Simpson Architects; Manchester City Art Gallery – Michael Hopkins & Partners; Manchester Piccadilly Station – Building Design Partnership; Timber Wharf, Castlefield, Manchester – Glenn Howells Architects; Urbis, Manchester – Ian Simpson Architects; Waulk Mill, Manchester – Total Architecture

8 The Civic Trust recognised the Millennium Quarter with the Urban Design Award, one of the Special Awards presented, while the City of Manchester Stadium, Cathedral Gardens, Manchester Art Gallery, Piccadilly Station, Manchester Museum, Box Works and Number One Deansgate each received an award. Commendations were given to Urbis, Piccadilly Gardens and Timber Wharf, making it a hugely successful awards event for the city.

9 In 1996 Westminster City Council won two awards, six commendations and three mentions

265

SUMMARY

PAUL FINCH

Interim Chairman, Commission for Architecture and the Built Environment

The late A.J.P. Taylor once remarked that, 'Manchester has everything but good looks'. One wonders what the great historian would have made of today's Manchester, a city that has been transformed by world-class architecture and urban design. Exchange Square, Piccadilly Gardens, Urbis, Manchester Art Gallery Extension, Number One Deansgate and the City of Manchester Stadium are just some of the buildings and spaces that now symbolise Manchester's post-industrial renewal, just as the great mills of Ancoats once symbolised its industrial might.

The Hilton Tower, Manchester Civic Justice Centre and Number One Spinningfields Square, to name but a few, will soon be added to the list. They will underpin ambitious efforts to regenerate whole quarters of the city. Spinningfields, Piccadilly Gardens and Great Northern are exercises in place-making that will open up previously neglected areas of the city centre. Creating a cohesive, permeable whole out of what Nikolaus Pevsner described as, 'one of the most confusing city centres in England'.

Such developments are the culmination of a physical regeneration process that has been ongoing for the past 15 years. In Castlefield, the creation of the first Urban Heritage Park, building on the fantastic, but almost forgotten physical legacy left by the canal network, led to a spate of warehouse conversions into apartments and offices, at a time when few would have thought that a northern city could lead the way in loft-living.

Barbirolli Square and the Bridgewater Hall soon followed. It seemed appropriate that the first architectural icon of the new era would be home to The Hallé, one of the city's most respected cultural institutions. Urban Splash's Smithfield Buildings meanwhile pioneered the way for mixed-use, city-centre development, while the regeneration of Hulme – where schemes such as Homes for Change rose from the ashes and rubble of the notorious Crescents – proved that a suburban renaissance was possible too.

While the 1996 bomb acted as a catalyst and spurred the regeneration process, the secret to today's success – strong and effective leadership from both the public and private sectors – was already in place. Never a city short of ambition and vision, all the key players, who'd cut their teeth on everything from Olympic bids to Urban Development Corporations, were quick to seize the opportunity created by the blast that destroyed a large swathe of the city centre: an opportunity to reconnect Victoria Station to the rest of the city, to rediscover the Cathedral, to create an exciting new public square and to attract some of the biggest names in retail. The city centre is once again a great place to visit, work and live.

The opportunities to continue this renewal lie to the north and east of the city centre, areas that are still very much suffering the social, economic and environmental effects of deindustrialisation. Physical improvements won't solve all these problems overnight, but there is no reason why the residents of Beswick, Openshaw, Miles Platting, Blackley and Harpurhey, shouldn't enjoy all the benefits that well-designed homes and streets can deliver. Developments such as New Islington and Central Park are exciting opportunities to capitalise on the success of the Commonwealth Games, and once again turn North and East Manchester into thriving residential and commercial districts.

Manchester's renaissance has inevitably led to comparisons with Barcelona. It is easy to see why; both have transformed themselves through an investment in physical infrastructure, prestige projects and quality architecture. Both also have a rich cultural heritage, and strong national and regional identity. And both face the same challenge in the future – to ensure that these physical improvements are used as a means of attracting and retaining investment and a skilled workforce, turning physical renewal into economic prosperity. The city once described by George Orwell as the 'belly and guts of the nation' now competes on a European stage with Lyon, Toulouse, Munich, Stuttgart, Milan and Turin.

The story of any city is one of flux and change, and the redevelopment charted over the preceding pages is just the beginning of the next chapter in Manchester's history. I see no reason why Manchester shouldn't take and keep its place amongst the key regional cities in Europe. There will undoubtedly be more hard work to come, but the city, and its leaders, have already proved that they have the right mix of ambition, confidence, pragmatism and stubbornness to get the job done.

CABE
Annual Report & Accounts 2003,
London, CABE (2003)

CMDC
Development Strategy for Central Manchester,
Manchester, CDMC (1990)

CMDC
Annual Report 1994/95,
Manchester, CMDC

CMDC
Eight Years of Achievementx 1988-1996,
Manchester, CMDC (1996)

FINTON, L; SYMES, M; NEARY, S; McKELVEY, J;
*Manchester: The Project of
Regeneration of District Hulme,*
Manchester, Urban Renewal Research Link,
University of Manchester (1994)

HARTWELL, C.
Manchester – Pevsner Architectural Guides,
London, Penguin Books (2001)

HASLAM, D.
Manchester, England: The Story of the Popcult City,
London, Fourth Estate (1999)

**HEMISPHERE DESIGN & MARKETING
CONSULTANTS**
A Brand Strategy for Manchester,
Manchester, Hemisphere (2003)

HETHERINGTON, K.
*Manchester's Urbis: Regeneration,
Interaction and Subjectivity,*
Lancaster, Department of Sociology, Lancaster
University (2004)

HILL, D.
The History of the Northern Quarter
(1996)

HULME REGENERATION LTD
*Rebuilding the City –
A Guide to Development in Hulme,*
Manchester, MCC (1994)

HULME REGENERATION LTD
Year 5 Action Plan Information Pack,
Manchester, MCC (1997)

HUNT THOPMSON ASSOCIATES
Creating the New Heart of Hulme,
Manchester, Community Planning Weekend Report
(1992)

HYLTON, S.
The History of Manchester,
Chichester, Phillimore & Co. Ltd. (2003)

KIDD, A.
Manchester,
Edinburgh, Edinburgh University Press, (2002)

MCC
*Manchester First: How to Become a
Cultured City, Vols 1 & 2,*
Manchester, Urban Cultures and Partnerships,
MCC (1992)

MCC
The Manchester Plan,
Manchester, MCC (1995)

MCC
Manchester in the Mid-90s,
Manchester, Environment and Development
Strategy (Planning Division, MCC) (1998)

MCC
Our Creative City, Manchester,
Manchester, Economic Initiatives Group,
MCC (2002)

MCC
Manchester Community Strategy 2002-2012,
Manchester (2002)

MCC
Manchester: Knowledge Capital Prospectus,
Manchester, MCC (2003)

MCC
Manchester: Knowledge Capital,
Manchester, MCC and the Knowledge
Capital Partnership (2003)

MCC
*Northern Quarter Development
Framework Final Report 2003,*
Manchester (2003)

PARKINSON-BAILEY, J.
Manchester, An Architectural History, Manchester,
Manchester, Manchester University Press (2000)

PECK, J. and WARD, K.
*City of Revolution,
Restructuring Manchester, Manchester,*
Manchester, Manchester University Press (2002)

RHEAD, E.
The 1945 City of Manchester Plan,
Manchester, Manchester Forum,
Edition No.31 (2004)